Whiplash

Whiplash
How to
Survive Our
Faster Future

Joi Ito
Director,
MIT Media Lab
and
Jeff Howe

Grand Central Publishing
New York & Boston

Grand Central Publishing
Hachette Book Group
1290 Avenue of the Americas, New York, NY 10104
grandcentralpublishing.com
twitter.com/grandcentralpub

First Edition: December 2016

Grand Central Publishing is a division of Hachette Book Group, Inc. The Grand Central Publishing name and logo is a trademark of Hachette Book Group, Inc.

The publisher is not responsible for websites (or their content) that are not owned by the publisher.

The Hachette Speakers Bureau provides a wide range of authors for speaking events. To find out more, go to www.hachettespeakersbureau.com or call (866) 376-6591.

Print book interior design by Michael Bierut and Aron Fay, Pentagram.

Library of Congress Cataloging-in-Publication Data

Names: Ito, Joichi, 1966– author. | Howe, Jeff, 1970– author.

Title: Whiplash : how to survive our faster future / Joi Ito and Jeff Howe.

Description: First edition. | New York, NY : Grand Central Publishing, 2016. | Includes bibliographical references.

Identifiers: LCCN 2016032313 | ISBN 9781455544592 (hardcover) | ISBN 9781455544585 (ebook)

Subjects: LCSH: Technological innovations—Economic aspects. | Technological innovations—Social aspects. | Technology and civilization. | Digital communications—Research—United States. | Massachusetts Institute of Technology. Media Laboratory

Classification: LCC HC79.T4 I8165 2016 | DDC 303.48/3—dc23 LC record available at https://lccn.loc.gov/2016032313

ISBNs: 978-1-4555-4459-2 (hardcover), 978-1-4555-4458-5 (ebook), 978-1-4555-9839-7 (international edition)

Printed in the United States of America

LSC-C

10 9 8 7 6 5 4 3 2 1

For M. and A. and A. and F.,
for demonstrating that
the best principles never change.

"Our journey so far has been pleasant, the roads have been good, and food plentiful....Indeed, if I do not experience something far worse than I have yet done, I shall say the trouble is all in getting started."

— Tamsen Donner, June 16, 1846

Contents

Introduction

On December 28, 1895, a crowd milled outside the Grand Café in Paris for a mysterious exhibition. For one franc, promoters promised, the audience would witness the first "living photographs" in the history of mankind. If that sounds a lot like a carnival sideshow to the modern ear, it wouldn't have deterred a Parisian of the late nineteenth century. It was an age of sensation—of séances, snake charmers, bear wrestlers, aboriginal warriors, magicians, cycloramas, and psychics. Such wonders shared headlines with the many legitimate scientific discoveries and engineering advances of the 1890s. In just the previous few years, Gustave Eiffel had erected the tallest man-made structure in the world, electricity had turned Paris into the City of Light, and automobiles had begun racing past carriages on the capital's broad boulevards. The Industrial Revolution had transformed daily life, filling it with novelty and rapid change, and a Parisian could be forgiven for thinking that anything might happen on any given night, because anything often did.

Eventually the first viewers of the first living photographs were ushered down a set of dark, narrow steps into the café's basement and into neat rows of folding chairs. In the middle of the room a man stood fiddling with a small wooden box on a raised platform. After a few awkward moments, light burst from this apparatus, illuminating a linen screen with a blurry image of women emerging from the shadows of a factory. This was an underwhelming spectacle; the patrons could see people leave a factory in half the districts of Paris. Then the image flickered strangely and sprung to life. The women onscreen began streaming out of the factory, in pairs or alone or in small, hurried clusters. The grainy footage is laughably primitive today, but in the Grand Café's basement in the middle of Paris that night the audience gasped and applauded and laughed. Some just sat dumbfounded at the sight. And then, exactly fifty seconds later, it was over. That was as much film—seventeen meters — as Auguste and Louis Lumière, the brothers responsible for the first movie screening in history — could fit inside their invention, the Cinématographe.

What was it like to be among the first people to see light transformed into a moving image, the first to look at a taut screen and see instead a skirt rustling in the breeze? "You had to have attended these thrilling screenings in order to understand just how far the excitement of the crowd could go," one of the first projectionists later recalled. "Each scene passes, accompanied by tempestuous applause; after the sixth scene, I return the hall to light. The audience is shaking. Cries ring out."[1]

Word of this most marvelous of sensations quickly spread. The crowds outside the Grand Café grew so chaotic that the police were required to maintain order.[2] Within a month the Lumière brothers had doubled their repertoire, shooting several dozen new "views," as the fifty-second films were called. Savvy businessmen as well as inventors, by that spring they were holding exhibitions of their work across Europe and America. And yet the Lumières are remembered less as the inventors of the motion picture — others, including Thomas Edison, were right on their heels — than for a single film, *L'Arrivée d'un Train*. Or, to be more accurate, they are remembered for the riot the film incited when it was first screened.

You don't need to be fluent in French to guess that *L'Arrivée d'un Train* features a train in the act of arriving. No one warned the first audience, though. Convinced, supposedly, that the train was about to trundle off the screen and turn them into ripped sacks of lacerated flesh, the tightly packed audience stumbled over one another in a frantic dash for the exits. The lights came up on a mass of humanity jammed into the narrow stairwell. The extent of the tragedy depends on whose telling you believe, and modern scholars question whether it really happened at all.

True or false, the story quickly passed into film lore, becoming what the critic Martin Loiperdinger calls "cinema's founding myth."[3] This urban folktale clearly served some kind of vital purpose:

Perhaps it was the most accurate way to convey the sheer, uncanny strangeness of witnessing the impossible happen, right in front of your eyes. Simple facts were not audacious enough to describe the sensation — we had to invent a myth in order to tell the truth. Technology had exceeded our capacity to understand it, and not for the last time.

One might reasonably anticipate the Lumières, with worldwide fame and a burgeoning catalog, to become fantastically rich, and instrumental to the evolution of the medium. Yet by 1900 they were done. Auguste declared that "the cinema is an invention without a future," and the brothers devoted themselves to creating a reliable technique for developing color photographs.

What's amazing about this pronouncement isn't that two bright entrepreneurs made a mammoth miscalculation. What's amazing is that it surely seemed like a smart bet at the time. By the turn of the century, the Lumières occupied a crowded field, their films having inspired countless imitators. Up to that point the early films were single scenes shot from one perspective. There were no pans or cutaways or even plots beyond man steps on rake; rake snaps up to hit him in the nose; hilarity ensues. Small wonder that, like the other sensations of the day, once the novelty wore off films became little more than boardwalk amusements. The technology of film had been created, but not the medium. When we watch these early films, we see pictures that move, but not a movie.

● ● ●

In failing to comprehend the significance of their own invention, the Lumières put themselves in excellent company. Some of our most celebrated inventors, engineers, and technologists have failed to understand the potential of their own work. In fact, if history is any guide, it's those closest to a given technology who are least likely to predict its ultimate use. In May 1844, Samuel Morse unveiled the world's first commercial telecommunications system. Standing in the basement of the U.S. Capitol Building, he tapped out a message to a train station in Baltimore some thirty-eight miles away. It consisted of a quote from the Old Testament: "What hath God wrought." Within a few years every major American city enjoyed instantaneous communication. Within the decade the first transatlantic cable was being laid.

As it appears in the Bible (Num. 23:23), "What hath God wrought" is understood to be an expression of gratitude — "Look at everything your dad's done for you!" At the time, Morse said the intention was to "baptize the American Telegraph with the name of its author," by which he meant the Almighty, not himself. Yet later in the day, when he recorded the phrase onto a small strip of paper for posterity's sake, he added a question mark, which changes the meaning altogether.[4] Morse had a reputation as something of a pious blowhard, but by introducing the question mark he emerges as a more thoughtful figure. For thousands of years information had never traveled faster than a horse, whether the messenger was the king or his cook. Now it would move with the speed of some cosmic force. How could he, or anyone else for that matter, really know what the world was in for?

He couldn't. Morse died in the secure belief that the next great step in telecommunications would not be the telephone — dismissed as "an electric toy" when Alexander Graham Bell first exhibited his invention — but instead telegraph wires capable of carrying multiple messages simultaneously. Decades later Thomas Edison showed scarcely more insight. He marketed the first phonograph, or his "talking machine," as he called it, as a device to allow businessmen to dictate their correspondence. He called it the "Ediphone," and for many years afterward insisted that few if any customers would want to use the thing to play music. It took a self-taught engineer named Eldridge Reeves Johnson to realize the phonograph's potential to bring music into every family parlor and saloon. Johnson founded Victor Records in 1901, and started hiring famous performers like Enrico Caruso to join his label. Edison may have invented the phonograph, but Johnson did something more significant: he invented the recording industry.[5]

It's easy to smirk at such strategic blunders, as if Edison was the stodgy straight man in a Buster Keaton movie, stumbling blindly into some historical pratfall, and that we, with our instantaneous communications systems and our command of vast stores of information, are immune from such epic failures of foresight. But like Tarzan in the city, humans are perpetually failing to grasp the significance of their own creations. The steam-driven engines used in late nineteenth-century factories were invariably arranged around the large central axle connected to the turbine. As the economist Paul David discovered when conducting research into the first electrified factories, factory planners continued to needlessly cluster electrical engines in a central location, even starting from scratch in a new factory. As a result, an innovation that should have increased productivity seemed to have no effect at all. It took thirty years before managers exploited the flexibility electrical engines allowed and organized factories according to work flow, doubling and sometimes even tripling productivity.[6]

Our own era isn't immune either. In 1977, Ken Olson, the president of one of the world's largest and most successful computer companies, Digital Equipment Corporation, told an audience that there was "no reason for any individual to have a computer in his home."[7] He stuck to this view throughout the 1980s, long after Microsoft and Apple had proved him wrong. Thirty years later, former Microsoft CEO Steve Ballmer told *USA Today* that there was "no chance that the iPhone is going to get any significant market share."[8]

● ● ●

These anecdotes, besides being funny and amazing in a nerdy kind of way, do have a point, and it's not to bring ridicule down on long-deceased American inventors. It's to recognize that we are all susceptible to misinterpreting the technological tea leaves, that we are all blinkered by prevailing systems of thought. As much as has changed — and our book is nothing if not a documentation of radical change — our brains, at least, remain largely the same organs that believed the automobile to be a passing fancy, or for that matter, that fire was just a technology for keeping us warm and producing interesting shadows on the cave wall.

Our book proceeds from the conviction that any given period of human development is characterized by a set of commonly held systems of assumptions and beliefs. We're not talking about opinions or ideologies. Beneath these lie another set of ideas, the assumptions that are unconscious, or more accurately, preconscious, in nature: Strength is better than weakness; knowledge is better than ignorance; individual talent is more desirable than difference. Imagine for a moment that your opinions, your political beliefs, and all your conscious ideas about the world and your place within it are the furniture inside a house. You acquire these quite consciously over a long period of time, discarding some, keeping others, and acquiring new pieces as the need arises. This book is about something else — the framework of joists, studs, and beams that support all your conscious ideas. In other words this isn't a book about what you know; it's a book about what you *don't know you know*, and why it's important to question these problematic assumptions.

The French philosopher Michel Foucault believed that this matrix of beliefs, prejudices, norms, and conventions makes up a set of rules that guide our thinking and, ultimately, the decisions we make. He called it the "episteme," and believed certain historical periods could be identified by these systems of thought, just as the archaeologist identifies layers of history by the type of pottery in use at that time.[9] In his classic work *The Structure of Scientific Revolutions*, the American philosopher of science Thomas Kuhn called such all-encompassing belief systems "paradigms."[10]

By carefully studying the evolution of scientific thought and practices over the preceding centuries, Kuhn identified patterns in how scientific disciplines like chemistry or physics accommodated new ideas. He observed that even the most careful scientists would regularly ignore or misinterpret data in order to maintain the "coherence" of the reigning paradigm and explain away the anomalies that are the first sign of fault lines in a scientific theory. For example,

Newtonian physicists performed impressive feats of intellectual acrobatics in order to explain away the anomalies in astronomical observations that would eventually lead to Einstein's theory of relativity. Such upheavals—scientific revolutions, or what Kuhn called paradigm shifts—were followed by brief periods of chaos that led, in time, to stability as a new scientific consensus formed around a new paradigm.[11]

Our book—targeted squarely to anyone with a lively curiosity — sidesteps the debate over terminology altogether. Alexis de Toqueville may have put it best way back in the 1830s. In trying to identify the source of the United States' singular strangeness and remarkable prosperity, he noted that Americans possessed unique "habits of the mind" (an earthy pragmatism, for example) that rendered us well qualified to play a leading role in the industrial revolution.

Our own habits of mind are different in content, but no less stubborn in character. And while our book deals with some complex subjects — cryptography, genetics, artificial intelligence — it has a simple premise: Our technologies have outpaced our ability, as a society, to understand them. Now we need to catch up.

We are blessed (or cursed) to live in interesting times, where high school students regularly use gene editing techniques to invent new life forms, and where advancements in artificial intelligence force policymakers to contemplate widespread, permanent unemployment. Small wonder our old habits of mind—forged in an era of coal, steel, and easy prosperity — fall short. The strong no longer necessarily survive; not all risk needs to be mitigated; and the firm is no longer the optimum organizational unit for our scarce resources.

The digital age has rendered such assumptions archaic and something worse than useless—actively counterproductive. The argument we develop in the following pages is that our current cognitive tool set leaves us ill-equipped to comprehend the profound implications posed by rapid advances in everything from communications to warfare. Our mission is to provide you with some new tools— principles, we call them, because one characteristic of the faster future is to demolish anything so rigid as a "rule."

It's no easy task. We can't tell you what to think, because the current disconnect between humans and their technologies lies at that deeper level—the paradigm, the basic assumptions behind our belief system. Instead our book is intended to help correct that incongruity by laying out nine principles that bring our brains into the modern era, and could be used to help individuals and institutions alike navigate a challenging and uncertain future.

One might think that such deeply held beliefs evolve gradually over time, just as a species of insect slowly develops attributes that help it compete in a given environment. But this doesn't seem to be how systems of belief change—in fact, it's not even how evolution among living organisms works. In both cases long periods of relative stability are followed by periods of violent upheaval triggered by a rapid change in external circumstance, be it political revolution, the rise of a disruptive new technology, or the arrival of a new predator into a previously stable ecosystem.[12] These transitions—evolutionary biologists call them "periods of speciation"[13]—aren't pretty. There's a strong case to be made that we're going through a doozy of a transition right now, a dramatic change in our own ecosystem. It is, in short, a helluva time to be alive, assuming you don't get caught in one of the coming cataclysms.

Our principles aren't a recipe for how to start an Internet business, or an attempt to make you a better manager—though both endeavors might benefit from them. Envision the principles as pro tips for how to use the world's new operating system. This new OS is not a minor iteration from the one we've been using the last few centuries; it's a major new release. And like any totally new OS, we're going to have to get used to this one. It runs according to a different logic. There isn't going to be an instruction manual, because, honestly, even if the developers issued one it would be outdated by the time you got hold of it.

What we offer is, we hope, more useful. The principles are simple — but powerful — guidelines to that system's new logic. They can be understood individually, but their whole is greater than the sum of their parts. That is because at the root level this new operating system is based on two irreducible facts that make up the kernel—the code at the very heart of the machine—of the network age. The first is Moore's law. Everything digital gets faster, cheaper, and smaller at an exponential rate.[14] The second is the Internet.

When these two revolutions—one in technology, the other in communications—joined together, an explosive force was unleashed that changed the very nature of innovation, relocating it from the center (governments and big companies) to the edges (a twenty-three-year-old punk rock musician and circuit-board geek living in Osaka, Japan). Imagine: Charles Darwin first conceived of natural selection while reviewing the specimens he had collected as the HMS *Beagle*'s botanist, a post he had accepted when he was twenty-three years old. He then spent more than thirty years gathering data to back up his claim, an act so patient and cautious that it strikes the modern mind as otherworldly in its monklike devotion to the scientific method.[15]

But then, it was another world. Reliant on the libraries of the Athenaeum Club, the British Museum, and professional organizations like the Royal Society, as well as shipments of books that could take months to arrive from abroad, he could only access a tiny fraction of the information available to the modern scientist. Without a phone, much less the Internet, collegial input was limited to that quintessentially Victorian communications network, the penny post. Research and discovery followed a glacier's pace, and real innovation required considerable sums of money, meaning family wealth or institutional patronage, and all the politics that went with it.[16] Today a geneticist can extract enough DNA from an ice core sample to develop a portrait of an entire Neolithic ecosystem, then refine the results with a global community of colleagues, all over the course of a summer break. That's no mere change in degree. That's a violent change to the status quo.

So, what's next? It's the perennial question of our era. But if our predecessors—living in simpler, slower times—couldn't answer the question, what chance do we have? It's hard to say. Nuclear fission represents one of mankind's most impressive achievements.

It simultaneously poses the greatest threat to survival our species has ever encountered. The Haber process led to synthetic fertilizers that increased crop yields. Its inventor, Fritz Haber, is credited with preventing the starvation of billions of people, and he won the Nobel Prize for his efforts. He also invented chemical warfare, personally overseeing the chlorine gas releases that resulted in sixty-seven thousand casualties in World War I.[17] So it goes. Marc Goodman, a security expert and the founder of the Future Crimes Institute, points out that some cybersecurity technologies are used by hackers as well as the people trying to protect against them. Thus has it ever been, writes Goodman: "Fire, the original technology, could be used to keep us warm, cook our food, or burn down the village next door."[18]

The truth is that a technology means nothing, in and of itself. Zyklon B, another product of Haber's research, is just a gas — a useful insecticide that was also used to kill millions during the Holocaust.[19] Nuclear fission is a common atomic reaction. The Internet is simply a way to disassemble information and reassemble it somewhere else. What technology actually *does*, the real impact it will eventually have on society, is often that which we least expect.

By the time you read this sentence, Oculus VR will have released a consumer version of its Oculus Rift, a virtual reality headset. How will we put it to use? Developers are already at work on video games that will take advantage of the intense immersion the Rift provides. Porn, that $100 billion industry, will not be far behind. It could allow doctors to perform remote surgical operations, or simply provide checkups for patients unable to get to a doctor's office. You'll visit Mars and Antarctica and that Denver apartment you might otherwise have to buy sight unseen. But the real fact is that we don't have any idea how humans will use the second, third, or tenth generation of the technology. The advances—the ideas—will come from the least likely places. If you had been tasked with finding someone to invent the telephone, you probably wouldn't have canvassed schools for the deaf. And yet in hindsight, Professor Bell—son of a deaf mother, husband to a deaf wife, and pioneering student of sound waves and methods of using vibrating wires as a system of communicating sound to those who could not hear it—seems like the perfect choice.[20]

The shock of the new would become a common refrain in the century of marvels that followed the telegraph: From the sewing machine to the safety pin, from the elevator to the steam turbine, mankind hurtled forward, ever faster, the technology always outstripping our ability to understand it. Will genetic engineering eradicate cancer or become a cheap weapon of mass destruction? No one knows. As Moore's law demonstrates, technology lopes along according to power laws of one or another magnitude. Our brains — or at least the sum of our brains working together in the welter of institutions, companies, governments, and other forms of collective endeavor — plod along slowly in its wake, struggling to understand just what God, or man, hath wrought.

"The future," science-fiction writer William Gibson once said, "is already here. It's just not evenly distributed."[21] This is less witty observation than indisputable truth. Even in Boston, the city both authors of this book call home, decades of progress seem to melt away in the time it takes you to drive from the humming laboratories of MIT to the cash-strapped public elementary schools just across the river.

Back to the Lumières for a moment, and their exhilarating but choppy stab at moving pictures. Things went along pretty much according to the status quo for nearly a decade. Then in 1903, George Albert Smith — hypnotist, psychic, and English entrepreneur quick to embrace the new medium — was filming two primly dressed children nursing a sick kitten. This was just the kind of domestic scene popular with Smith's middle-class Victorian audiences. But a viewer would have had difficulty seeing the detail of the girl spoon-feeding the swaddled kitten. So Smith did something radical. He scooted his camera closer to his subject until only the kitten and the girl's hand were in the frame. Up to that time conventional wisdom held that such a composition would throw the moviegoing public into an ontological quandary: What happened to the girl? Has she been sliced in two? Smith tempted fate and edited the shot into the final cut. Viewers responded positively, and like that, Smith had invented the close-up.[22]

Ponder this for a moment. It took eight years, hundreds of filmmakers, and *thousands of films* before someone conceived of the new technology as anything other than a play in two dimensions. This simple innovation helped jump-start a period of experimentation and progress in the cinema. Yet it would take another twelve years before a film appeared — D. W. Griffiths's *Birth of a Nation* — that a modern audience would recognize as such.[23] Not because the technology didn't exist, but because in the end, technologies are just tools — useless, static objects until they are animated by human ideas.

● ● ●

For most of Earth's history, change has been in rare supply. Life appeared 4 billion years ago. It took another 2.8 billion years to discover sex, and another 700 million years before the first creature with a brain appeared. The first amphibian squirmed up onto land about 350 million years after that. In fact, complex life is a fairly recent phenomenon on this planet. If you were to condense Earth's history into a single year, land-dwelling animals come onstage around December 1, and the dinosaurs don't go extinct until the day after Christmas. Hominids start walking on two feet around 11:50 p.m. on New Year's Eve, and recorded history begins a few nanoseconds before midnight.

And even *then*, change moves at a glacial pace. Now let's pretend that that last ten minutes — the era of the "behaviorally modern" human — is a year. Not a thing happens until December. The Sumerians begin smelting bronze in the first week of December, the first recorded languages pop up around the middle of the month, and Christianity starts spreading on December 23. But for most people life is still nasty, brutish, and short. Just before dawn on December 31, the pace finally begins to pick up, as mass production ushers in the industrial age. That morning, train tracks blossom across the land, and humans finally start moving faster than a horse. The rest of the day is action-packed: Around 2:00 p.m., infant mortality and life expectancy — both largely unchanged since the exodus from Africa last January — are improved with the introduction of antibiotics. Planes are circling the earth by late afternoon, and well-heeled companies begin buying mainframe computers around dinnertime.

It took us 364 days before a billion humans walked the earth. By 7:00 p.m., there are three billion people on the planet, and we just uncorked the first bottle of champagne! That number doubles again before midnight, and at the rate we're going (roughly another billion people every eighty minutes) we'll reach Earth's expected capacity for humanity by 2:00 a.m. on New Year's Day.[24] At some recent point—the geological equivalent of a hummingbird's single heartbeat—everything from the speed of travel to population growth to the sheer amount of information our species now possesses started to metastasize. In short, we entered an exponential age.

But the "big shift," as an influential 2009 *Harvard Business Review* article termed it,[25] occurred around 10:00 p.m. with the twin revolutions already mentioned: the Internet and the integrated circuit chip. Together the two heralded the beginning of the network age, a more distinct break from the industrial era than anything that has occurred before it.

What seems increasingly evident is that the primary condition of the network era is not just rapid change, but *constant* change. In the space of a few generations—since 10:00 p.m., to stick to our one-year metaphor—the periods of stability have grown shorter, and the disruptive shifts to new paradigms have come with greater frequency.[26] Imminent breakthroughs in fields like genetics, artificial intelligence, manufacturing, transportation, and medicine will only accelerate this dynamic. "What if the historical pattern—disruption followed by stabilization—has itself been disrupted?" ask the authors of "The Big Shift" in another article, "The New Reality: Constant Disruption."[27]

If you work in cybersecurity or software design, you don't need a book to discover what it's like to grapple with an industry in which change itself seems pegged to Moore's law, doubling then doubling again. It's a quantitative phenomenon with qualitative implications. When chips get that small, that fast, we get wearable computers. Robots building robots. Computer viruses that can trigger financial panics. Are you ready for brain implants? Wait, don't answer. Change doesn't care if you're ready. Change outpaced humans sometime late in the last century. These are exponential times. And they have given rise to three conditions that define our era.

Asymmetry

In the analog age, a sort of rough, Newtonian physics held sway in the realm of human endeavor. Large historical forces could only be counteracted by a force of equal size and strength. Capital was held in check by labor, and both were restrained (however imperfectly) by government. Large armies defeated small armies. Coke worried about Pepsi, and not much else. While there was friction—often bloody, cataclysmic friction—where these massive forces came into contact, the outcomes conformed to a sort of order everyone understood.

And then, in the space of little more than twenty years, all that changed. The most dramatic example, of course, has been the rise against powerful players on the world stage of terrorist organizations with memberships smaller than a midwestern farming town. But other examples abound: Small teams of hackers have wreaked havoc by infiltrating U.S. government databases;[28] one man—Craig Newmark—single-handedly crippled the American newspaper business with the release of Craigslist;[29] in 2010 an unemployed day trader named Navinder Singh Sarao installed a "spoofing" algorithm on the computer in his London flat that wound up obliterating nearly $1 *trillion* in the U.S. securities market.[30]

It would be simplistic to say that small is the new big, but what's indisputable is that the Internet and rapidly improving digital technologies have leveled the field in ways that can be used for good as well as nefarious purposes. It's not so much a question of whether any of this is good or bad. Whether you're operating a small business or running a department of a government agency or merely hold any position of responsibility inside an organization of any scale, the simple fact of asymmetry is what's important. The point is that you can no longer assume that costs and benefits will be proportional to size. If anything, the opposite of that assumption is probably true: Today, the biggest threats to the status quo come from the smallest of places, from start-ups and rogues, breakaways and indie labs. As if that fact wasn't daunting enough, we are having to deal with this swirl of new competitors as the problems we are grappling with are more complex than ever.

Complexity

Complexity, or what scientists generally call complex systems, is anything but new. In fact, complex systems predate *Homo sapiens* by more than three billion years. The immune response in animals is a complex system, as is an ant colony, and the climate on planet Earth, and the brain of a mouse, and the intricate biochemistry within any living cell. And then there's anthropogenic complexity, or the kinds of systems—like our climate, or the chemistry of our water sources—made vastly more complex by man's unwitting interventions. Put another way, we may have created climate change, but that doesn't mean we understand it.

The economy bears all the classic hallmarks of complexity. It is composed of a vast number of individual parts that obey a few simple rules. (That would be a broker, for instance, executing a sell order, setting off a dizzying chain reaction of moves and countermoves.) Millions of these few simple actions—buy, sell, or hold—form the basis for a market's tendency to self-organize.[31] This is why an ant colony can almost be thought of as a single "super-organism," since it behaves far beyond the capacity of any one ant within the system. Many complex systems are also adaptive—markets, for instance, constantly change in response to new information, just as ant colonies immediately respond en masse to new opportunities or threats.[32] In fact, it is in the very nature of some complex systems to process and produce information.[33]

The study of complexity has become one of the most promising areas of scientific inquiry. It is inherently interdisciplinary, a product of physicists, information theorists, biologists, and other scientists teaming up to understand what cannot be grasped by any single field of study.

The quantity, or level, of complexity is influenced by four inputs: heterogeneity, a network, interdependency, and adaptation. "Imagine these as four knobs," says Scott E. Page, the director of the Center for the Study of Complex Systems at the University of Michigan. At one point, Page says, all these knobs were turned to zero. We lived in isolated, homogeneous communities that were ill-equipped to adapt to rapidly changing conditions, but for thousands of years this mattered little. The Roman Empire, for instance, took centuries to unravel. "We've cranked the volume on all these knobs to 11 in recent years," says Page.[34] "And we can't begin to know what the consequences of that will be."[35] It is not knowing that brings us to our third contributing factor.

Uncertainty

Again we return to the million-dollar—no, billion-dollar—question: What comes next? No one knows. Not the pricey consultants at McKinsey & Company, not the analysts burrowed inside some highly classified NSA facility, and certainly not the authors of this book. As we saw in the beginning of this introduction, over the last few hundred years humans have racked up a deplorable record when it comes to predicting the future. In fact, experts and futurists have some of the worst records of all, underperforming random selections.[36] (The *Wall Street Journal* for years ran a popular feature in which expert stock pickers were pitted against random throws of a dart against the stock pages; the darts almost always won.) If it was a mug's game before, it's even more futile now that we've turbocharged the world's complexity quotient.

Global warming, climatologists have taken to pointing out, is a bit of a misnomer. Not every region will experience a rise in temperature. What many regions will experience is an increase in extreme weather events."[37] This is because the broad rise in temperature introduces more variability into any given weather pattern, with the result that some areas will be drier, some wetter, and almost every region will experience more storms. Far from simply producing warmer temperatures across the board, global warming has dramatically increased the volatility of the climate system; warming is really just the beginning of more meteorological uncertainty.

For much of our history, humans' success was directly related to the ability to create accurate forecasts. A medieval merchant didn't know much, but if he knew there had been widespread drought in the Rhineland, he could predict that his wheat might fetch the best price in that district. In an age of complexity, though, unforeseen development can change the rules of the game in the space of a few days.

And here's where our book pivots from merely observing the conditions of asymmetry, uncertainty, and complexity to prescribing something to do about them. Not knowing is okay. In fact, we've entered an age where the admission of ignorance offers strategic advantages over expending resources—subcommittees and think tanks and sales forecasts—toward the increasingly futile goal of forecasting future events.

How do you rebuild a company, a government agency, a university department, or even a career around the principle of not knowing? It sounds like some perplexing Zen koan—mysterious and ultimately unanswerable. But we can draw some lessons from the people who, to go back to William Gibson's way of thinking, arrived at the future while still inhabiting the present. People in areas as diverse as the military, the life sciences, technology, and even the news media have begun creating organizations hardwired for complexity and unpredictability. They have more in common than you'd think.

● ● ●

As it happens, the Media Lab is a pretty good outpost from which to glimpse this future mind, since the principles are more or less baked into its DNA. The term "media" has always been interpreted liberally, as in a "way of communicating information," or "the material or the form that an artist, a writer or a musician uses," but also "a substance that something exists or grows in" or simply "something that is used for a particular purpose."[38]

The Lab needs this capacious umbrella, since it's always been something of an island for misfit toys, a place for artists who create new technologies and engineers who work in genetics and computer scientists trying to reinvent our educational system. The culture isn't so much interdisciplinary as it is proudly "antidisciplinary"; the faculty and students more often than not aren't just collaborating between disciplines, but are exploring the spaces between and beyond them as well.

It is an approach that began with Lab cofounder Nicholas Negroponte. The Media Lab emerged from the Architecture Machine Group that Negroponte cofounded, in which architects at MIT used advanced graphical computers to experiment with computer-aided design and Negroponte (along with Steve Jobs, out in Silicon Valley) envisioned an age when computers would become personal devices. Negroponte also predicted a massive convergence that would jumble all of the disciplines together and connect arts and sciences together as well— the Media Lab's academic program is called "Media Arts and Sciences."

Luckily for Negroponte and the Media Lab, the world was ready for this message and the Lab was able to launch a unique model in which a consortium of companies — many of them competitors — would fund the work and share all of the intellectual property. This created a space for undirected research with tremendous freedom for the students, faculty, and guest researchers, with the consortium model allowing everyone to share with everyone else inside the Lab.[39]

The early years of the Media Lab helped chart the course for the world in advanced display technologies, touch screens, virtual reality, holography, user interfaces, sensors, haptics, learning, personal robots, artificial intelligence, software and computing, 3-D printing and fabrication, and more. John Sculley, Apple's CEO through much of the 1980s, was a member of the Media Lab's Visiting Committee for about a decade. He recently said that "many of the ideas that we ended up doing at Apple came out of the MIT Media Lab."[40]

As many of Negroponte's predictions came true, the world became digital and computers empowered people and things to connect to each other effectively, cheaply, and in a sophisticated way; the world became more open, networked, and complex, pushing the Lab into new fields such as social networks, big data, economics, civics, cities, cryptocurrencies, and other areas that became more concrete and accessible as the Internet, computers, and devices opened these domains to new thinking and innovation.

Meanwhile, the Internet and computers also dramatically lowered the cost of invention, sharing, collaboration, and distribution, which substantially increased the places where interesting work was going on and the interconnectedness of this work.

More recently, the Lab has moved into "hard sciences," with an increasing number of projects and people working on biology.[41] It turns out that the fiercely pragmatic, "antidisciplinary" ethos of the Media Lab — in which computer scientists might borrow freely from architecture, and architecture from electrical engineering, so long as the threads all come together — works surprisingly well when applied to science, and may in fact be uniquely suited to that increasingly complex, interdisciplinary, and fast-paced world. That pragmatism inherent in antidisciplinary approaches has proven especially valuable in scientific fields on the frontier of human understanding. Ed Boyden runs the synthetic neurobiology group — with forty-five researchers, it's the largest in the Media Lab. Rather than focus on clinical studies or theoretical work Boyden's team is focused on building tools that a generation of brain scientists can use to jump-start our nascent understanding of our nervous system. Such a mission would never succeed without utilizing expertise from well outside the field of neurobiology.

The Media Lab has been successful at adapting to changes that have crushed many businesses (remember the Palm-Pilot?), or, for that matter, research labs (Xerox famously neglected many of the best innovations to emerge from Xerox PARC).[42] The Lab owes its adaptability to the strong core values and principles that Negroponte and others put in place when it was established; while the world and the Lab have changed in many substantive ways, the core principles remain solid.

The principles are designed to overlap and complement one another. (They are not ranked in order of importance.) In fact, the principle that might be closest to the core of the Media Lab's mission isn't listed here at all, though you will find it running through every chapter of the book. It's the notion of putting learning over education. Learning, we argue, is something you do for yourself. Education is something done to you. The pedagogical spirit of the Media Lab owes much to Mitch Resnick, whose mentor, Seymour Papert, helped start the Lab. Resnick runs the Lifelong Kindergarten research group, and his dedication to what he calls the "four Ps" of creative learning—Projects, Peers, Passion, and Play — animated much of the spirit behind this book. We firmly believe that for the principles to find a fertile soil in the years ahead, our educational system must embrace some of the same philosophy.

In many ways the nine principles of this book represent our interpretation of the core principles of the Media Lab. They've become the Lab's guiding principles, and the director's job has been to nudge and tweak the direction of the Lab—its ecology, in a sense, because the Lab is a self-adapting complex system as much as any tundra or rain forest. The director, then, tends the garden and fosters the emergence into the world of something beautiful and new.

That, too, is the point of this book, though our guess is that the process will at times be more tumultuous and trying than a spring afternoon in the garden. But these are the times in which we live. These principles offer a blueprint for how to shape that new world, and to thrive.

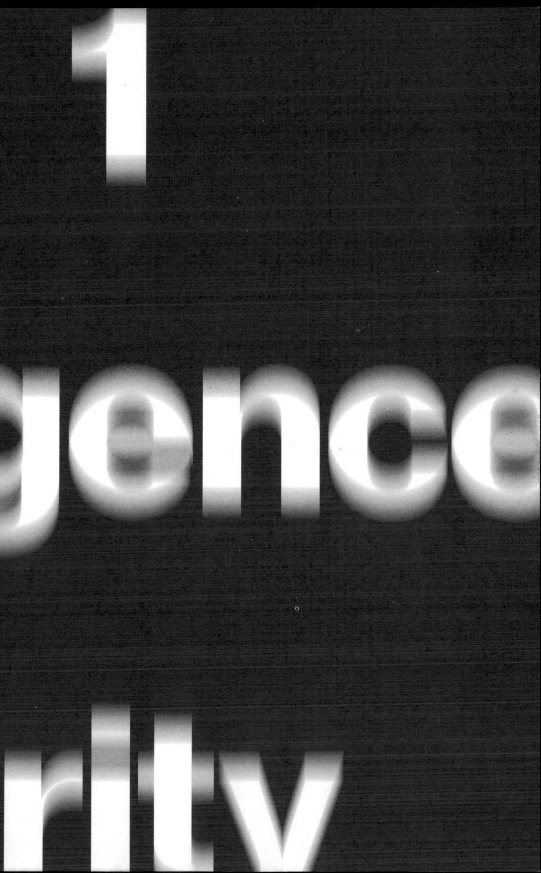

1   Emergence over Authority

We once had a very linear notion of how knowledge was produced and disseminated: It originated with God and was divulged to a variety of clerics, prophets, priests, and theocratic leaders, at which point it took the form of dogma (or in a more secular vein, policy) that would be disseminated through antiquity's version of middle management until it reached a largely unquestioning populace.

This all sounds terribly archaic — redolent of pharaohs and the Old Testament. While we can start to see cracks in this system with Martin Luther and the radical notion that religious truths emerged from a community of brethren rather than from the Church, with a capital C, as a basic pattern of knowledge production, organization, and distribution, the model remained largely unchanged.

Now that system is on the way out; a new system, emergence, is on the way in. Emergent systems aren't *replacing* authority. We aren't going to start policing ourselves, or repairing en masse to lawless communes. What has changed is a basic attitude toward information — its value and its role in channeling the many over the desires and dictates of the few. The Internet has played a key role in this, providing a way for the masses to not only make their voices heard, but to engage in the kind of discussion, deliberation, and coordination that just recently were the province of professional politics. In 2007, a point at which amateur-written blogs were suddenly able to contest the authority of venerable news institutions, Joi wrote a paper online predicting that the Internet was giving rise to a new political phenomenon, a kind of collective intelligence that, like honeybees or other colonial organisms, would possess qualities far beyond the capabilities of a single individual within it. Such "emergent democracy" can be seen in certain aspects of the Arab Spring that roiled Middle Eastern authoritarian governments in 2011, though it sadly failed to move beyond the coup to the creation of a government. The hacktivist group Anonymous—highly potent, yet completely leaderless—may be the purest expression of emergent democracy. Elements of emergent democracy were a prominent feature in the 2016 presidential campaign; one could easily sense that neither Bernie Sanders nor Donald Trump "led" their respective movements so much as surfed them, hoping and praying the electorate's collective id would eventually lead safely back to shore.

The science writer Steven Johnson, whose book *Emergence* introduced many of these ideas to a general audience, compares the evolution of new ideas to slime mold—a single-celled organism that gathers together to form a kind of super-organism when food is in short supply. How do slime mold cells know to do this, given that they lack a brain? Like ants in a mound, they follow a set of simple rules and leave pheromone trails wherever they go. If enough individual organisms leave the pheromone that says, "I'm *starving!*" the alarm goes out for all parties to convene at the nearest rotting log. Ideas are no different, Johnson writes. Individual slime mold cells spend most of their lives in isolation, perpetually exploring their immediate environment for food. But when the cells begin to gather en masse the strength of the collective signal triggers the formation of something else entirely, something no slime mold cell planned or can ever even understand. The same phenomenon, Johnson writes, occurs with ideas. "Plug more minds into the system and give their work a longer, more durable trail— by publishing those ideas in bestselling books, or founding research centers to explore those ideas—and before long the system arrives at a phase transition: Isolated hunches and private obsessions coalesce into a new way of looking at the world, shared by thousands of individuals."[1] We are now in the midst of that phase transition—the point at which a solid, say, suddenly melts into liquid, or airborne moisture cools just enough to become a rainstorm.

Emergence is what happens when a multitude of little things—neurons, bacteria, people—exhibit properties beyond the ability of any individual, simply through the act of making a few basic choices: Left or right? Attack or ignore? Buy or sell? The ant colony is the classic example, of course. This meta-organism possesses abilities and intelligence far greater than the sum of its parts: The colony knows when food is nearby, or when to take evasive action, or, amazingly, just how many ants need to leave the colony to forage for the day's food or ward off an attack.[2]

Our own brains are another amazing example of emergence. Somehow, approximately one-third of the twenty thousand or so different genes that make up the human genome are expressed in the brain and direct the development of tens of billions of neurons. Each neuron, while relatively complex, isn't conscious or very smart. Somehow these neurons, when connected, together create an amazing network that is not only greater than the sum of its parts, but is able to be so conscious that we can even think about thinking. While the question of how the brain actually works is still hotly debated, it is clear that thinking and consciousness—the mind—can emerge from networks of less sophisticated parts connected together in the right way.

The natural world abounds in other demonstrations of collective cognitive processes too. Schooling fish, flocking birds, swarming locusts—all display emergent properties. Life itself is an emergent property, the result of molecules—carbohydrates, lipids, proteins, and nucleic acids—going about their business. A lipid never turned to a protein and said, "We need to get organized. We should all get together in the form of an awkward, hairless biped named Jeff." The lipid just wants to store energy or link up with other lipids to create a cell membrane.

Emergent systems aren't new, of course, and their study goes back to the ancient Greeks. And emergence isn't just a natural phenomenon. From the scale of an entire city, humans are just like ants, scurrying to and fro making small-scale decisions without a thought to civic consequences. Which in fact is what makes cities such magical environments. No single intelligence could have orchestrated the ferment of the Bywater in New Orleans, or the complex styles of Tokyo's Shibuya district. The traffic roundabout relies on emergence, as does the continual evolution of human communication. Again, no single mind—except possibly William Shakespeare's—could create the constant stream of linguistic innovations that cohere into the myriad forms of any single language. The most obvious example of an emergent system created by humans is the economy, which clearly exhibits attributes that no individual could control. We tend to think of markets as little more than the site at which buyers meet sellers to conduct their business. But as Austrian economist Friedrich Hayek observed in a 1945 paper regarded as one of the foundational texts of information theory, markets do something far more valuable: They gather and utilize knowledge which is "widely dispersed among individuals," Hayek writes. "Each member of society can have only a small fraction of the knowledge possessed by all, and...each is therefore ignorant of most of the facts on which the working of society rests." The market, in Hayek's view, is the accidental aggregation machine that humans created in order to "conquer intelligence."[3]

By Hayek's reckoning, the price of a stock is the encapsulation of all the information known about that company at any time, compounded by what is understood about the relative stability of the world itself. The stock market was the greatest information system of all time, until the Internet came along. In our own era, the Internet gives billions of people[4] access to the same ability the market has to aggregate vast amounts of information and use it to make informed decisions. As the relative stability of the world itself is derived more and more from the fear or confidence of those billions of people, stock prices have become less linked to the underlying material value of the companies. As a result, fluctuations have become dangerously amplified.

But this shift from authority — when organizations charted whatever course those lofty few up on the quarterdeck deemed wise — to emergence, in which many more decisions aren't *made* so much as they emerge from large groups of employees or stakeholders of one type or another, is changing the future of many organizations. Having originally greeted the phenomenon with fear and disdain, companies are now realizing that emergent systems may render their services unnecessary. Of course, they may also be exploited for great gain, as we've already begun to see.

Comparing the shifting of authority from the *Encyclo-pedia Britannica* to Wikipedia—an authoritative collection of experts vs a self-organizing community of bookworms for the common good—is a great indicator of this phase change. In 2005, *Nature* published a study that revealed that the two were comparable in quality.[5] Since then, we have witnessed the steady ascension of Wikipedia. Capable not only of instantly responding to new information (a celebrity's death, the onset of hostilities between two rival factions) but fostering dissent, deliberation, and ultimately consensus on how that information should be presented.

● ● ●

Although the Arab Spring uprising and the hacktivist group Anonymous may seem like exceptions in a world still rife with authoritarian power structures, they're really just discrete, colorful manifestations of a well-established phenomenon. Paradigms, belief systems, prejudices—all exhibit the hallmarks of an emergent phenomenon. An individual can have a breakthrough, but an entire system of ideas, what we called an episteme, these emerge from the multitude, none of them conscious of the act. Gravity is an idea. Isaac Newton, with a hat tip to Galileo, was its author. But the scientific revolution was a gut renovation of mankind's epistemological beliefs—how we acquire knowledge and justify our beliefs. In short, it was a new set of principles, the brainchild of no one and everyone.

It's no accident that this newfound fascination with emergent systems has coincided with our current historical moment. We've made great progress in understanding how emergent properties evolve in natural systems, which has in turn helped inform how we approach the emergent systems on which we've come to so heavily rely. Remember the ants? Two Stanford professors, a computer scientist and a biologist, recently collaborated on a research project studying how ants forage for food. They discovered that ant colonies had effectively invented TCP/IP—the core method by which information is distributed over the Internet — untold millions of years before humans.[6]

That humans unknowingly replicated a pattern already present in nature is not unusual. In fact, the tendency of certain irreducible patterns — the fractal curve that defines the snowflake — to repeat themselves over and over is itself an emergent property. For nearly twenty years we've used the language of profound change to describe the growth of the Internet — a "radical" and "revolutionary" new medium. This was not an exaggeration. But it should not surprise us that the growth of the network — the very architecture of which comprises an emergent system of nodes and neurons that defy any obvious, linear order — would have an effect on us at the deepest levels of how we think.

● ● ●

Biology is the original emergent system, a fact that is as self-evident as it is difficult for us to grasp on an intuitive level. We are naturally disposed to believe that behind every Oz lies a wizard, a single entity that directs the action. Nearly every culture has at its core the story of how Earth and its most persistent species came to be. In the beginning there was only God — or Gaia if you hail from ancient Athens, or Pangu according to the classical Chinese tradition.

This central cognitive assumption shaped how we structured our "knowledge" about the world. We believed that ant colonies took orders from their queen and that some organizing force — obviously — was responsible for the overwhelming complexity of the world around us. We inscribed this basic misunderstanding into our social organizations — every tribe with its own leader, every company with its own CEO. Only recently have we come to understand the seemingly less plausible explanation that the queen, metaphorically speaking, has no more agency than her lowliest drone. And that contrary to centuries of commonly held belief, there is no central authority behind speciation, the relentless production of variety and difference in the life forms around us. This principle—emergence over authority—precedes the others because it provides the cornerstone on which the others rest. What if we built institutions and governments that reflected that reality, instead of reinforcing a bygone fallacy? The fact is, we already do. Consider the fight to eradicate tuberculosis.

Mycobacterium tuberculosis is spread through airborne particles—a single sneeze can contain forty thousand infectious droplets, but it takes only ten to contract the disease. The tubercle bacilli lodge inside the victim's lungs. The human immune system dispatches the local cops, who trap the bacilli. Most of the cells die, but the tricky *M. tuberculosis* can bide its time. It's estimated that a full third of the human population is infected with the disease, which may remain latent for a month, a year, or a lifetime. In about 10 percent of cases, however, the bacilli escape the protective barrier our immune system sets up around them and rapidly reproduce, eventually filling the lungs and killing about half of all people infected.[7]

As old as mankind itself, tuberculosis didn't become an epidemic until the eighteenth century,[8] following the great migration of its hosts into dense urban slums in which a single sneeze could infect an entire family.[9] By 1820, "consumption," as it was known, took the life of one in four Europeans. After World War I the disease went into a steep decline, the result of improved sanitation and sophisticated antibiotics. By 1985 there were fewer than ten cases per one hundred thousand in the United States.[10] It seemed to be on the verge of elimination.

Then *M. tuberculosis* outwitted us again. Sometimes the antibiotics were incorrectly prescribed. Some patients forgot to complete their regimen. Prison inmates and tuberculosis patients in developing countries were especially likely to get incomplete doses. A miniature version of *Survivor* ensued, as these partial treatments knocked out the weakest *M. tuberculosis* and allowed the strong—those that possessed genetic mutations immunizing them against the antibiotics—to flourish. This drug-resistant strain prospered and had many offspring, all sharing the same mutation.[11]

Tuberculosis isn't the only pathogen to follow this evolutionary path. According to the World Health Organization, drug-resistant diseases pose one of the greatest public health crises in years. "Without urgent, coordinated action by many stakeholders," says Dr. Keiji Fukuda, WHO's assistant director-general for health security, "the world is headed for a post-antibiotic era, in which common infections and minor injuries which have been treatable for decades can once again kill."[12]

In 2013 one urgent coordinated action was taken by a group of researchers from nine countries across Europe. "To defeat a modern disease," they declared, "you need modern weapons."[13] And one of those weapons was a new, emergent way of organizing research.

Enter the bacteriophage, a virus that targets bacteria. A sort of lunar capsule with long spindly legs, it might well haunt your nightmares were it not, in this case, in the employ of the good guys.

The European researchers, who call themselves Team Bettencourt after the Paris institution where the project is based, have reprogrammed the phage to do something beneficial. The phage inserts a protein that has been instructed to home in on the genetic mutation that makes the *M. tuberculosis* strain immune to antibiotics. The protein snips the strands of double helix that bookend the offending sequence, as easily as one of us might delete this sentence after writing it. With this small tweak to the DNA of *M. tuberculosis*—its source code—the bacterium is again susceptible to a standard drug regime. The Bettencourt group has also demonstrated how they could make a special tissue that can diagnose the disease on the spot, a great advantage in those regions worst affected by tuberculosis outbreaks. With the tweaking of a few lines of code within the bacteria's DNA, one of the most prolific killers of the human species could go the way of smallpox.

It might be a few years before Team Bettencourt's therapies are available to the public. So far the intercellular warfare described above has been restricted to test tubes using a "safe" bacteria designed to mimic *M. tuberculosis*, and Team Bettencourt developed its groundbreaking treatment for the International Genetically

Engineered Machine, or iGEM, competition.[14] Most of the researchers were still working on their degrees.

iGEM isn't your traditional science fair, but then, synthetic biology—creating new genetic sequences to program living things with new properties and functions, like new forms of chocolate or a yeast that produces an antimalarial drug—isn't your traditional scientific discipline. "There was a time when science advanced by locking small teams of researchers up in their labs until they produced some minor breakthrough," says Randy Rettberg, the former MIT scientist who helped start iGEM. "Science won't work that way in the future, and synthetic biology doesn't operate that way now.[15] Having emerged in the era of open-source software and Wikileaks, synthetic biology is becoming an exercise in radical collaboration between students, professors, and a legion of citizen scientists who call themselves biohackers. Emergence has made its way into the lab.

As far as disciplines go, synthetic biology is still in its infancy, but it has the potential to impact humanity in ways we can scarcely imagine. Molecular computers could pick up where the silicon chip leaves off, packing a supercomputer onto the head of a pin. The entire human race could be reprogrammed to be immune to all viruses. Reengineered *E. coli* could poop out enough jet fuel to power an airliner across the Atlantic.[16] Imagine giant collecting ponds of the bacteria capable of satisfying the global thirst for fossil fuel. Maybe you'll want an exotic pet? Try one of the boutique, pint-sized elephants on offer at the local GeneFab, or program your own.

"You can't predict the future of a scientific field," says George Church, a geneticist at Harvard and MIT. Church is often criticized for hyping the field of synthetic biology—he has promoted the idea of "de-extincting" the Neanderthal and the woolly mammoth[17]—but in person he seems less a provocateur than a realist. Asked whether some of the more outlandish ideas around synthetic biology were far-fetched, he shrugged and pointed out that no one could have predicted the emergence of an easy, high-speed technology that would allow us to map the human genome. "Gene sequencing is declining in price and increasing in speed at a rate six times that of Moore's law," Church says. "Ten years ago no one could have predicted that would happen."[18] (Moore's law holds that computer processing speeds will double every two years.)

While Team Bettencourt's project was brilliant, it was also largely theoretical—it *should* be possible, given extensive expertise, time, and funding, to create a virus that reprograms tuberculosis. The realistic odds of instituting such a therapy received a major boost with the rapid adoption of genetic editing, now standard operating procedure for the bio-curious, as civilians attending the community biohacking labs springing up around the world are called. "The science is moving very quickly," says Church, who pioneered many of the techniques employed in synthetic biology. "Many wonders might come to pass well within our lifetimes....Or," he says with a mordant smile, "some bored thirteen-year-old could engineer a virus that wipes out the human race. It's all possible, and the question is, do we feel lucky?"

● ● ●

Exotic scientific disciplines aren't the only areas of human endeavor undergoing a transition to new ways of generating discoveries or promoting innovation. Call it citizen science or crowdsourcing or open innovation, but what the rise of synthetic biology shows is that soon we'll simply call it standard operating procedure. The triumph of emergence — expertise and knowledge emerging out of distributed networks like the Internet — over authority amounts to a tectonic shift in the way knowledge is produced and distributed. The age of emergence has replaced the age of authority. Institutions like iGEM aren't peripheral to the academic discipline, but integral to it.

In traditional systems, from manufacturing to government, most decisions are made at the top. While employees may be encouraged to suggest products and programs, it's the managers and other people in authority who consult with experts and decide which of the suggestions to implement. This process is usually slow, encrusted in layers of bureaucracy, and encumbered by a conservative proceduralism.

Emergent systems presume that every individual within that system possesses unique intelligence that would benefit the group. This information is shared when people make choices about what ideas or projects to support, or, crucially, take that information and use it to innovate.

This shift has become possible because the cost of innovation has plummeted as new tools have become widely available. Cheap, effective 3-D printers have made prototyping a breeze; knowledge once accessible only inside large corporations or academic institutions can now be found through online courseware or within communities like DIYbio, a collection of citizen scientists who engage in the kind of genetic experiments that were only recently the stuff of expensive, exclusive laboratories.[19]

Finally, crowdfunding sites like Kickstarter and Indiegogo have built nearly frictionless platforms for raising money to develop anything from small art projects to major consumer appliances. These are real-time examples of emergence in action. They allow creators to test the validity of that unique information — a water bottle turned Super Soaker! — with a large group of potential customers. This built-in social aspect makes crowdfunding useful even for projects that have venture capital or other sources of funding, and invaluable for those that don't. Early success on crowdfunding sites also signals to professional investors that a project resonates with the public, giving innovators an opportunity to access sources of capital that might otherwise have remained out of reach.[20]

Capital in hand, our innovators-slash-entrepreneurs can easily extend their resources, and discover some they didn't know they were missing, through crowdsourcing. Rather than hiring large teams of engineers, designers, and programmers, start-ups and individuals can tap into a global community of freelancers and volunteers who can provide the skills they lack.[21]

Another important component in the move toward emergence over authority has been the proliferation of free and low-cost online and community education. This not only includes formal classes, such as edX, but also educational websites like Khan Academy, hands-on classes at maker- and hackerspaces, and informal peer tutoring conducted online or in person. The more opportunities people have to learn new skills, the more innovative they become.[22]

All of these advances are creating a de facto system in which people worldwide are empowered to learn, design, develop, and participate in acts of creative disobedience. Unlike authoritarian systems, which enable only incremental change, emergent systems foster the kind of nonlinear innovation that can react quickly to the kind of rapid changes that characterize the network age.

● ● ●

Among the most underappreciated qualities of a great scientist is the willingness to look foolish. In the fall of 1995, Tom Knight was a senior research scientist at MIT, the inventor of several key technologies in the development of computing, and the founder of a public company. Yet he found himself one September day in an intro-level biology course surrounded by sophomores. "I think they were wondering who this weird old man was," says Knight with a chuckle. "But I had to learn one side of the pipette from another."[23] (The pipette is like a highly refined eyedropper.) Knight had realized a central fact of the coming century: Biology *is* technology. But he was one of only a handful of people who knew it.

Knight had received his PhD designing integrated circuits, the technology that operates everything from your car to your computer to your alarm clock. By 1990 he realized that he was likely to outlive the silicon chip. "You could predict that by 2014 or so Moore's law would hit a ceiling." The observation that the number of transistors on a given chip will double every two years has held steady for more than fifty years, but "eventually you could see it would run into the laws of physics." In other words, a transistor can only be so many atoms wide. As it happens, Knight's prediction has occurred; in recent years Moore's law has begun to plateau.

"It was clear we would have to switch from assembling things physically, which is how we had been making semiconductors, to assembling them chemically." And the best chemistry in the world, he realized, took place at the cellular level. The most likely successor to the integrated circuit, Knight decided, would be the living cell. "I decided I would basically become a grad student in biology."

Knight had always regarded biology as impossibly messy. "The assumption I made — and that I think all the engineers in the world made — was that life was so incredibly complicated that anyone with any sense would just throw up their hands and say, 'No hope.'" A chance discovery changed his mind. A colleague handed him a paper by the biophysicist Harold Morowitz.[24] There's a pecking order in biology: "My organism is much more complicated than your organism." Funding and prestige tend to be arranged on the same basis. But Morowitz wasn't interested in eukaryotic, or multicellular, life forms. Instead he had spent his long career studying the origin of life on Earth, and that meant looking at the very simplest of life forms, the humble, single-celled *Mycoplasma*.

To put this in perspective, the human genome contains about 3.2 billion base pairs (the smallest fundamental units of our genetic code). Science has made great strides in sequencing, or reading, the genome. But given the size of the text, we still don't understand much of what we've read. *M. tuberculosis*, by contrast, contains as few as half a million base pairs. "It's about three thousand times simpler," Knight says. "So you can at least fool yourself into thinking you know everything there is to know about it."

In the summer of 1996, Knight attended a conference hosted by DARPA, the Department of Defense R&D group. He proposed to study what he called "cellular computing," the idea that cells might be programmed to do useful things, including pick up where the silicon chip would eventually leave off. Within a few years he had constructed an entire lab, complete with incubators and test tubes and an autoclave, in his perch at MIT's computer science department. "My colleagues thought I was nuts," he says with a laugh. "Here's all this mysterious biochemistry equipment in the middle of a computer lab."

Knight isn't an engineer by vocation. It is his calling, a passion, a discipline, a system of belief. Engineers think differently than biologists, he says. "My biologist friends would say, 'We've learned everything there is to learn about *E. coli*, Tom. Why study them?' The translation of that is, 'I've learned everything that I'm going to learn... from studying *E. coli* and all of the rest of it is detail which I'm not interested in.'"

Engineers, Knight says, think differently. "If your goal is to study complicated biology, that's fine. But if your goal is to take these very simple biological systems and understand everything there is to know about them with the intention of going in and being able to modify them, and to build on that and to do something different, that's an entirely different perspective and it requires a different degree of understanding," says Knight. "And that's very much more profound than what they have." To an engineer, understanding means taking it apart and putting it back together again.

In 1998, Knight had started studying *Vibrio fischeri*, a bioluminescent bacteria found inside the bobtailed squid. The squid feeds the bacteria sugar and amino acids. In exchange, the bacteria emanate just enough light to match the moon's rays, rendering the squid virtually invisible at night.

But what interested Knight was how the bioluminescence is triggered, because *Vibrio fischeri* only illuminate inside the squid. "The bacteria excrete small amounts of a certain chemical," he explains. "Out in the ocean that chemical just washes away, but inside the squid it builds up, and when it hits a certain density it triggers the bioluminescence." In other words, the cells are sending each other signals. Knight figured that he could isolate the genetic sequences that control the bioluminescence and "use it in a way that nature had never intended." Reproducing cellular communication on command proved to be a tall order.

By this time Knight had begun to attract a cadre of similarly minded young scientists. Two of his collaborators from this era, Drew Endy and Ron Weiss, would go on to make crucial contributions to the development of synthetic biology. (That is why Knight is sometimes called the "father of synthetic biology.") Like Knight, Endy and Weiss were drawn to the intoxicating prospect of applying the principles of programming to genetics, and like Knight, neither scientist had trained as a biologist. Endy originally intended to be an environmental engineer. Weiss, a programming prodigy, came to biology from his work on "smart dust," in which nanoscale computers are embedded into pliable materials like paint or roads. "I think it's fair to say we were rank amateurs at this point," Knight says with a laugh. "But we were learning fast."

As the millennium dawned, synthetic biology was an engineering discipline in theory more than practice. A small but growing number of computer scientists, engineers, and physicists were recognizing the revolutionary applications that might one day result from synthesizing genetic material, but there was little in the way of a proof of concept.

This changed in January 2000, when the Boston University bioengineer James Collins and his colleagues demonstrated a "genetic toggle switch" in E. coli.[25] By sending an external signal, the scientists could trigger a gene to begin the process of transcription (the first step of gene expression, where DNA is transcribed to RNA, then usually translated into protein). Send the signal again and the cell turned off, like a light switch, but in bacteria.

In the same month, another landmark paper was published in the journal Nature. Scientists had engineered an oscillatory circuit that produced proteins at ordered intervals. They called it the "repressilator," for the repressor gene that helped control the alternating genetic expression.[26] The two papers showed that complex biological processes could be synthesized from scratch.

And then the next year Knight and Weiss succeeded in engineering the intercellular communication between *Vibrio fischeri*, which is to say, they were able to turn on the lights. Such a project can now be conducted at a high school science f, and even then, Knight says, it wasn't significant within the field of biology. "It was, however, seminal in the engineering sense. A biologist looked at what we did and said, 'Why would you do that?' But engineers looked at it and saw we were taking a baby step in an entirely new direction."

Yet reproducing any one of these experiments was an incredible chore. Fabrication labs had sprung up that would synthesize the necessary genetic sequences, allowing Knight and his team to focus on the experiment at hand. But these were prohibitively expensive. And besides, engineers that they were, Knight and his collaborators didn't want to reproduce an experiment once, but over and over again with the same level of consistency one found in any other realm of engineering. And that meant creating a set of standardized parts.

The idea was to create a collection of DNA sequences that performed set, well-understood functions. These could be combined in infinite varieties. They were like bricks, and so in 2003 Knight published a paper that laid out a plan to create a catalog of the building blocks of the genetic code.[27] These "BioBricks," as he called them, would be gathered in a Registry of Standard Biological Parts. One, a "promoter," might initiate transcription of a segment of DNA. Another brick might generate a certain protein. These predictable parts would have predictable functions, again and again and again.

Inspiration was drawn from two disparate sources. One was a list of circuit components called the TTL Data Book, which cataloged thousands of circuit components and their functions. "You'd look up your part, write down the part number, and call it in. Presto." The other inspiration was considerably more down-to-earth: "The early thinking, the early metaphor, people who like to tinker and pull things apart like LEGOs. And so the metaphor was centered around the idea of these reusable parts, these LEGO blocks that you could put together."

One could say that Knight and his collaborators were approaching the study of biology like any engineer might: Take the object apart; discover its constituent parts; then see how it might be improved by reconfiguring it. But this neglects the far more audacious goals embedded within iGEM. The creation of a library of standardized BioBricks is above all an act of *social engineering*. With LEGOs, you don't have to be an architect to express a unique vision of the intersection between form and space. And while synthetic biology remains in its infancy, it already bears the unmistakable imprint of this egalitarian vision. Knight, Endy, and Rettberg didn't so much "create" or "launch" a new scientific discipline; from the earliest days their efforts were spent in creating the conditions by which it might grow organically, fed by people and ideas they couldn't begin to anticipate. Far more than any field before it, synthetic biology has been the product of emergence.

This isn't unexpected, says David Sun Kong, a promising young scientist who participated in some of the first iGEM competitions as a PhD student at the MIT Media Lab. After all synbio got started because, in a sense, someone's chocolate landed in someone else's peanut butter. "The pioneers were civil engineers, computer scientists, and electrical engineers." The pioneers might not appreciate the analogy, but just as with individual slime mold cells, synthetic biology is the whole that is greater than the sum of its parts.

By lowering the bar of entry and emulating the context of play, Knight and others encouraged a more diverse and creative set of minds to contribute to the field. "There's a fundamental belief that biology should be incredibly democratic. How it works, that knowledge, but also an understanding of how to manipulate it," says Kong, who also runs EMW, an art, technology, and community center near MIT. One of its programs, Street Bio, explores the interface between engineered biology and the street—the people, culture, and products that will shape how biology leaves the lab and enters our everyday lives. "There's an idea pretty common to our field that biology in general, and biotechnology in particular, is too important to be left up to the experts."[28]

It was far easier to propose the registry than to actually create it. Unlike rebar or servo motors or integrated circuits, there is no standardization to the parts that compose living creatures. Every BioBrick would consist of a genetic sequence whose traits—the ability to trigger nearby cells to glow luminescent, for instance — are well known. This sequence would then be synthesized from nucleotides, base by base. At the time, very little of the genome — even the fairly straightforward genome of prokaryotic life forms — was "characterized," or established and understood. Knight and his collaborators didn't need more time in the lab or more funding. They needed an army. Soon they would have one.

PS:
Pushing the
Pendulum Back

In 2003, several years after the Internet birthed blogging, I wrote a paper on "emergent democracy," with the help of an optimistic community of bloggers. I and my coauthors firmly believed that this revolution would fundamentally and rather quickly change the nature of democracy for the better.

When "The Arab Spring" erupted in 2010, we thought we were proven right. What soon became clear, however, was that we had helped created the tools for the emergent overthrow of governments, but not necessarily the emergence of responsible self-governance. Our hopes turned to dismay as we watched the region turn from the optimism of the Jasmine Revolution in Tunisia to the emergence of ISIS.

Further dismaying is the trend for these tools to be used less for an open and "democratic" network of blogs often run on self-hosted servers, to the walled garden of Facebook and short-form chatter on Twitter. Unfortunately, it has become quite clear that the hateful and uncaring side of the Internet is now as organized and effective—if not more so—at using this new social media to further its causes and voices than the side that saw the Internet as a new-found avenue for open discourse and democratic movements.

We are now in a phase of emergent democracy that is quite distressing. But witnessing this has given those of us who held such optimism a decade ago even greater resolve to develop both the tools and momentum to fulfill our original dream of the technology advancing democracy in a positive way.

As a step in this direction, we have established a new Scalable Cooperation research group at the Media Lab, run by Associate Professor Iyad Rahwan, a Syrian. When I was interviewing Iyad for the faculty position he now holds, he said that he was inspired by both the success and failure of the emergent democracy movement, and remains committed to building the tools for scalable cooperation to advance new forms of democracy.

I look forward to working with Iyad and others in a concerted effort to push the pendulum back in the other direction and show that the arc of the Internet can indeed bend toward justice.

—Joi Ito

2   Pull over Push

The Pacific Plate is something of a sprinter, as far as geological bodies go. Every year it moves three and a half inches in a northwesterly direction. About a hundred miles off the coast of Japan, this giant slab of oceanic crust rams into the far slower Okhotsk Plate, sliding beneath it in a process geologists call subduction. This creates a lot of unresolved tension. The Pacific Plate doesn't slide smoothly down into the Earth's mantle. Instead, the upper plate catches on the lower one, bending to its superior force. Eventually, about every thousand years, like the steel teeth inside a music box, the Okhotsk Plate springs back into place.

That's what happened shortly before 3:00 p.m. on March 11, 2011. The resulting earthquake measured 9.0 on the Richter scale—so powerful that it shifted Earth's axis, and moved Japan nearly eight feet closer to the United States. The quake itself damaged thousands of buildings, destroyed highways, and caused one dam to fail. But the worst was yet to come.

The Fukushima Daiichi nuclear plant lies just 110 miles from the epicenter of the quake. The initial shock waves reached the engineers within thirty seconds. "Suddenly I heard the earth rumble, like a fierce growl," a general manager at the plant told a TV interviewer. "It was an extremely intense earthquake, but it wasn't only strong, it was also terribly long." Even a moderately severe earthquake rarely lasts longer than forty seconds. The 3/11 earthquake, as it became known in Japan, lasted six minutes.

Like most buildings in the immediate vicinity of the quake, the nuclear plant lost all power after the first few temblors. A set of diesel generators automatically kicked into gear, but it meant Fukushima was now operating without a safety net. Inagaki and his staff had shut down the reactors as soon as the initial quake passed, but the uranium would remain extremely hot for days. Electricity powered the pumps that kept cool water passing continuously over the fuel rods. Stop the flow, and the water quickly boils off, leading with terrifying speed to a full-blown meltdown.

As of 3:00 p.m., fifteen minutes after the initial jolt, this still seemed like a remote possibility. In a nation accustomed to the violent consequences of plate tectonics, Fukushima was designed to withstand the effects of both an earthquake and any tsunami that might result. The facility's six reactors sat thirty feet above sea level and behind a thirty-three-foot seawall. By 3:02 the government's tsunami warning center predicted that the region would soon be hit by ten-foot waves.

At 3:25, airborne tsunami spotters reported the first set of waves approaching Fukushima. As 650 employees made a mad dash up the hill behind the nuclear plant, the first of seven waves crashed into the seawall. Some were nearly twice its height. Two workers drowned within minutes, and seawater swamped the turbines, the generators, and all of the wiring for four of the six reactors as Inagaki and his team were thrown into complete darkness. Even the clamor of alarms from the initial quake went quiet, leaving the control room in a terrifying silence. Without power to cool the fuel rods, a meltdown was now inevitable.[1]

Tokyo Electric Power Company, or TEPCO, had long held that the maximum height of any possible tsunami would fall well below twenty feet. And Fukushima wasn't the only area to suffer from this tragic failure of imagination and planning. This estimate was shared up and down the northeast coast of Honshu, Japan's main island. The mistake was inscribed into emergency drills, evacuation shelters, and physical impediments. Japan built most of its seawalls, levees, and other tsunami safeguards after 1960, when the great Valdivia earthquake—the most powerful ever recorded, at magnitude 9.5—struck Chile. In twenty-two hours a tsunami traveled across the Pacific and struck Japan with great force. Waves fourteen feet high were reported, and more than 150 people died.

These precautionary measures conformed to a kind of unassailable industrial-age logic. Earthquakes capable of generating such massive tsunamis are incredibly rare. Is it even possible to plan for so-called black swan events (incidents whose very rarity lull people into the false belief that the terminal disease will never strike their family, the market will never fail, and the government will not be overthrown)?[2] In fact, if you adjust your field of observation, Japanese tsunami preparations constrained their view to recent history. There hadn't been a quake larger than 8.5 in that part of Japan for over four hundred years. A 2010 map of seismic activity in Japan didn't even highlight the area.

A geologist, however, has a different frame of reference from a utilities executive. In 2009, Yukinobu Okamura, the director of Japan's Active Fault and Research Center, told TEPCO that the subduction zone just off the Fukushima coast had been the site of the Jogan earthquake, a catastrophic tectonic event in the year 869.[3] We know about the Jogan quake from the Japanese emperor's official records, and when scientists took core samples of earth from the surrounding areas, they not only discovered abundant evidence that the 869 quake had produced waves far greater than those anticipated by TEPCO, but that such quakes had occurred every five hundred to eight hundred years.[4] Since it had been more than eleven hundred years since the Jogan earthquake, Okamura told TEPCO, the coastline near Fukushima was overdue for a major tsunami.

Officials ignored the warning, and despite heroic efforts by Inagaki and his team, who were on-site in the weeks after the tsunami, by March 12 three of the plant's cores had melted down, releasing significant radioactive material into the air and the ocean in the worst nuclear disaster since Chernobyl. Just how much radioactive material wasn't immediately clear. In the aftermath, the Japanese government had evacuated 134,000 people from a twenty-kilometer radius around the plant. The United States, however, told its citizens to avoid anywhere within a eighty-kilometer radius.[5] The Japanese government, its resources stretched thin, seemed to have lost control of the situation. Over the next several days it failed to inform the public about radiation levels, in part because there were few people capable of measuring them in the first place.

But like TEPCO's failure to prepare for an earthquake that scientists considered a matter of when, not if, the government was struggling with a crisis of its own way of thinking. Like most institutions that evolved in a pre-Internet era, the Japanese Nuclear Safety Commission was built for a command-and-control management style. Information from the front lines, like from the Fukushima plant, had to work its way up through many tiers of management. Decisions would then follow the same route back down.

The approach by Fukushima, and the disastrous results that stemmed from it, give us a case study in two divergent views of decision making. The result in this case was that resources—expertise in the measurement and analysis of radiation contamination—were *pushed* to where the decision-makers believed they could be used best. It's a cumbersome, command-and-control approach in the best of times; in a nuclear emergency, it can have fatal consequences. And yet for hundreds of years it was the best any of us had. In the network era that's no longer true. The best use of human resources is to *pull* them into a project, using just what's needed, when it's needed most. Timing is key; while emergence is about the use of the many, over the few, to solve problems, pull takes that notion one step further, using what's needed only at the precise moment it's needed most. The idea would have sounded utterly foreign to the executives at TEPCO. A pull strategy requires transparency and a two-way flow of information in and out of the organization; TEPCO's institutional culture emphasized minimum disclosure. But a group of concerned citizens from every corner of the globe were about to give them an object lesson in the power of pull.

● ● ●

When the quake hit, Joi was struggling to fall asleep in a Boston hotel room, trying to overcome his jet lag after a long day of interviews to become the director of the Media Lab. Having never received his undergraduate degree, Joi was an unusual choice to lead a prestigious academic institution. Of course, that may have been part of his appeal.

After Nicholas Negroponte took a leave of absence in 2000, MIT offered an interim appointment to Walter Bender, a fellow traveler from Negroponte's days in the Architecture Machine group. Bender maintained a steady hand on the tiller until 2006, when the Institute hired Frank Moss, a successful entrepreneur and MIT PhD. The Lab had entered an awkward transition—at twenty, it was no longer a radical start-up able to get by on the brilliance of its extraordinary founder and faculty. Moss had deep experience and success managing complex, ambitious organizations, but with the Media Lab he faced a series of unique challenges.

There was a perception — among journalists if not their readers—that the Internet and the waves of technological innovation that followed in its wake had left the Lab flat-footed. Lacking Negroponte's charisma and vision, and with a focus on running the Lab more like a business with an eye to advancing research of interest to the Lab's corporate sponsors,[6] many felt Moss failed to kindle the kind of excitement that had once thrummed through the Media Lab, inspiring faculty, funders, and the public alike. By 2011, the Lab was widely seen as having lost both the focus and the edge that once gave it such cultural cachet. When Moss decided to leave at the end of his term, the faculty and staff were determined to bring in someone who could both return the Lab to its founding principles and lead it in uncertain times.

After an initial conversation to gauge Joi's interest in the position, the search committee had recommended that he not apply, due to his lack of academic credentials. But after the selection committee burned through a long list of more likely suspects, Negroponte was asked to go back to see if Joi might still be interested. A flurry of calls followed, and a few days later Joi was boarding a flight to Boston.

Around 2:00 a.m., Joi finally surrendered to his jet lag and reached for his laptop. It had been an exhausting day—nine back-to-back interviews with some of the brightest scientists, artists, and designers in America. It left him giddy and nervous and supremely awake. As soon as he opened his email it was evident that something terrible had happened. His inbox was overflowing with anxious messages full of questions about an earthquake and a tsunami and, most confusing of all, explosions at a nuclear plant. Joi flipped on the hotel television, and quickly got a sense of the scale of the disaster.

The next few hours passed in a blur. The Internet still seemed to function in most parts of Japan, but cell service did not. First Joi tried to reach his wife, who had been in their home outside Tokyo. That part of the country had weathered the quake and the tsunami with relatively little damage or loss of life. Joi's extended family, however, lived on the coast not far from the Fukushima plant.

As night gave way to a blustery, rainswept morning, Joi still hadn't managed to reach his wife, and he was facing another thirteen interviews at the Media Lab. In stolen moments between interviews he tracked down his friends and family in an overlapping series of emails, online chats, and Skype calls. Over the course of the day, two facts emerged: One, all of Joi's loved ones were safe. Two, the visit had been a success. Joi was now the leading candidate to fill Negroponte's big shoes. Not that he had much time to think about career prospects.

All Japanese caught outside the country when the quake hit faced a kind of survivor's guilt. The big topic among Joi's far-flung, frequently flying friends was whether they could help more by returning to Japan—which was still being racked by aftershocks and transportation snafus—or by doing what they could from wherever they happened to be. This group of bright minds quickly settled on the troubling question of how much radiation had been released and where it had gone. TEPCO and the Japanese government continued to follow their outdated (and ultimately self-defeating) playbook and released virtually no information at all. Joi and his friends developed their own plan.

Within days, a group of volunteers and advisers had emerged from those online conversations, forming the core of what would become Safecast.[7] Their first order of business was to obtain as many Geiger counters as possible. Dan Sythe, whose company, International Medcom, produced them, provided some. Pieter Franken, an executive director of Monex Securities, tried to buy more, as did Joi and Sean Bonner, an entrepreneur in Los Angeles who had been working with Joi to produce a conference with Tokyo's Digital Garage. Within twenty-four hours of the tsunami, though, they had become nearly impossible to find—in part because people in California and Washington were concerned about radiation reaching the West Coast of the United States.[8]

If the team was going to secure enough Geiger counters to take accurate readings throughout the affected area, it was going to need to build its own. Bonner provided connections to Tokyo Hacker-Space and Chris Wang, better known as Akiba, who is now a researcher at Keio University Internet Research Lab and the founder of Freaklabs. Andrew "bunnie"[9] Huang, an old friend and Joi's hardware guru, came on board as well. Huang is an MIT alumnus and astute chronicler of the Chinese hardware industry, who's probably best known for hacking the Xbox,[10] creating the Chumby—an open-source networked hardware appliance—and helping people around the world with their hardware, firmware, and software designs.

Members of the team reached Fukushima by mid-April and started taking measurements a week later. They quickly realized that readings could change dramatically from one side of a street to the other, but the available data averaged readings over a wide area. Some six months later, the team learned that evacuees had been sent into neighborhoods more contaminated than the ones they had left. The government's data, much of which had been collected in helicopter flyovers, seemed to be less accurate than the volunteers'.

Now that the team had begun collecting information, it needed a way to distribute it. Aaron Huslage, an engineer in North Carolina, introduced Joi to Marcelino Alvarez, whose Portland, Oregon–based Web and mobile company, Uncorked Studios, had already launched a website to map aggregated radiation data. Ray Ozzie— the creator of Lotus Notes and former chief software architect of

Microsoft—volunteered his expertise in data analysis. He turned over the name Safecast and its URL to the project. Ozzie also made the suggestion that Geiger counters strapped to cars could collect more data, more quickly, than those carried by hand. Bonner, Franken, and a team at Tokyo HackerSpace set to work designing and building a new type of Geiger counter, the bGeigie, which fits in a container about the size of a bento box and includes a GPS receiver.

All of the pieces were now in place. With nearly $37,000 from a Kickstarter campaign and additional funding from Reid Hoffman, Digital Garage, and The John S. and James L. Knight Foundation, Safecast began deploying Geiger counters and gathering data from citizen scientists across Japan. By March 2016 the project had collected more than fifty million data points, all available under a Creative Commons CC0 public domain dedication, which places them in the public domain. Researchers around the world have used the Safecast dataset not only to learn more about how the radiation from Fukushima Daiichi has spread, but also to learn what the normal levels of background radiation in different areas are. This information gives scientists and the public a useful baseline in the event of another nuclear accident.[11]

● ● ●

Safecast points the way to a radically more efficient way of organizing intellectual and physical capital. "Pull" draws resources from participants' networks as they need them, rather than stockpiling materials and information. For a manager within an established firm, this can mean reducing costs, increasing the flexibility to react to quickly changing circumstances, and, most important of all, stimulating the creativity needed to rethink the way his or her job is done.

For the entrepreneur—and we use the term loosely, to include anyone with a good idea and a passion to find an audience for it—pull means the difference between success and failure. As with emergence over authority, pull strategies exploit the reduced cost of innovation that new methods of communication, prototyping, fund-raising, and learning have made available.

So-called "push-pull" strategies originated, aptly enough, in the fields of logistics and supply chain management, but in 2005 John Hagel, a management consultant, and John Seely Brown, the former chief scientist at Xerox Corp., wrote a series of articles apply-ing the concept to a much broader array of fields. It has a particularly dramatic potential in hardware, since pull could ostensibly transform the entire supply chain in that industry. The logic of pull would be that supply shouldn't even be generated until demand has emerged.[12]

In the upside-down, bizarro universe created by the Internet, the very assets on your balance sheet—from printing presses to lines of code — are now liabilities from the perspective of agility. Instead, we should try to use resources that can be utilized just in time, for just that time necessary, then relinquished. Amazon allows customers to rent a cozy little corner in one of their nine gargantuan server farms. How much depends strictly on demand. Traffic to a site hosted on Amazon's cloud might spike, then decline just as rapidly, and the system adjusts automatically.[13]

From its earliest days, the Internet has been, in tech-nologist David Weinberger's words, built from "small pieces loosely joined."[14] This is antithetical to the traditional corporate model, but it has allowed a variety of niche organizations to thrive online by providing products and services that fulfill specific needs. Together, they make up a complex ecosystem that relies on open standards and interoperability rather than central, top-down control.

As Daniel Pink noted in his TEDGlobal talk "The Puzzle of Motivation," this is a key difference between Microsoft's failed *Encarta* encyclopedia, an expensive, professionally designed, push-based product, and Wikipedia's amateur-led, pull-based platform, which was infinitely more successful.[15] In this environment, no one person or organization controls the network. Instead, it is built on a platform of "rough consensus and running code," the motto of the

Internet Engineering Task Force, itself a loosely organized that addresses engineering problems with the Web as they arise.[16] Companies like AOL, which originally took a more traditional approach to doing business, have faltered in these conditions, while companies like Twitter have flourished.

The early AOL model was push-based. It attempted to provide consumers with a full range of services, while controlling their access to the network. Because its products were often incompatible with Internet standards, it effectively locked its customers into a walled garden. As AOL later learned—though not nearly as well or as fast as its shareholders would have liked—push is antithetical to the inherent attributes of the network itself, its DNA, if you will. Online gaming companies like Blizzard Entertainment embraced a pull strategy early, and in Blizzard's case, quickly turned it to their great advantage. Blizzard treats its players and its community of fans as part of its organization—in fact, many players have become employees. Player-generated ideas have been incorporated into the game. The developers often share the inner workings of the game and even allow fans to use copyrighted content to create videos or other derivative goods. It's very hard to see where the company ends and the customer begins in these systems.

You see pull at work not only with parts and labor, but with financial capital as well. Kickstarter allows people to raise what they want in a fashion that's far more agile and responsive than traditional fund-raising methods. Crowdfunding demonstrates that the same logic behind Amazon Web Services—the "distributed computing" division—works for the aggregation of financial capital as well. People often associate crowdfunding with dubious ideas for new products, but Experiment.com shows that the same system can be used to fund serious scientific research.[17]

Beyond crowdfunding, crowdsourcing also provides independent creators with affordable options for extending their resources. Rather than hiring large teams of engineers, designers, and programmers, start-ups and individuals can tap into a global community of freelancers and volunteers who can provide the skills they lack. This is, of course, also related to emergent systems, because none of the principles exist in a vacuum — they all feed into and inform each other.

The Safecast project showed that a dedicated group of volunteers guided by the ethos of the open software and hardware movements could build tools that were more accurate and more useful in a rapidly changing environment than the official tools provided by the government. They were able to provide people in the affected communities with actionable data, empowering them to look after themselves and their neighbors and inspiring them to create a foundation to help them help other people worldwide.

One of the reasons the Safecast team was able to mobilize so quickly was its access to social media and other online tools, which help like-minded innovators build communities that can provide knowledge, encouragement, and other intangible resources. These extended networks can also help locate tools, workspaces, and manufacturing facilities, further lowering the cost of innovation and allowing new ideas and projects to emerge without direction from a central authority.

Many of these projects have also benefited from modern prototyping technologies and supply chains, which are beginning to enable the same kind of rapid, low-cost innovation in hardware that has already occurred in software. This has allowed independent creators to develop sophisticated consumer products that would have been out of their reach even a few years ago. As this trend accelerates, we can expect to see ever more innovative hardware produced by small start-ups and individual inventors.

As the cost of innovation continues to fall, entire communities that have been sidelined by those in power will be able to organize themselves and become active participants in society and government. The culture of emergent innovation will allow everyone to feel a sense of both ownership and responsibility to each other and to the rest of the world, which will empower them to create more lasting change than the authorities who write policy and the law.

• • •

When most of us say we're not good at math, we mean something slightly different than does Jeremy Rubin, a recent MIT graduate whose hobbies include longboarding and radically re-inventing the medium of exchange we generally call money. "I don't feel I have a natural facility with numbers, so I was worried about falling behind," says Rubin, explaining why he had run through all the problem sets for a semester's worth of math curriculum in a weekend during high school. "One of the most important lessons I've learned here is about working hard, and that if you want to learn something—anything—you just force yourself to sit down and do the work."[18]

In the fall of 2013, his sophomore year, on top of the five courses he was taking, Rubin and some friends had started Tidbit, a company based around the digital currency Bitcoin. The project had already caught the attention of the venture capitalists who perpetually circle universities like MIT hoping to get in on the next next big thing. It was, Rubin recalls, welcome attention, but it left him frazzled and overworked.

It was about to get worse. On the morning of December 9, Rubin found a thick manila envelope crammed into his mailbox. It held a subpoena and interrogatories from the attorney general of New Jersey—a demand for Tidbit's source code, the Bitcoin accounts associated with it, and any other information pertaining to the formation of Rubin's company, including "all documents and correspondence concerning all breaches of security and/or unauthorized access to computers by you."[19] It was not, Rubin thought, a good way to start finals week.

Like so many other new digital ideas, Tidbit originated at a hackathon, a product of the epiphanies induced by mixing youthful optimism and generous doses of mild stimulants like Red Bull under a high-pressure deadline. The only requirement behind this particular hackathon, an annual competition called Node Knockout, was that it be written using the popular Javascript server Node.js, and be ready to submit at the end of a forty-eight-hour period.

What Rubin and his friends created over the next two days says a great deal about the power of pull over push, the still largely misunderstood cultural clash between the two, and why the students were as unlikely to anticipate that their idea would draw the ire of the authorities as the authorities were to imagine a software program that would allow people to trade a few spare cycles of their computer's processing power for the quintessentially modern luxury of not having to suffer obnoxious, buggy Web advertising.

Like the other principles in this book, the advantage of push over pull is more of an intuition than an idea. Tidbit cleverly exploited one of Bitcoin's basic properties: The currency itself is created by its users. These "miners" set their computers to perform the task of recording every Bitcoin transaction that ever occurs into a central ledger, or blockchain. Such is the mathematical complexity of this job that it requires enormous computing power—there are, for instance, vast server farms in China that do nothing but mine bitcoins around the clock.

With his skateboard and faded T-shirt and chino shorts, Rubin fits right in with the other aspiring programmers and scientists and entrepreneurs who make up much of MIT's undergraduate population. But there's a ferocious intelligence at work in Rubin, an intensity not everyone finds agreeable. Like all good hackathletes, he and his friends had started by identifying an existing problem that could be solved using technologies they were already excited about. The problem was that the primary business model for the news media—advertising—didn't work online. What if instead of subjecting readers to increasingly invasive and offensive ads, readers donated some spare CPUs—excess computing power—instead? For however long they were on the site their computers would perform some of that laborious math that goes into the creation of each bitcoin. By the end of the hackathon, Rubin and the rest of his team had not only demonstrated the basic business logic behind the idea, but they had also built an elegant little app that websites could install to make it happen. And it would all take place in the background; once the reader opted in, they wouldn't even know their computer had entered the mine.

The Node Knockout hackathon awarded them the top prize in innovation. Rubin and his friends hadn't quite solved the greatest crisis in the news media's history, but their ingenious approach to it gained the attention of the venture capitalists, and they were looking into creating an LLC and launching a company. And why not? Tidbit would hardly be the first innovative young company to spring from a hackathon.

Then New Jersey came calling. The attorney general hadn't accused Rubin or Tidbit of a committing any specific crime, but the subpoena's language could have been lifted from the state's computer fraud act, which carries some stiff penalties. The previous year the state had accused E-Sports Entertainment, a company that organized competitive video gaming contests, of embedding malicious code in its anticheating software. As a result, New Jersey alleged, some fourteen thousand subscribers unknowingly had their computers hijacked and turned into virtual slaves mining bitcoin. (The E-sports case was eventually settled, though the owner has admitted to participating in the scheme.)

In January 2014 the Electronic Frontier Foundation, a digital rights advocacy group, took on Rubin's case. On one hand, Tidbit indeed consisted of software that could in theory be used to mine bitcoins. On the other hand, as Rubin was quick to point out, users would have to opt in to such a program. More to the point, *the Tidbit code had never been functional.* It was a "proof of concept" that demonstrated that it worked in a contained environment for the purposes of showing off the idea. New Jersey claimed to have found the code surreptitiously mining away on the computers belonging to three separate New Jersey residents. And so Rubin spent much of his sophomore and junior years wondering whether he would be prosecuted for a project that was neither fraudulent nor functional.

● ● ●

Scientists and inventors are often all too ready to claim credit for an important discovery. So it is one of our age's more baffling mysteries that the man — or woman, or group of men and women — behind the biggest financial innovation since the ATM remains stubbornly, sincerely anonymous. It started on November 1, 2008, when someone calling himself Satoshi Nakamoto posted "Bitcoin: A Peer-to-Peer Electronic Cash System" to a cryptography mailing list.[20]

In his introduction, he wrote, "I've been working on a new electronic cash system that's fully peer-to-peer, with no trusted third party....The main properties: Double-spending is prevented with a peer-to-peer network. No mint or other trusted parties. Participants can be anonymous. New coins are made from Hashcash style proof-of-work. The proof-of-work for new coin generation also powers the network to prevent double-spending." Unless you're a cryptographer, much of that may fly well over your head. So let's bring it down to ground level.

To begin with, Bitcoin, unlike so many other technological innovations, deserves the hype. It could lift billions out of poverty, turn our modern banking system into a quaint relic, and generally perform no less magical a feat than creating money that functions without, well, money. It's also entirely possible that Bitcoin itself, the currency, collapses and becomes little more than an answer to a Trivial Pursuit question. So the second and far more important reason to pay attention is that the blockchain — the technology that makes Bitcoin possible—has implications far beyond the future of currencies and financial services. The blockchain is, in our estimation, likely to change the very relationship between individuals and institutions, a revolution in the nature of authority.

The importance of Bitcoin and the blockchain — in simple terms, the public ledger in which every Bitcoin transaction that has ever taken place is recorded—lies in its architecture, a structure based on the understanding that the network will *pull* the resources necessary to its formation and maintenance, without the need for a central director orchestrating, *pushing* the organization of those resources.

Satoshi's Bitcoin paper described a decentralized method for sending electronic payments without involving a third party—no central bank to issue the currency, no intermediaries needed to guarantee the transaction. Instead, the network itself would provide the assurances that humans have historically expected from their currency. To ensure that each bitcoin is wholly unique—that a user can't, in effect, double-spend a bitcoin by making more than one purchase with it—the details of the transaction are broadcast across the network, where they are entered into the public ledger, the blockchain.

If Satoshi (generally referred to by his pseudonymous first name) had tried to create a system by which individuals would be tasked with recording these transactions, Bitcoin would have remained little more than another obscure academic paper in the annals of cryptography. Instead, he leveraged people's acquisitiveness to do the work for him.

In order to create a functioning currency, Satoshi had to create artificial scarcity. The number of bitcoins had to be finite, or they would be worth less than a German mark during the 1920s. Gold is naturally scarce; dollars are scarce because the U.S. Treasury Department controls the monetary supply. Bitcoins, Satoshi determined, would be scarce because considerable computing effort would be needed to create each one. Each coin is in reality a long chain of digital signatures, and the work of creating new ones involves recording each and every transaction into blocks that are then added to the blockchain at a rate of roughly six per hour. These "proof of work" formulas are constructed so that it's exceedingly easy to verify a transaction, but nearly impossible to fake one. That's because every bitcoin transaction contains the "hash," or numerical identifier, of every transaction that came before it.

Because the total number of bitcoins is limited — no more than twenty-one million can be produced with the current code—and the rate of block creation stays fairly constant, the number of bitcoins created by each block must decline over time. Thus, the system is designed so that the proof-of-work functions used to verify transactions become increasingly difficult, making it harder to mine new bitcoins. The number of bitcoins created by the blockchain is set to decrease by 50 percent every four years. As a result, while the earliest bitcoin miners could use their personal computers to validate the blockchain, today's miners use specialized, high-end server farms. In late 2014, one of those operations comprised six sites in China that collectively produce eight petahashes of computation per second, creating 4,050 bitcoins per month. It's an indicator of how large the bitcoin market has grown that this massive effort claimed only 3 percent of global bitcoin mining operations.[21]

In fact, as this book went to press, Bitcoin underwent its second halving — meaning that the number of bitcoins generated per second decreased by one-half. Just before the first halving, a bitcoin was valued at around twelve dollars. Within a few months, it jumped in price by more than an order of magnitude. Before the halving occurred, there were any number of theories about what would happen — speculators anticipate a sudden spike spurred by smaller supply; game theorists feared that miners would fight for the last higher-rewarded block, or shut their machines off entirely; and many users, blissfully unaware of Bitcoin's economic policy, had no expectations at all. And when it did come, the halving was relatively uneventful. Considering the complexity of Bitcoin's economics, we won't try to predict the future, but will note that there will be sixty-four halvings before the subsidy fades to zero, spaced out over many years to come — or, put another way, sixty-four opportunities to debate how the halving will impact the Bitcoin ecosystem.

Bitcoin's decentralized design, which relies on CPUs and cryptographic algorithms rather than central banks and government authority, was apparently inspired by Satoshi's distrust of traditional financial transactions. In an essay describing the system, he wrote, "The root problem with conventional currency is all the trust that's required to make it work. The central bank must be trusted not to debase the currency, but the history of fiat currencies is full of breaches of that trust. Banks must be trusted to hold our money and transfer it electronically, but they lend it out in waves of credit bubbles with barely a fraction in reserve." He may have embedded another comment on his motivation for creating the cryptocurrency into the genesis block, in a parameter that reads, "The Times 03/Jan/2009 Chancellor on brink of second bailout for banks."[22]

Just days after the creation of the genesis block, which produced fifty bitcoins, Satoshi released the first version of the open-source Bitcoin software platform. Written in C++, it was, according to Dan Kaminsky, the Internet security guru, nearly impenetrable. In a 2011 interview with the *New Yorker*, Kaminsky said, "When I first looked at the code, I was sure I was going to be able to break it. The way the whole thing was formatted was insane. Only the most paranoid, painstaking coder in the world could avoid making mistakes." And yet every time he thought he'd found a gap in the code, he'd discover that Satoshi had already sealed it. "I came up with beautiful bugs. But every time I went after the code there was a line that addressed the problem."[23]

By making trust and authority the province of the network—a literal peer-to-peer solution—instead of a bank or a government, Satoshi created a milestone in our development as a society. And by fashioning a system that is at once so complex yet also so elegantly simple, he created something close to a work of art.

Tidbit, the system Jeremy Rubin set up to rid us of noxious advertising and put the Fourth Estate back on a firm financial footing, was constructed along similar lines. Both presume that the best possible way to organize and allocate resources is to create an appealing proposition—Make your own money! Get your ad-free news here!—and let people organized into complex and deeply linked networks do the rest. The idea runs counter to several hundred years of organizational thinking, so the New Jersey attorney general's office might be forgiven for not entirely understanding how Tidbit was intended to function.

In May 2015, New Jersey agreed to drop its subpoena in exchange for Rubin's commitment to, in essence, continue obeying the same sets of laws he had never stopped adhering to. "Whether or not browser-based bitcoin mining was a viable replacement for advertising-supported content, New Jersey sent a signal that they might lash out at any technology that attempted to enlist a user's machine in mining, even if the user consented to the exchange," noted Ethan Zuckerman, a longtime civic media scholar and one of Rubin's advisers at the Media Lab.[24]

In the meantime, Rubin has found himself at the center of a new controversy. Satoshi may have solved many of the technological hurdles facing a digital currency, but there was little he could do to solve human nature. A schism—ostensibly over the size of each block in the blockchain, but also touching on core issues of decentralization and governance—has emerged between two factions within the Bitcoin community, showing one of the downsides to the leaderless organization. Rubin has stepped into the breach. "Both sides accuse the other of trying to 'own' Bitcoin," he notes. "The problem is they're both right. If either one succeeds it could be the worst thing that ever happened to the currency. Bitcoin should belong to everyone, not just a small group of insiders."

● ● ●

Nearly a month after the 3/11 earthquake, the Japanese government had still not released radiation data stemming from the Fukushima meltdown. Rumors of a volunteer network of DIY radiation monitors had begun to work their way around the Internet. On April 25, Joi and a core group of designers, entrepreneurs, and, of course, hackers of both software and hardware met in Tokyo to brainstorm. By the end of the day they had built the raw framework of what would become Safecast.

Just as Safecast would use the power of pull to attract the intellectual capital the project required, so would the founders attract the financial capital. Launched on crowdfunding site Kickstarter, Safecast met and exceeded its $33,000 goal to purchase and distribute Geiger counters.

Recall our AOL example? Contrast it with companies like Twitter, which allow their users to gather information and build relationships that will benefit them across the network. These relationships grow out of diverse networks that let participants engage with a broad range of people and sources of knowledge. John Seely Brown drew attention to the natural efficiencies these networks offered, so long as the company is willing to think differently, and popularized the strategy in a 2010 book, *The Power of Pull.*[25]

A robust web of relationships will include both weak and strong ties. In his seminal 1973 paper "The Strength of Weak Ties," Dr. Mark Granovetter argued that weak ties — those that connect casual acquaintances and friends of friends — have the potential to bridge communities and create a sense of trust and connection between people who know each other only slightly or not at all.[26] People with a wide range of weak ties therefore have more opportunities to pull resources from their networks. As Malcolm Gladwell has noted, "Our acquaintances—not our friends—are our greatest source of new ideas and information."[27]

While we draw inspiration from our weak ties, our strong ones may have the greatest impact on our performance. A group of researchers from the Media Lab and the Technical University of Denmark, led by Yves-Alexandre de Montjoye, has discovered that for teams engaged in complex problem solving in a competitive environment, the strength of the members' ties is the most important predictor of their success.[28]

Strong ties are also vital for participants in dangerous or revolutionary social movements. During the Freedom Summer of 1964, a Stanford sociologist named Doug McAdam discovered that volunteers who had strong personal ties to other volunteers were more likely to remain in the South for the duration of the Mississippi Summer Project, despite physical threats and daily intimidation.[29] Researchers have noted similar patterns in other social movements, including the Arab Spring. Participants may be drawn into political action by their weak ties, but their strong ties help keep them in the movement.

Although Gladwell and others have been skeptical that online communication platforms like Twitter and Facebook can foster strong ties, Dr. Granovetter, citing the work of Ramesh Srinivasan and Adam Fish at the University of California, Los Angeles, recently noted that online social networks may be useful in maintaining strong ties between people separated by geography or politics.[30] In 2007, Srinivasan and Fish discovered that activists in Kyrgyzstan use social media platforms to communicate with sympathetic networks worldwide, creating strong ties that cross national boundaries.[31] Ethan Zuckerman, who oversees the Center for Civic Media at MIT, has also noted that unlike the local neighborhood networks Dr. Granovetter studied, these international networks may include strong ties that also serve as bridging ties, helping to ensure that as your network grows larger, you will have more resources at your disposal.[32]

The story of Safecast illustrates this dynamic. Perhaps in Margaret Mead's day the only thing that could change the world was a "small group of thoughtful, committed citizens," as the anthropologist famously claimed.[33] Safecast, however, was less the product of that group of committed citizens than it was the product of that group's extended network of loose ties. Safecast quickly grew into a major citizen-science initiative. Those initial emails between Joi and two of his well-connected friends were not so much the founding of a movement as simply the lighting of a match. While many of the participants were experts in their fields, they received no extrinsic rewards for their work — only the intrinsic satisfaction of contributing to the public's health and safety. As Daniel Pink has noted, intrinsic rewards lead to higher levels of motivation and performance than extrinsic motivators do.[34]

This is the power of pull over push — it leverages modern communications technologies and the decreased cost of innovation to move power from the core to the edges, enabling serendipitous discoveries and providing opportunities for innovators to mine their own passions. At its best, it allows people to find not only the things they need, but also the things they didn't know they needed.

PS:
Serendipity Is Not Luck

Ever since I was a small boy, everyone has told me to focus. Focus focus focus. I'm very good at being hyper-focused, but I'm not good at sustained focus. Everything excites me, and generally I end up focusing on everything. My peripheral vision is overdeveloped.

When John Seely Brown first told me about "the power of pull," it helped me think about my own thinking. As we described in this chapter, the world is changing, and instead of stocking resources and information, controlling everything, planning everything, and pushing messages and orders from the core to the edge, innovation is now happening at the edges. Resources are pulled as needed: the world is going from "stocks" to "flows."

I try to set a general trajectory of where I want to go, but I also try to embrace serendipity and allow my network to provide the resources necessary to turn any random event into a highly valuable one. I embrace sociologist Mark Granovetter's theory of the "strength of weak ties": it's those connections outside of your normal circle that often provide the most value.

But serendipity is not luck. It is a combination of creating a network and an environment rich with weak ties, a peripheral vision that is "switched on," and an enthusiasm for engagement that attracts and encourages interaction.

When mushroom hunters or others engage in tasks that require highly sensitive peripheral-vision work, they have to become extremely mindful and present and allow their eyes and their minds to become aware of the patterns and movements that we normally filter out. It is only then that the mushrooms—or any otherwise unperceivable opportunities—become visible.

In our lives, the ability to switch between peripheral-vision mode and focus-and-execution mode is probably one of the most essential skills for empowering serendipity, but then the trick is to turn those "lucky" events into real opportunities.

One of the problems is that our traditional educational system — and most of our business training — reward focus and execution, limiting the opportunity to become a "visionary." Too much of our training is focused on solving known problems rather than imagining and exploring.

In "pull over push" you need to be fully aware, fully present, and able to develop a very broad network through exploration and curiosity. You need a portfolio of interests and the ability to quickly respond to both opportunities and threats as they emerge. Focusing too much on the past—or the future—narrows your vision and makes you less able to respond to changes, opportunities, and threats. In many ways, it is like Zen or martial arts training that requires dedication and an open mind.

—Joi Ito

3   Compasses over Maps

Zach, a boy living in the suburbs of New York City, views algorithms as a kind of compass. His ability to see the hidden patterns that make the world work is a talent he picked up a few years ago, a talent that has become one of the organizing principles of the twenty-first century: A great many of the objects in our life, exceptional and mundane, obey a precise set of instructions that determine their behavior. Push the button on a flashlight, the thing turns on. Push it again and it gets brighter. Wait five seconds before the next application of pressure, and the flashlight turns off. This moment, when a child realizes that humans can convert intent into logic, and that this logic, however complex, can be analyzed, tested, and understood, is either the end of a child's belief in magic or, depending on your view on such things, its discovery.

"It was pretty remarkable," says David Siegel, Zach's father. "Whenever he'd look at anything he'd want to understand the algorithm behind it."[1] Soon after starting to program with Scratch—an application that lets kids create animations and video games—Siegel says, Zach became the de facto IT guy in his classrooms, troubleshooting computer systems and smart boards for his teachers.

As it happens, David also sees algorithms. Like his son, Siegel is always looking for the hidden algorithms that govern human behavior, and he makes a good living—a *very* good living—applying those insights to that complex and idiosyncratic system, the global financial market. Unlike his son, Siegel has billions of dollars with which to test his theories.

After graduating from Princeton, Siegel studied computer science at MIT. He received his PhD in 1991 and immediately took a job working for a new financial services firm called D. E. Shaw. Its founder, a Columbia computer scientist named David Shaw, used his training in quantitative analysis to find signals within the chaotic noise of the stock market. Alongside another hedge fund legend, James

Simons, D. E. Shaw ushered in the era of quantitative investing, which uses complex mathematical models to rapidly analyze and execute trades. Instead of hiring business school graduates, these funds recruited physicists, computer engineers, and mathematicians. Highly secretive, even paranoid, the quants ruthlessly protect their mathematical formulas.[2] In corporate style they are closer to Silicon Valley tech companies than Wall Street firms, and in fact call themselves technology companies. Jeff Bezos and John Overdeck, a math prodigy with a Stanford PhD in statistics, passed through D. E. Shaw.[3] Overdeck joined Bezos at his new start-up, Amazon, and is rumored to have been responsible for some of the very complicated—and very lucrative—algorithms that instantaneously told Amazon's customers, "If you liked *that*, then you might also like *this*."

In 2001, Overdeck and Siegel launched their own quantitative investing company, Two Sigma. The company doesn't disclose its returns, but while Wall Street banks are shrinking staffs and scaling back their operations, Two Sigma is growing. Its office culture, befitting the quant ethos, bears more resemblance to a San Francisco start-up than to a financial services firm. On a recent Friday morning, young men wearing hoodies and untucked oxford shirts milled about the spartan lobby eating bagels and lox. "It's a Friday morning tradition," said one of them, standing in line for a cappuccino. In 2013 the number of software and data specialists hired by Two Sigma exceeded the firm's hires for analysts, traders, and portfolio managers.[4]

Siegel doesn't regard technology merely as a tool for making money. Computer science is an abiding passion, and when he returns to his Westchester home after spending much of his day analyzing data and tweaking code, he spends time with his family, then devotes the last few hours of the day indulging in his favorite hobby, analyzing data and tweaking more code. When Zach announced, at the age of six, that he wanted to learn to program computers too, Siegel remembers smiling with the great pleasure any father feels in such a moment.

"Okay," he said. "Let's figure out how to do this."

● ● ●

> "Would you tell me, please, which way
> I ought to go from here?"
>
> "That depends a great deal on where
> you want to get to," said the Cat.
>
> "I don't much care where — " said Alice.
>
> "Then it doesn't matter which way you
> go," said the Cat.
>
> " — so long as I get *somewhere*," Alice
> added as an explanation.
>
> "Oh, you're sure to do that," said the Cat,
> "if you only walk long enough."
>
> — Lewis Carroll,
> *Alice's Adventures in Wonderland*

Of all the nine principles in the book, compasses over maps has the greatest potential for misunderstanding. It's actually very straightforward: a map implies a detailed knowledge of the terrain, and the existence of an optimum route; the compass is a far more flexible tool and requires the user to employ creativity and autonomy in discovering his or her own path. The decision to forfeit the map in favor of the compass recognizes that in an increasingly unpredictable world moving ever more quickly, a detailed map may lead you deep into the woods at an unnecessarily high cost. A good compass, though, will always take you where you need to go.

This doesn't mean that you should start your journey without any idea where you're going. What it does mean is understanding that while the path to your goal may not be straight, you'll finish faster and more efficiently than you would have if you had trudged along a preplanned route. Favoring the compass over the map also allows you to explore alternate paths, make fruitful use of detours, and discover unexpected treasures.

These factors have long made compasses over maps one of the guiding principles of the Media Lab, which emphasizes undirected research—research that dances in the white spaces between disciplines. For example, Neri Oxman's Silk Pavilion — a complex dome cocooned in the silk of more than six thousand silkworms — began as an exploration of the boundaries between digital and biological fabrication.[5] As the project evolved, Oxman and her team developed a system they called CNSilk, which used a computer numeric control (CNC) robot to lay out a web of silk threads that guided the silkworms' movements.[6] This both mimicked and extended the silkworms' ability to create three-dimensional cocoons out of thin single strands of silk. The overall shape of the dome was planned, but the details of the fabric surface emerged from the natural action of the silkworms. The often unexpected, sometimes chaotic interplay between the rigid CNC framework and the fluid overlay of organically produced silk created a hybrid structure that the director of the Museum of Arts and Design, in a feature in *Metropolis* magazine, called one of the most important art projects of 2013.[7]

The development of Oxman's Silk Pavilion also illustrates the utility of a strong compass in guiding the trajectory of antidisciplinary research. In this case, a detailed map would likely have failed to account for the complex behavior of the silkworms, whose reactions to environmental conditions such as lighting variations and crowding required a responsive, flexible approach that respected their life cycle. However, proceeding without so much as a compass heading might well have ended in a tangle of silk and wire, rather than an internationally recognized design and engineering project.

In addition to enabling innovators to explore and control serendipitous discoveries, and helping learners find their way to a holistic understanding of difficult subjects, the principle of compasses over maps also allows individuals and companies to respond rapidly to changing assumptions and environments. When faced with a roadblock, innovators with good compasses can navigate around the obstacle rather than have to go back to the beginning of the journey to redraw the map. This not only enables them to change direction quickly, it also saves them the time and expense of creating multiple plans to deal with multiple contingencies, some of which they may not have foreseen.

The principles are not meant to chart your path to a specific destination. They are meant as a compass that will guide your steps through the landscape of innovation, whatever your chosen field.

● ● ●

For such a smart country, America can be awfully dumb. The United States continues to generate the kinds of revolutionary technological advances that lead to millions of new jobs, but judging by the latest round of grim education statistics, it's doubtful there will be enough people with the skills to fill them.

Every three years the Organisation for Economic Co-operation and Development administers a reading, science, and math test to fifteen-year-olds in sixty-five of the world's richest countries. In 2009, twenty-three countries scored higher in basic math literacy than the United States. Kids in thirty-five countries— including Spain, Ireland, and Russia—scored higher than the United States in 2012.[8]

"Improving our achievement has huge economic ramifications," says Stanford economist Eric Hanushek. As one of the authors of a 2011 paper, "Globally Challenged: Are U.S. Students Ready to Compete?" he argues that failing to improve our math scores to the level currently obtained by, say, China, already costs America an entire percentage point in annual growth rate, or roughly $1 trillion a year.[9] The trend lines, projected forward, look worse.

For years now, very talented education reformers have been working to change things, and their efforts have shown limited though encouraging progress. Unfortunately, it may be the wrong kind of progress. The Knowledge Is Power Program, founded in 1994, now runs 183 public charter schools in mostly disadvantaged communities around the country. KIPP schools, as they're commonly known, have achieved admirable results in communities saddled with failing public schools. They focus on discipline, longer school days, and a steady diet of math, reading, writing, and homework. In 2013, a Mathematica Policy Research Study found that KIPP students on average are ahead of their peers by eleven months in math and fourteen months in science.[10]

And then there's the latest nationwide innovation, the Common Core Standards. Some forty-five states have begun implementing the new goals developed by the National Governors Association.[11] They have also rolled out batteries of standardized tests intended to measure what students are learning. But the problem, according to a growing chorus of experts from a diverse range of fields, is that while we're fixing the engine in our old Dodge, the rest of the world is tweaking the cold fusion engine on their new landspeeder. Finland, for instance, doesn't conduct any kind of standardized testing, and has little in the way of common curriculum, allowing individual teachers almost total autonomy.[12]

"The problem is that we're solving the wrong crisis," says Scott Hamilton, who once served as KIPP's CEO. "I've accomplished amazing things in the last few years," he says. "I grew KIPP, I helped quadruple the size of Teach for America. I've been happy about all those things and the fact I got to play a role in them, but the bottom line is that we've doubled what we're spending per child over the last few decades and the needle isn't moving."[13]

Hamilton believes America's schools will be no better at teaching to the even tougher Common Core Standards, and says they are missing the boat. He currently operates an initiative called Circumventure, which uses focus groups, field tests, and interviews to determine what parents and kids really want from their schools. He's spent much of the last year traveling the country talking to some two thousand parents and their kids. "What I learned is that there was actually a strong interest in learning, and a very weak interest in most classes at school. In other words, a low correlation between learning and school.

"One girl asked me, 'I'm going to be a clothes designer. Why do I need to learn algebra?' I didn't know what to tell her." Hamilton called Dan Willingham, a cognitive scientist focused on education, and asked him why high school students study algebra, since it so rarely applies to their lives. "First," Willingham told him, "because algebra is gymnastics for the brain." But, he went on, there's something more important. "Algebra is how we teach the brain to apply abstract thought to practical things." It's the bridge, in other words, between the Platonic world of idealized shapes and the messy one we inhabit. Students—all of us, really—need that bridge.

Hamilton had his answer. Algebra's not important. The bridge is important. Abstract thinking is important. It's a compass we can use to navigate the world. "So are we using the best method to teach that?" he asks. "Because if there's some other method, something that would be fun and student-driven, I could have them lining up at the door."

As it happens, there's an app for that.

● ● ●

Like a lot of coders of a certain generation, David Siegel had warm memories of using Logo as a child. The granddaddy of educational programming languages, Logo was simple but powerful. In the words of its creator, the late Seymour Papert, it was designed to have a "low ceiling" (it was easy to learn) and what Mitch Resnick calls "wide walls" (there were no limits to what a kid could create on it). But that was decades ago. Surely, Siegel figured, thirty years of explosive progress had wrought great advances in how children interfaced with the greatest technology of our age.

Or not.

"We found this simple little program, kind of a variant on Logo," says Siegel. "But I could tell it wasn't very good. I continued to poke around a little bit, and finally I discovered Scratch."

Aimed at eight- to fourteen-year-olds, Scratch looks nothing like Logo, but shares its DNA. The commands are written in simple English—"Move 10 steps"—and categorized into brightly colored blocks that snap together like LEGO bricks. It is friendly, colorful, fun, and engineered to infatuate instead of intimidate.

While the underlying logic of Scratch — variables, conditionals—comes from computer programming, there isn't a line of traditional code in sight, which suited Zach's dad fine. "Remember, he's in first grade at the time. He's never thought of what a 'program' might be. I showed him a few tricks, but, lo and behold, before long he was writing his own little games."

In the spring of 2012, Zach was finishing third grade. Two years had passed. His interest in Scratch was undiminished. Siegel would say, "Why don't you write a version of Hangman for Scratch?" and Zach would come back a day later and he'd made Hangman. Zach had also discovered the real engine behind the program's popularity, a worldwide community of kids who shared suggestions, criticisms, and, in support of a special Scratch function called "Remix," the source code behind their creations.

Online, Zach learned that other Scratchers were descending on MIT's campus for Scratch Day and asked his dad to drive him up to Boston for the event. Siegel's a busy man, but of course he said yes. ("What am I going to do, tell him no?")

On a warm Saturday morning in May, father and son arrived at the sixth floor of MIT's Media Lab to discover hundreds of other youthful Scratch devotees dashing between the various workshops and demonstrations. The Fifth Annual Scratch Day had been organized to resemble a carnival of delights. One entire wall had been set aside for Scratch-based graffiti. There were scavenger hunts, a "press corps" running around conducting interviews, workshops for building and programming robotics projects, and a show-and-tell session at the end of the day. The best attraction of all was simply the solidarity the event engendered among the kids. "It was inspiring," Siegel says, looking back. "Zach got to see he wasn't the only little kid who liked to code."

Near the start of the event, a tall, slender man with a halo of gray curls stepped up to a podium to welcome the attendees. To Siegel's surprise, he recognized the speaker. It was Mitch Resnick, a colleague from his graduate days in MIT's computer science program in the late 1980s. Later in the day, as the proceedings were winding down, Siegel approached Resnick and introduced himself.

"I just wanted to thank you for what you've done for me," Siegel told him. "You've really inspired my kid in an unimaginably good way."

Resnick smiled and nodded politely, but instead of reminiscing about the old days, he bent down to talk to Siegel's son. He asked Zach what he liked to make in Scratch, and how he got involved with the community, and what his favorite things were about the program, and what he would like to see Scratch do better.

"I paid more attention to Zach," remembers Resnick. "There's so much diversity in the program, so I'm always interested in different pathways in and what engages the kids."

On the drive back to New York, Siegel decided to make a financial contribution to Scratch. "It's a nonprofit," he thought. "They could use the money." Then he had another thought: Perhaps he had more to offer than just a check.

● ● ●

In 1864 an enterprising machinist named William Sellers delivered a paper to fellow inventors at Philadelphia's Franklin Institute. He proposed that all screws should have a flattened tip and a thread profile of precisely 60 degrees. The U.S. government adopted the "Sellers Thread," and the railroads followed suit. This simple proposal — the standardization of that most modest of industrial components — inspired the development of interchangeable parts.[14]

"He helped spark the second Industrial Revolution," says Tom Knight, the MIT synthetic biologist. "You can't overstate the importance of standardization to the creative process. An inventor wants to invent, not worry about the threading of his screws."

Tom Knight, Drew Endy, and Ron Weiss were in a quandary. By 2004 scientists at MIT and a handful of other institutions were demonstrating the ability to synthesize simple genetic sequences. Weiss had even created the rudiments of a biological computer, breathing life into Knight's original vision of DNA replacing silicon. To anyone drinking the same water as Knight, they were closing a circle that stretched back to Mendel and ran through Watson and Crick to the modern era of genetics.

Yet the mainstream scientific community was skeptical. Or, worse, they weren't paying attention at all. What Knight, Weiss, and Endy were proposing was much more than genetic engineering, which involves making fairly minor tweaks to a cell's DNA. Synthetic biology, as it was now called, involved building sequences of DNA from scratch. The biologists thought they were amateurs and the engineers thought they were nuts. It was a lonely time for the programmers who had traded their circuit boards for incubators and centrifuges.

The problem, Knight believed, came down to a lack of parts. The previous year he had written a paper proposing a system of BioBricks—LEGO-like parts that could be used in synthetic biology.[15] But he and Endy were still fine-tuning the proposed standard, and "it had very little uptake at that point." He pauses. "Which was disappointing. You want to create a vibrant community that is motivated to move in the same direction. What we tried to do was to create some leadership, in terms of creating the standard and the enabling technology."

There are BioBricks for synthesizing proteins—the energetic molecules responsible for most of the work that keeps you alive—and BioBricks for promoter genes, which kick the rest of a DNA sequence into action. Plug one brick into another, like some nanoscopic LEGO set, and soon you're creating a de novo—entirely new to this planet—kind of life form. It's the modularization of biology, and if it sounds like what happens when a couple of computer nerds get hold of a cell culture and a benchtop laboratory, you're not far from the truth. In fact, synthetic biology didn't come from a biologist at all. As Knight says, "Everything interesting happens because one field has crashed into another."

Fittingly enough, around the same time that Knight's work was getting off the ground, a movement toward "open biology" slowly began forming, inspired in large part by the open-source software movement. At a convention of computer scientists, Meredith Patterson, a polymath with degrees in computer science and linguistics,[16] purified a strand of DNA in front of a large audience. "I think it blew people's minds," says Mac Cowell, a fierce advocate of open biology. "This was a convention of software and hardware geeks. No one had even contemplated biology as a space for experimentation."[17]

By 2008, "community bio labs" had sprung up in New York, London, and San Francisco. To a large degree the participants knew each other, and a well-articulated ethos emerged, which Cowell characterizes as "Do no harm. Work for the common good." The cost of sequencing — reading the instructions, as opposed to writing them — was falling at a rate of six times Moore's law. Or to put it in absolute terms, Craig Venter's privately funded version of the Human Genome Project was estimated to cost a quarter of a million dollars.[18] (The federally funded HGP, by contrast, cost $2.7 billion,[19] including administrative and other expenses.) By the time this book is published, anyone should be able to sequence his or her own genome for a mere $1,000. The goal of all of this is to give scientists the building blocks they need to experiment and to play, much like we give a kid blocks and watch him or her build a house or a dinosaur or a banana.

Yet the lack of standards — the fact that every researcher who had begun to dabble in synthetic biology was, in a sense, using a screw of a different thread — was slowing the growth of the nascent discipline. "A field only progresses when it has a community surrounding it," notes George Church, the Harvard molecular biologist.

Unable to coax more than a handful of university scientists to explore this intersection of biology and engineering, Knight, Endy, and Randy Rettberg, who went on to found iGEM, recruited a different cohort: undergraduates. MIT's winter semester begins in February, and the university has a long tradition of allowing faculty, students, or even unaffiliated outsiders to host courses on diverse, even playful curricula in January, as part of the Independent Activities Period (IAP).[20] So in January 2003, Knight and his colleagues hosted a course in synthetic biology. "We taught them how to design biological systems. The idea was, we would build systems that exhibited 'oscillatory behavior,' like a bacteria that turned on and off like a traffic light." Knight pauses, then says drily, "I think it's fair to say that we demonstrated a certain level of naiveté with that." With access only to rudimentary tools and the few BioBricks Knight had created up to that point, the students were not able to create anything resembling a genetic circuit.

That didn't bother their instructors. "We don't know how to engineer biological systems," Endy later said. "You can't teach something you don't know how to do, so the students are helping us to figure it out." As indeed they did, adding new components to what Endy and Knight were now calling the Registry of Standard Biological Parts. Knight was encouraged enough to teach the course again the following summer. Word about the class began to spread, not only to other MIT students but among academics as well. In the fall of 2003, Knight was approached by a program director from the National Science Foundation. "Look, I've got some extra money in my pocket this year, and I love what you're doing," she told Knight. "We want to help you do more of it. Have you considered holding a competition with other universities?"

The following summer, MIT hosted the inaugural iGEM competition, welcoming teams from Boston University, Caltech, Princeton, and the University of Texas at Austin.[21] Each group of students was sent a package of freeze-dried DNA samples—an early version of the BioBricks. They could order additional "parts" as needed, though as Knight freely admits with a chuckle, the catalog was "somewhat limited."

And yet surprising projects were unveiled that year. The group from UT Austin was able to create the first "bacterial photograph," stitching together a range of genes from across the (very small) animal kingdom, then inserting them into *E. coli*, which gamely began reproducing and forming a culture of *E. coli* capable of recording an image when suddenly exposed to light. The project wound up being published in the pages of the prestigious journal *Nature*, an almost unprecedented coup for undergraduates.[22] The "jamboree," as the actual annual event is called—"We don't like to call them contests," Rettberg says—performed another nifty trick. Many groups wind up synthesizing new genetic sequences out of simple necessity. These were then added to the Registry of Standard Biological Parts, which now numbers more than ten thousand distinct sequences, all capable—in theory, anyway—of performing a well-understood function within a living system.[23]

Team Bettencourt won the Grand Jury prize in 2013, and has since teamed up with the Indian nonprofit Open Source Drug Discovery to continue developing its tuberculosis therapy.[24] That year's runners-up were no slouches either. These included a new species of bacteria that would protect bees from the fungus that has been killing off colonies around the world[25] and a new species of *E. coli* that can be programmed to transport medicines to a specified target location anywhere in the body.[26] (It's called—wait for it—Taxi.Coli.)

iGEM has categories for high school, college, and "aftergrads," a catchall for teams composed of people who have already obtained their baccalaureates. In 2014 they opened the competition to the burgeoning "community lab" movement, in which groups of biohackers working from public labs with names like Genspace and BioCurious compete alongside the young academics.

● ● ●

In 2012 a group of students from MIT's Sloan business school were doing a paper, trying to understand how the Media

Lab was organized. They interviewed many people, faculty as well as students. After a while, Joi received word that the project had been abandoned because after the interviews everyone had such a different view of what the Media Lab did and how it did it that the researchers couldn't actually map it.

Trying to understand the Lab in some sort of structure is sort of futile. Like a random walk in a vibrant natural ecosystem with a random group of people, some people will see how the geology is working, others will note the way the plants are working together, others will focus on the microbial flora, and still others will focus on the rich culture of the people who live there.

Everyone in the Media Lab is, metaphorically speaking, running his or her own algorithms, and they interact with each other and various internal and external systems. Some algorithms work better than others, but each person and each group looks at the Lab slightly differently. There is a "Lab Culture," but each research group and each unit of staff has its own culture. Each group buys into some or all of the Lab Culture and interprets this its their own way. This creates an impossibly complex but very vibrant and, in the end, self-adapting system that allows the Lab to continue to evolve and move "forward" without any one piece entirely understanding the whole of it or any one thing controlling all of it—it is a system that is impossible to map, but where everyone is generally on the same compass heading. If the system were mappable, it wouldn't be as adaptable or as agile.

The Media Lab has had many faculty meetings to discuss its vision — its compass heading. The only true consensus they've reached since Joi got to the Lab—and it happened at a faculty meeting in his first year as director—was an agreement that the Lab is about "Uniqueness, Impact, and Magic." Uniqueness: The Lab works on things no one else is working on, and if someone else is working on it, we move on. As George Church says, if you're competing, it's not interesting. Impact: Many who work in the pure sciences are trying to discover knowledge "for science." While this is important, the Media

Lab works in the service of impact, a concept that has evolved over the years. Nicholas Negroponte allegedly coined the phrase "Demo or Die."[27] It's a reference to the Lab as build-oriented and impact-oriented. In a faculty meeting, Joi tried to push beyond "demo" because more and more of the Lab's work could be deployed into the real world through the Internet, decreasing the costs of manufacturing and increasing the role of start-ups. Joe Jacobson, head of the Molecular Machines group, proposed "Deploy or Die," which the Lab adopted as its new motto. (After President Barack Obama said Joi might need to "work on his messaging," he shortened it to "Deploy."[28])

These compass headings create a framework for thinking about our own work and leave open enough flexibility and interpretation to allow each group and individual to have an identity and a direction without reducing the wonderfully rich diversity of the place. "We want to be less a solid mass and more like a liquid or a gas."

● ● ●

In 1978, Mitch Resnick was just another college graduate looking for a job. He had studied physics at Princeton, but also wrote for the school paper. College journalism led to an internship at *BusinessWeek* magazine, which turned into a full-time job when the editors discovered he had a flair for translating the baffling new world of computers into clear, concise prose. "It was great," he says. "I could pick up the phone and call Steve Jobs. I could pick up the phone and call Bill Gates, and they would talk to me. Every week I could learn about something new."

After several years, though, he grew restless. As a journalist, he was exposed to some of the greatest technical challenges of the day, but he began yearning for a chance to work on projects that he found more personally meaningful. In the spring of 1982 he chanced to hear a keynote by computer scientist and educator Seymour Papert, the creator of Logo. The speech entirely changed the way he thought about computers.

"The way we wrote about computers at *Business-Week*, the way most people talked about computers, were as tools, a way to get jobs done," he says. "But Papert saw computers as something that could help you see the world in new ways and as a medium for kids to express their ideas." The next year Resnick landed a yearlong fellowship at MIT. He signed up for one of Papert's seminars, and was hooked. MIT became his new home. More than thirty years later, he's still there.

Seymour Papert derived many of his early ideas about educating children from the pioneering Swiss philosopher and psychologist Jean Piaget, with whom he had worked at the University of Geneva from 1958 to 1963.[29] Piaget spent much of his eighty-four years striving to understand how children—and by extension, adults—develop an understanding of the world. He believed that from the earliest age humans build mental models to explain the phenomena—a speeding car, a cat's raspy tongue—that surround us. As we grow older our experiences collide with these models, forcing us to adjust the models to accommodate our ever-changing reality. As such, child's play is the act of a child inventing and reinventing his or her own model of how the world works.[30]

To Papert, computers were where models rub up against experience, a perfect vehicle for play and learning both. Papert encoded these ideas into Logo; children learned that a few simple lines of code could induce an onscreen cursor to, say, build a square ("repeat 4 [forward 50 right 90]") or even a flower ("repeat 36 [right 10 square]"). If this, then that. Most valuable of all, sometimes this might not lead to that, requiring the nascent coder to troubleshoot—to form a hypothesis, test it, then refine the hypothesis. With Logo, every child became an empiricist.

By 1984, classrooms around the country were running Logo on their primitive PCs. A generation of computer scientists wrote their first lines of code on Logo. More to the point, a generation of artists and accountants and insurance salesmen used Logo to write their first (and quite possibly their last) lines of code.

"Computers can be carriers of powerful ideas and the seeds of cultural change," Papert wrote in his seminal manifesto, *Mindstorms*.[31] "They can help people form new relationships with knowledge that cut across the traditional lines separating humanities from sciences and knowledge of the self from both of these." For a few golden years, the purpose of the computer seemed clear: It was to facilitate the act of creation. To Papert, the fact that programming, even with Logo, was difficult to do represented "a challenge, not an obstacle."[32] And challenges were what made learning fun.

But just when Logo was at the height of its popularity, the world tacked away from Papert's vision of the computer as a means of creation. During a time-out in the third quarter of Super Bowl XVIII, Apple Computer televised its iconic ad—"On January 24 you'll see why 1984 won't be like *1984*"—to tens of millions of Americans.[33] Two days later the Macintosh 128K introduced the graphical user interface, forever transforming our relationship with technology. Computers were cute. They were friendly, easy to use, no longer so challenging. Children went from being budding programmers to passive users. Separately, as Papert later lamented, the computers themselves were moved into special rooms at school called computer labs. Programming became a specialized activity, an elective practiced by the few, the lonely, the nerdy (and much later, the rich).

By this point, Resnick had started as a graduate student at MIT, well on his way toward a PhD in computer science. He was working closely with Papert, his mentor, on the development of LEGO Mindstorms, a collection of programmable robots that helped catapult the toymaker into the digital era. (Resnick continues to collaborate with the LEGO company to this day.)

Resnick and the rest of Papert's team remained determined to show that kids could create their own games and software, not just consume games and software created by others. After finishing his PhD and joining the MIT Media Lab faculty in 1992, Resnick started a research group now known as the Lifelong Kindergarten, which generally furthered Papert's vision of children using technology to expand their knowledge and powers of expression. In 1993 he co-founded the Computer Clubhouse, an Intel-funded afterschool program for inner-city youth, which has grown, with support from Intel, into a global network with one hundred locations around the world.

By 2003, Resnick had spent nearly two decades in the fertile intersection between toy robots, the computer code that controlled them, and the children writing the code. He had set out to solve hard problems, and he had. But once again he was restless. "The Web had just entered its first truly social phase," he says. "But you can't really share a robot."

Unless, of course, you "bring the robot into the computer," as Natalie Rusk, a research scientist at the Media Lab and one of Resnick's longtime collaborators, puts it. Rusk and Resnick began to sketch out a programming language that would in some ways pick up where Logo had left off. It would encourage kids to learn by designing and creating, but it would also tap into the immense power of community to aid and abet the process of learning. Marvin Minsky, the pioneer of artificial intelligence, once said that "the problem with Logo is that it has a grammar but no literature," by which he meant that there was no method by which great works could be recognized, celebrated, and—coders being coders—copied.[34] Scratch would take Logo into the future.

"I remember having a retreat with my research group," Resnick recalls, "and saying, 'This has the potential to reach more people than anything we've ever done.'" It took four years of programming and prototyping and testing—much of that involving gaggles of children at various computer clubs around Boston—before Resnick and his collaborators launched Scratch in May 2007. The product of many minds and hands, it remained true to Papert's original vision: It allowed anyone, regardless of experience or age, to sit down at a computer and immediately make things happen. More important, it had community woven into its very core.

Resnick and his students designed Scratch so that a reasonably intelligent eight-year-old could sit down and begin programming, with the help of the online tutorials. Just the kid, the perky orange Scratch Cat mascot, and the code. This is central to the digital learning philosophy, which puts much of its emphasis on motivation. Children should—and do, intuitively—*want* to learn. It's up to us, the blundering, wrongheaded adults, to frame the lessons correctly.

● ● ●

Since its 2007 launch Scratch had grown slowly but steadily to become something of a juggernaut. By the time David Siegel encountered it, it was receiving more traffic than any other site at MIT, and the number of projects online had grown to hundreds of thousands. New comments to the Scratch forums were being posted every two to three seconds, and Resnick's team was working on a complete overhaul and upgrade. But the sheer volume of work was threatening to consume Resnick and his entire staff. "I knew that for Scratch to reach its potential we would need a new organizational structure," he recalls. "The Media Lab alone wouldn't be enough."

On the Tuesday following his trip to the Media Lab, Siegel sent a short email to Resnick saying he would be back in the Boston area at the end of the month. "I would be excited to stop by and say hello, and to drop off a contribution to the Scratch effort. I'd also like to discuss ways that I could be involved in helping this program going forward."

That summer, a correspondence sprung up between the two men who had both devoted their lives to computer science, albeit for different ends. They discovered a shared passion for not only making programming accessible to elementary school children, but making it fun as well. Siegel noted that he had had a hard time homeschooling Zach in programming. "I can only imagine that a parent without my sort of background would have a great deal of trouble keeping a child motivated," he wrote. But Scratch, he mused, could serve as the perfect vehicle. "It would even be useful in elementary and middle schools, as so many do not have qualified instructors in this area."

In August, Siegel was back at the Media Lab, ready to push things forward. He picked his way around the experimental bicycles, soldering kits, and, of course, LEGO blocks that filled the Lifelong Kindergarten lab. Sitting in Resnick's office, the two laid the conceptual framework for a project far more ambitious than developing a new programming language: transforming the ways people think about learning and education.

Resnick and Siegel both agreed that learning to code wasn't just about training the computer engineers of the future. It was a terrifically efficient method to learn how to learn. "Learning to code helps you organize, express, and share your ideas—just like learning to write," says Resnick. "That's important for everyone."

Siegel warmed to the concept. "It's not about learning to code," he said. "It's about coding to learn." The idea stuck, and when Siegel returned to New York, he filed the paperwork to create a new nonprofit: the Code to Learn Foundation, now known as the Scratch Foundation.[35]

PS:
Think Mythology
Not Mission

In 2011, Nicholas Negroponte sent me an e-mail that said, "Now and then, I may send little tips that you are welcome to ignore, but they will be the kind of things that only parents tell their children....For example, I never referred to the faculty as 'my faculty,' and I always said that so-and-so worked with me, not for me. These little things are part of the difference between the corporate world and your new job, which is more that of a civil servant."

The only thing I would disagree with Nicholas about is that I believe that even in the corporate world, companies are no longer well served by the traditional top-down leadership style of the pre-Internet era.

In this chapter we discussed the importance of having a direction — a compass — and the pitfalls of trying to map or plan in a world of complexity and change. It is nearly impossible to have a detailed plan when leading a complex and creative organization like the Media Lab. In fact, in many ways, the word *leading* probably invokes the wrong image, since we often think of our leaders as having a tremendous amount of control and direct power. Leading the Media Lab is more like being a gardener than being a CEO — watering the plants, tending to the compost, trimming hedges, and getting out of the way so that the explosion of creativity and life of all of the plants and wildlife in the garden are allowed to flourish.

The Media Lab, and organizations like it, can be "led" by working on our compasses and converging on a common heading. It is impossible to understand the details or to anticipate all of the ideas and challenges that the hundreds of bright, curious and independent people who work with me might encounter. We have to become comfortable with the idea that we are not in control, that we can't anticipate or even know everything that is going on, but we can still be confident and courageous. This also allows us to embrace a diversity in thinking, approach, and timescales, and not force everything to be oversynchronized.

Instead of rules or even strategy, the key to success is culture. Whether we are talking about our moral compass, our world view, or our sensibility and taste, the way that we set these compasses is through the culture that we create and how we communicate that culture through events, e-mail, meetings, blog posts, the rules that we make, and even the music that we play. It is more of a system of mythologies than some sort of mission statement or slogan.

—Joi Ito

4   Risk over Safety

Julia Hu has no business being in an Apple Store, and yet she somehow found herself in 361 of them.[1] The reason why says a lot about why big things—companies, governments, universities, for instance—struggle to compete in an age of complexity that favors little things like terrorist cells and hackers and, really, any individual with a bright idea and a fast Internet connection.

A few years ago Hu, a recent Stanford grad, had an idea to create an iPhone app that would use a wristband to measure its users' sleep patterns as well as gently nudge them awake in the morning. After a few weeks, the app would analyze the biometrics it had gathered to become a virtual sleep coach, offering advice to legions of the overworked and underslept.

The idea was good. Her friends liked it. Her family liked it. Venture capitalists liked it. And if the wristband hadn't required hardware to make it work, our story would have ended there. Like thousands of other software entrepreneurs, Hu would simply have hired a coder or two and gone into business. But there's a big difference between an Apple Store and an App Store. It takes roughly $5 million to get a product, even a wristband, into enough retail outlets to turn a profit. By the end of 2009, Hu had raised less than $1 million in seed money—enough to develop a prototype, but not a product. She had to hope that more venture capitalists were willing to back her entry into the high-risk, thin-margin market for smartphone accessories.

Then she met Liam Casey, the founding CEO of PCH International. Casey's company had plenty of money on hand. That year, his privately held firm was on track to make $410 million. But Casey didn't offer Hu capital, because from his vantage point, she didn't need it. He offered her something better: access to his supply chain.[2]

It turns out that the supply chain is a crucial battle line between Big Things and Little Things, and as we'll see, Little Things are beginning to win. Casey is like a master conductor, except that his orchestra is composed of thousands of factories around the world that hum away 24/7, cranking out everything from the circuit boards inside your desktop computer to the cardboard packaging that will surround it. Just like Hu, Casey is also a creator.

In 1996, Casey moved to Shenzhen, the booming factory town that was fueling China's emergence as a manufacturing powerhouse. He started a trading company, and for years, he says, all he did was match Western companies with Chinese factories. By 2003 that business was dying. The West had met the East, and they had decided they could do business. Casey had to offer something more than an introduction. "When I got here, China was a good place to make cheap products. It quickly became a cheap place to make good products. Then it became the only place to make that product."

Casey took his accumulated knowledge — what factory could make which chip in how much time using raw materials from which airport — and created a database. Displayed at his headquarters across enormous multiple computer monitors, it allows him to take an article of commerce — earbuds, say — and highlight every node in this global network that produces the components for that most ubiquitous species of headphone. If he drills down further, Casey can see data on management, workforce, even the specs for the products they make.

The database allows him to offer his clients (which include some of the world's largest companies) to outsource just about everything. Fabrication, yes, but also design, packaging, warehousing, and fulfillment. In the process, Casey has removed one of the biggest risk factors in a traditional business: inventory. As sales pick up, he can ratchet up production. If it slows, he tweaks his global network accordingly. Those big warehouses in Nashville and eastern Washington? They're as outdated as an old Pennsylvania iron mill.

Because of his database, because of his skill at tweaking the global economy, Casey has brought us to the logical conclusion of outsourcing. "You don't need to own anything anymore," he says.

"Not a factory, not a warehouse, not even an office." In other words, Casey allows a company to move the atoms offshore. What's left? "You need an idea, and you need to be able to market it. That's it." It's a far cry from the kind of business created by Vanderbilt, Ford, or even Jobs.

It's capitalism without capital, and the implications for the Fortune 500 shouldn't be underestimated. Because when all you need is an idea, anyone can play the game. Anyone, in this instance, being Julia Hu. "We took her design, modified it for mass production, picked the materials, made sure it was sized to ship in the most efficient way possible, then helped her design the packaging," says Casey. And when the earthquake in Japan threatened to derail Hu's launch date? Casey's supply chain self-heals, like some fecund wetland moss. "We found someone else to supply the part in two days. It wasn't even a hiccup." In the end, Hu and Casey even collaborated on the branding and the marketing. They called the smartphone wristband the Lark,[3] and Casey moved it from raw idea to finished product in a stunning six months.

The consumer electronics industry is valued at around $1 trillion a year,[4] and it's just the kind of world where Big Things strode around like Gigantasaurs, alternately squashing (i.e., suing) or eating (i.e., buying) the Little Things. What Casey and so-called just-in-time supply chains have done is make it a lot more like the software business, where individuals and small companies have generally provided an endless font of innovation.

● ● ●

So what happens when the hardware business becomes a lot more like the software business? The rules change. When the cost to bring a product to market—or to simply bring an idea to a large audience—could drive an institution into bankruptcy, it made sense to privilege safety over risk. But this is, quite dramatically, no longer the case. The Internet actually reversed the dynamic: It's more expensive to keep secure an idea, or even the rough blueprint for a product, than it is to let it go wander the world in the form of the bits that it is.

The new rule, then, is to embrace risk. There may be nowhere else in this book that exemplifies how far our collective brains have fallen behind the state of our technology.

We mean this not in the sense that everyone should go engage in the kind of extreme sports that will render his or her life insurance policy null and void, but in the sense that we should get our heads around the scale of change that has occurred, that is occurring even more quickly every day. That an ambitious high schooler can engineer new life forms isn't just interesting; it has implications for the entire structure and logic of capitalism, which, lest we forget, was built largely on presumptions that have no longer been true for three decades. That an unhinged individual could design an ingenious weapon that can be distributed online, fabricated on a 3-D printer, then taken onto an airplane isn't just scary, it requires a complete rethinking of how we approach the idea of risk.

Taking advantage of the opportunities our sometimes confusing and scary new world provides requires decision makers to work quickly, without the layers of permissions and approvals required by the traditional command-and-control management model. One company, which for obvious reasons will go unnamed, ordered a feasibility study on whether or not to invest $600,000 in one of Joi's projects. It didn't blink an eye at the fact that the study had cost $3 million. This company's rigid procedures and failure to embrace risk over safety led it to exchange a $3 million theory for a $600,000 fact; even if the project had failed, the company would have lost only a fifth of what it spent deciding not to invest.

Like putting practice over theory, the principle of risk over safety may sound irresponsible, but it is essential for unlocking the full potential of the modern, low-cost innovation that enables it. It has long been an integral part of the software and Internet industries, and helped shape the landscape of venture capital. Increasingly, it is also an important tool for innovation in manufacturing, investment, art, and research.

Implementing risk over safety does not mean blinding yourself to risk. It simply means understanding that as the cost of innovation declines, the nature of risk changes. As we'll see in a later chapter on resilience, the Internet freed—and in some cases forced—software companies to abandon the risk-averse, bureaucratically approved protocols of their predecessors in favor of an agile, permissionless approach to innovation. Of course, many of these companies failed, but those that succeeded did so before their competitors even made it to market.

As the companies that built the early Internet changed their business practices to more closely reflect the realities of their industry, the investors and venture capitalists who helped fund their efforts also had to master a new approach. Rather than reading business plans, talking to MBAs in suits and ties, and ordering expensive feasibility studies, they learned to bet on great people and great ideas. Each of the bets was relatively small, and few of them were successful —but because they were small, and because the ones that were successful were often *very* successful, the results asymmetrically favored those who were both willing and able to embrace these high-risk investments.

Investors who embrace risk over safety also have to change their approach to failing investments. When you make numerous risky investments, rather than a few safe ones, you have to be willing to walk away from the ones that don't succeed. The very thing that makes it possible to privilege risk over safety also makes it *impossible* to pour resources into an investment that's dying—and that's the low cost of innovation.

If you spend $200,000 trying to save your investment rather than walking away from it, you're in the same position as the company that spent $3 million deciding not to make a $600,000 investment. At the same time, you have to be willing to lose your initial investment rather than try to recover it from innovators who should be left alone to develop their new ideas, with or without your money.

Even mature companies like Facebook and Google have leveraged risk to remain agile and resilient, changing their strategies and product focus as their environments have changed. As Google cofounder Larry Page told *Wired*, "[Most] companies decay slowly over time [because they] tend to do approximately what they did before, with a few minor changes. It's natural for people to want to work on things that they know aren't going to fail. But incremental improvement is guaranteed to be obsolete over time. Especially in technology, where you know there's going to be non-incremental change."[5]

Dramatic changes of the kind Page is talking about both drive innovation and result from it, accelerating over time. Taking advantage of this curve requires innovators to embrace risk, and requires investors to seek and recognize opportunities and encourage innovation by not requiring that the people they bet on ask them for permission.

The potential benefits of focusing on risk over safety go well beyond monetary gain. As the cost of innovation falls, enabling more people to take risks on creating new products and businesses, the center of innovation shifts to the edges. This provides a host of new opportunities for people who were shut out of the old, hierarchical model of investment and product development.

Organizations that allow their employees to pursue risk also encourage greater creativity. Neri Oxman's Silk Pavilion, an award-winning project that bolstered Oxman's career and attracted a wealth of interest in the Media Lab's antidisciplinary research, required both Oxman and the Lab to embrace risk over safety. For Oxman, there was a risk that the unpredictability of the silkworms would destroy the project. There was also a risk that it wouldn't be well received, or that its unconventional combination of art and science would endanger her academic standing. For the Lab, there was a risk inherent in hosting a community of more than six thousand silkworms that spent their short lives clinging to lengths of wire and thread that spanned the main lobby of a very public building. The safe thing to do when Oxman presented her proposal would have been to say no. The right thing, as it turned out, was to say yes. The Silk Pavilion was a risk worth taking.

This focus on risk over safety has always been part of the Media Lab's DNA, just as it's always been part of the Internet. It informed Nicholas Negroponte's admonition to "Demo or Die," and it also informs Joi's call to "Deploy." It doesn't require a blind rush to support every risky proposition, but it does ask innovators and investors to weigh the cost of doing something now against the cost of *thinking* about doing something later. Those who best understand this equation will win as the pace of innovation continues to accelerate.

● ● ●

America, with its long history of innovation, should already be on top of this, right? Aren't we home to Silicon Valley? Liam Casey is the first to say that the West enjoys an edge when it comes to branding, marketing, and simply coming up with ideas for gadgets everyone wants to shove in their pockets. But before you curl up with that cozy thought, consider this: not only does nearly every major electronics manufacturer make products in Shenzhen, but those Chinese factories are increasingly equipped to produce their own precision-crafted, high-end goods.

We don't need a crystal ball to see what occurs when making an awesome new camera phone is no more difficult than creating a cool new app for the Android, because it's already happening: It's called *shanzhai*, and it's taking place in Shenzhen. Shanzhai literally means "guerrilla fortress," but over time it became the slang appellation for cheap Chinese-made knockoff brands. You've seen them on the streets of New York or L.A.: North Faith jackets. Nckia cellphones. Guuci purses.

About five years ago there was a shift. First the quality improved. Nckia and Samsing were soon rivaling the quality and durability of Nokia and Samsung. Then something rather amazing happened: The clones started improving on the originals. Specifically, they started innovating. Freed from the grips of patent lawyers and restrictive regulations, shanzhai manufacturers began cranking out weird and wacky features — a phone with an HD wall projector, for instance. And why shouldn't they? Using the same ultra-fast, ultra-flexible supply chain that Casey employs, a wily entrepreneur can produce small runs of a wide range of products, gauge demand, and then ramp up production on whatever sells.

"They are doing to hardware what the Web did for rip/ mix/burn," bunnie Huang told *Wired UK*.[6] Caught flat-footed, the big consumer electronics firms scrambled to catch up: That LG phone with two SIM-card slots? The built-in counterfeit money detector Samsung offers in its phones? Both features were shanzhai innovations. Of course, by the time Samsung rolled them out, the pirates had already moved on to further features, further innovations. The big firms can't keep up — it takes months to respond to market demand, and unlike the shanzhai, they have to negotiate thickets of international patents before every product release.

The result is that the shanzhai captured 20 percent of the global market for cell phones by 2009,[7] and are rapidly extending their reach into other genres of consumer electronics. It's a large slice of an almost incomprehensibly large pie: If the global market for black-market goods were a country, its GDP would rank second in the world at $10 trillion.[8] It pays to take risks.

Seventy million years ago it was great to be a dinosaur. You were the complete package: big, thick-skinned, sharp-toothed, cold-blooded, long-lived. And it was great for a long, long time. Then, suddenly — possibly, some paleontologists believe, in a matter of hours[9] — it wasn't so great. Because of your size, you needed an awful lot of calories. And you needed an awful lot of room. So you died. You know who outlived you? The frog.[10]

The script we're reading here in America is as worrisome as it is familiar: China on the rise, the American Imperium in decline. The frog leaping past the dinosaur. But this storyline exhibits a fundamental misunderstanding of the new age. American companies and Chinese companies are in the same boat. The dinosaurs don't need to be worried about other dinosaurs. They need to start thinking like, acting like, the frogs.

• • •

This attitude toward risk goes a long way toward explaining how Bitcoin could come into being at all. Until 2010, when he gave Gavin Andresen the keys to the Bitcoin SourceForge project, Satoshi Nakamoto—the pseudonymous creator of the software that enabled the creation of Bitcoin—himself made nearly all of the modifications to the software. According to Andresen, former chief scientist of the Bitcoin Foundation, Satoshi's original code still made up about 30 percent of Bitcoin Core in late 2015.[11] In the same talk, Andresen noted that the core developers — the individuals with authority to accept changes to Bitcoin Core—were "cranky and risk-averse," but not as cranky and risk-averse as Satoshi was. In fact, Andresen believes that one of the reasons Satoshi stepped away from the project in April 2011 was that his desire to control the code was incompatible with building the community of developers it needed, some of whom have contributed enormously to the source code in the past five years. (It's worth noting that Andresen himself had his commit access—his ability to make changes to the Bitcoin Core source code—revoked in May 2016.)[12]

Even as Satoshi's presence began to fade, other members of the Bitcoin community were building an infrastructure around the cryptocurrency. New Liberty Standard established an exchange rate in October 2009 (1,309.03 bitcoins to the dollar, based on the cost of the electricity needed to mine bitcoins at the time).[13] In February 2010, the Bitcoin Market became the first Bitcoin currency exchange— a place where bitcoins could be purchased with fiat currencies, or converted into more traditional forms of money. May 2010 saw the first real-world Bitcoin transaction, when Laszlo Hanyecz of Jacksonville, Florida, offered 10,000 BTC for two pizzas. Though the price seemed reasonable at the time, amounting to about $25, the same 10,000 bit-coins would have been worth more than $2 million in early 2015.[14]

That pizza purchase came the same year as the rise of the most famous, or infamous, Bitcoin exchange—Mt. Gox. Originally established in 2007 as "Magic: The Gathering Online eXchange," a trading site for *Magic: The Gathering Online* cards, Mt. Gox gathered digital dust for several years before its founder, Jed McCaleb, read a Slashdot post about Bitcoin and rewrote the site as a Bitcoin exchange. McCaleb moved on in 2011, but he transferred Mt. Gox to Mark Karpelès, a French developer living in Japan.[15] Over the next two years, as Bitcoin became more visible and more popular, Mt. Gox grew along with it, eventually handling more than 70 percent of the global trade in bitcoins.[16]

While Mt. Gox's business suffered from a number of security breaches and software bugs along the way—including a massive, fraudulent transfer of bitcoins to a hacker who then dumped the coins on the exchange, driving the price to nearly zero for several minutes[17]—the debacle for which it will be most remembered occurred in 2013, when a cascade of legal and regulatory problems drove it into bankruptcy.[18]

It started when the U.S. Department of Homeland Security seized $5 million from a Mt. Gox subsidiary in the United States, alleging that the company was operating as an unregistered money transmitter. Although Mt. Gox soon obtained a license from the Financial Crimes Enforcement Network (FinCEN), which regulates money services business in the United States, its ability to transfer money to customers in the United States was severely restricted.[19]

In late February, Karpelès resigned from the board of the Bitcoin Foundation, the Mt. Gox website went offline, and the company filed for bankruptcy protection in the United States and Japan.[20] In its filings, it claimed to have lost nearly 750,000 bitcoins belonging to its customers, as well as 100,000 bitcoins of its own. Although it later found about 200,000 bitcoins in "an old-format wallet which was used prior to June 2011," approximately one-twentieth of the total bitcoins in existence at the time had simply disappeared.[21] The bitcoin market reacted much as traditional financial markets once responded to the loss of ships carrying gold from the New World to the Old—the price of bitcoins fell, and a series of lawsuits and critical think pieces followed.

Mt. Gox issued a statement suggesting that hackers were to blame. However, in December 2014 the *Yomiuri Shimbun* newspaper of Japan reported that Japanese police believe only about 1 percent of the missing bitcoins ended up in hackers' wallets.[22] As for the rest, *Yomiuri Shimbun* said that police found discrepancies between customer accounts and pools of bitcoins assembled by unknown parties, implying that fraudulent transactions accounted for the disappearance of most of the missing bitcoins.[23] Karpelès was arrested and charged with embezzlement in 2015.[24]

The Mt. Gox implosion also touches on another Bitcoin-related scandal that broke in 2013—the seizure of Silk Road, a shrouded online marketplace for everything from illegal drugs to murder for hire. Because its operator, known as the Dread Pirate Roberts (DPR), was unusually willing to grant interviews, the market's existence had been well reported since *Gawker's* Adrian Chen first profiled it in 2011.[25] By 2012, the Department of Homeland Security had started an investigation, and a year later, DHS special agent Jared Der-Yeghiayan had secured a position as a Silk Road moderator.[126] His work led to the arrest in October 2013 of Ross William Ulbricht, who had helpfully kept a diary detailing his adventures as DPR on the same laptop that held 144,342 bitcoins allegedly obtained through Silk Road transactions.[27]

The U.S. Marshals Service has auctioned nearly 30,000 bitcoins seized during the investigation—the buyer, venture capitalist Tim Draper, loaned them to Vaurum, a Bitcoin start-up focused on developing "new services that can provide liquidity and confidence to markets that have been hamstrung by weak currencies."[28] The remaining bitcoins—the ones found on Ulbricht's laptop—were sold in batches, with the last auction taking place in November 2015.[29]

The Silk Road investigation and Ulbricht's trial highlight one of Bitcoin's paradoxes—the cryptocurrency's apparent anonymity invites the attentions of criminals and terrorists, while its intentionally transparent architecture renders it entirely open to examination. This isn't a flaw—it's part of the platform. As Bitcoin. org explains, "Bitcoin is designed to allow its users to send and receive payments with an acceptable level of privacy as well as any other form of money. However, Bitcoin is not anonymous and cannot offer the same level of privacy as cash. The use of Bitcoin leaves extensive public records."[30]

It's also compatible with the original *Cypherpunk's Manifesto*: "Privacy is not secrecy. A private matter is something one doesn't want the whole world to know, but a secret matter is something one doesn't want anybody to know. Privacy is the power to selectively reveal oneself to the world."[31] Bitcoin requires something of its users— that they decide how much they're willing to reveal, and to whom.

● ● ●

Last year, a group of Media Lab students visited Shenzhen with Huang. He kept the Media Lab group small, since it would be going to places with limited space and had to stay nimble. The tour also included Reid Hoffman, who is the founder of LinkedIn and another friend of Joi's, as well as the provost of MIT, Marty Schmidt.

The first stop was a small factory run by AQS, a manufacturer with operations in Fremont, California, as well as Shenzhen. They mostly focus on putting chips on circuit boards, and their factory is full of surface-mount technology (SMT) machines that use computer-programmed pneumatics to pick and place chips and other components onto the boards. In addition to the rows of SMT machines, there were lots of factory workers setting up the lines, programming the equipment, testing the results using X-rays, computers, and eyeballs, and performing those parts of the process that—for technical or economic reasons—are still better done by hand.

AQS works closely with start-ups and other projects that would otherwise have a hard time finding manufacturing partners in China, because of the small volume, high risk, and usually unconventional requests that go hand in hand with working with entrepreneurs.

But it isn't the technology that makes factories like AQS impressive. It's the people. From the factory boss to the project managers and engineers, they were hardworking, experienced, trustworthy, and excited about working with Huang and his friends. They were also willing and able to design and test new processes to create things that had never been manufactured before. As Joi wrote soon after the tour, "Their work ethic and their energy reminded me very much of what I imagined many of the founding entrepreneurs and engineers in Japan must have been like who built the Japanese manufacturing industry after the war."[32]

After AQS, the group visited King Credie, which makes printed circuit boards (PCBs). The PCB manufacturing process is difficult and highly sophisticated; it requires the manufacturer to add layers while etching and printing materials such as solder, gold, and various chemicals. There are many steps and complex controls needed for a successful result. At King Credie, they were working on some very sophisticated hybrid PCBs that included ceramic layers and flexible layers—processes considered exotic anywhere else in the world, but directly accessible to the Media Lab thanks to a close working relationship with the factory.

The next stop was an injection molding plant — Huang had been helping Joi with a project that required some relatively complicated injection molding. Most of the plastic parts for everything from cell phones to baby car seats are made using an injection molding process, from huge steel molds that the plastic is injected into. The procedure is difficult, because if you want a mirror finish, the mold has to have a mirror finish. If you need one-thousandth of an inch tolerance in production, you have to cut the steel molds at that precision. Also, you have to understand how the plastic is going to flow into the mold through multiple holes and make sure that it enters evenly and cools properly without warping or breaking.

The factory the group visited that day had a precision machine shop and the engineering expertise to design and machine the injection molding tools Joi needed, but his initial production volume was too low for them to be interested in the business. They wanted orders of millions of units and he only needed thousands.

In an interesting twist, the factory boss suggested that Joi could have the precision molding tools built in China, and then send them to a U.S. shop that would run the production. Due to the requirement for clean-room processing, he thought it would be cheaper to run production in the United States, but the American shops didn't have the expertise or capability of his shop in China to produce the tools, and even if they did, they couldn't touch his cost for such value-added services.

This role reversal is an indicator of how the technology, trade, and know-how for injection molding has shifted to Shenzhen. Even if the United States had the manufacturing capacity, key parts of the knowledge ecosystem currently exist only in Shenzhen. Which is also where the tolerance for experimentation, for failure—for risk—far outpaces ours.

Next, Huang took the group to the market. They spent half of a day there and only saw a small part of the huge network of buildings, stalls, and marketplaces. The market was several large city blocks of multiple-story buildings with stalls packed into each floor. Each building had a theme, ranging from LEDs to cell phone hacking and repair. The entire place had a *Blade Runner* feel.

The tour started in the section of the market where people take broken or trashed cell phones and strip them down for parts. Any phone part that has conceivably retained functionality is stripped off and packaged for sale in big plastic bags. Another source of components is rejected parts from the factory lines that are then repaired, or sheets of PCBs in which only one of the components has failed a test. iPhone home buttons, Wi-Fi chipsets, Samsung screens, Nokia motherboards, everything. Huang pointed to a bag of chips that he said would have a street value of $50,000 in the United States selling for about $500. These chips were sold not individually, but by the pound.

Who buys chips by the pound? Small factories that make the cell phones we all buy "new." When they're short on parts, they'll run to the market to buy bags of them so that they can keep the line running. It's very likely that the "new" phone you just bought from AT&T has "recycled" Shenzhen parts somewhere inside.

The other consumers of these parts are the people who repair phones. Phone repair ranges from simple stuff like replacing the screen to full-on rebuilds. You can even buy whole phones built from scrap parts—"I lost my phone, can you 'repair' it for me?"

After this market where phones were "recycled," the group saw equivalent markets for laptops, TVs, everything, then went to another kind of market. When they walked in, Huang whispered, "*Everything* here is fake." There were "SVMSMUG" phones and things that looked like all kinds of phones everyone knows. However, the more interesting phones were the ones that weren't like anything that existed anywhere else. Keychains, boom boxes, little cars, shiny ones, blinking ones—it was an explosion of every possible iteration of phone that you could imagine. Many were designed by the so-called shanzhai pirates who had started by mostly making knockoffs of existing phones but had become agile innovation shops for all kind of new ideas because of their proximity to the manufacturing ecosystem. They had access to the factories, but more important, they had access to the trade skills (and secrets) of all of the big phone manufacturers, whose schematics could be found for sale in the shops.

The other amazing thing was the cost. The retail price of the cheapest full-featured phone was about nine dollars. Yes, nine dollars. This could not be designed in the United States—this could only be designed by engineers with tooling grease under their fingernails who know the manufacturing equipment inside and out, as well as the state of the art of high-end mobile phones.

While in Shenzhen intellectual property seems to be mostly ignored, tradecraft and trade secrets are shared selectively in a complex network of family, friends, and trusted colleagues. This feels a lot like open source, but it's not. The pivot from piracy to staking out intellectual property rights isn't a new thing. In the nineteenth century, American publishers blatantly violated copyrights until the country developed its own publishing industry. Japan copied U.S. auto companies until it found itself in a leadership position. It feels like Shenzhen is also a critical point where a country/ecosystem goes from follower to leader.

When the group visited DJI, which makes the Phantom line of aerial UAV quadcopter drones, they saw a company that was ahead.[33] DJI is a start-up that is growing fivefold every year. It has one of the most popular drones ever designed for the consumer market, and it's one of the top ten patent holders in China. It was clearly benefiting from the tradecraft of the factories but also very aware of the importance of being clean (and aggressive) from an IP perspective. DJI had the feel of a Silicon Valley start-up mashed together with the work ethic and tradecraft of the factories the group had been visiting.

The tour also visited a very high-end, top-tier mobile phone factory that made millions of phones. All of the parts were delivered by robots from a warehouse that was completely automated. The processes and the equipment were the top of the line and probably as sophisticated as at any factory in the world.

Then there was the tiny shop that could assemble very sophisticated boards in single-unit volumes for a price comparable to a typical monthly cable TV bill, because they make them by hand. They place barely visible chips onto boards by hand and have a soldering technique that Americans will tell you can only be done by a $50,000 machine. No microscopes, no magnifying lenses. Huang posits that they do it mostly by feel and muscle memory. It was amazing and beautiful to watch.

Joi and his friends then visited PCH International, where they saw supplies coming in just in time to be assembled, boxed, tagged, and shipped. What used to take companies three months from factory to store now only took three days — to anywhere in the world.

They also went to HAX Accelerator, a hardware incubator in the middle of the market district, which is run by a pair of French entrepreneurs.[34]

What the group experienced at all of these companies was an entire ecosystem. From the bespoke little shop making fifty blinking computer-controlled Burning Man badges to the guy rebuilding a phone while eating a Big Mac to the clean room with robots scurrying around delivering parts to rows and rows of SMTs—the low cost of labor was the driving force to pull most of the world's sophisticated manufacturing here, but it was the ecosystem that developed the network of factories and the tradecraft that allows this place to produce just about anything at any scale.

Just as it's is impossible to make another Silicon Valley somewhere else, although everyone tries, after spending four days in Shenzhen, Joi is convinced that it's impossible to reproduce this environment anywhere else. Both Shenzhen and Silicon Valley have a "critical mass" that attracts more and more people, resources, and knowledge, but they are also both living ecosystems full of diversity and a work ethic and experience base that any region will have difficulty bootstrapping. Other places have regional advantages—Boston might be able to compete with Silicon Valley on hardware and bioengineering; Latin America and regions of Africa might be able compete with Shenzhen on access to certain resources and markets. However, Joi believes that Shenzhen, like Silicon Valley, has become such a "complete" ecosystem that we're more likely to be successful building networks to connect with Shenzhen than competing with it head-on.

But we'll only be able to compete with Shenzhen if we embrace the ethos that has helped to form it: an acceptance, even celebration, of risk and experimentation, and a willingness to fail and start again from scratch. For a country like the United States and for the companies that have grown up here, it feels like a backslide, a reversion to a more seat-of-your-pants time in our economic history. And maybe it is. But it is also critical to surviving and thriving in an age where safety in innovation is no longer a virtue and where taking chances is critical to keeping companies, and economies, afloat.

PS:
Buy Low, Sell High

How do you make money investing? Buy low, sell high. I once asked a Japanese government fund manager investing in stocks how he picked his investments. He said, "I invest in big companies, the ones without risk." I had to explain to him that everything has risk and that what you needed to understand was what the risks were and their probabilities so that you could assess the value of the stock.

For instance, if I know that Jeff is a good entrepreneur and he's working in a space that I know well, I can value the opportunity and risk of the venture better than others. I can afford to pay more for the stock than someone who doesn't know Jeff or the field because it will look riskier to them than it might look to me. Later, when Jeff's company is a huge success, goes public, and is on the front page of the *New York Times*, it might be time for me to sell. Everyone, including my Japanese government fund manager friend, will be saying, "Gee, what an amazing company! How could anything go wrong now?" The price will be surging. We often say, "The information is in the price." The company may be in better shape than when I first invested, but people may be underestimating the risks and overestimating the opportunity. The stock could be overpriced.

In other words, use the information that you have to understand risk, take risk, but buy low, sell high. Understanding the risk allows you to more accurately value the risk—and there is always risk.

People who want to take over projects when they are doing really well and stick around until they are disasters are people who are "buying high and selling low." Students who start studying a field that is peaking as they enter college are often faced with extreme competition for jobs and a declining industry by the time they graduate. People often tease the admissions of some of the top universities in Japan as a trailing indicator of where an industry is going.

The "buy low, sell high" version of higher education is to try to find emerging fields where you have an unfair advantage and a passion. It might be risky, but you're much more likely to find yourself at the top of an emerging field with less competition, and in the worst case, you still end up doing something you enjoy.

In addition to "buy low, sell high," another important lesson from venture investing is that when the cost of innovation becomes very low, trying to reduce losses is less important than trying to amplify your wins. In this chapter we discussed the idea of not spending more on due diligence than the price of the investment, and the importance of not pouring in "good money after bad" in order to save an investment. In addition to this, it is important to focus your energy on the upside and nurture the winners in your portfolio.

As the cost of innovation goes down, the early rounds of investment required to get the company going can often be quite small. When funding was scarce and start-up costs were high, the people with the money had more power. But today, serial entrepreneurs with a good product and a good team often get their pick of investors in Silicon Valley.

—Joi Ito

5

Resilience over surveillance

5   Disobedience over Compliance

In 1926, Charles M. A. Stine, the director of DuPont's chemical department, convinced the executive committee to fund what he called "pure science or fundamental research work." It sounds obvious now, but this was long before the age of corporate R&D. In fact the idea was downright radical.

He had, he said, four good reasons why DuPont should pay scientists to engage in basic science:

1
The scientific prestige would bring "advertising value."

2
The chance to do groundbreaking research would improve morale and provide new opportunities to recruit chemists with PhDs.

3
The new scientific knowledge could be traded for interesting research from other institutions.

4
And finally, if least importantly, pure research might lead to practical applications.[1]

One of the first scientists to work at Purity Hall, as the researchers began to call the DuPont research lab, was a young organic chemist from Harvard named Wallace Hume Carothers. At DuPont, Carothers focused on polymers — large, complex molecules composed of lots of smaller units. Stine knew that there was tremendous industrial potential for polymers, but the chemistry behind them — specifically, the forces that bind the molecules to each other — was poorly understood. Enter Carothers, whose research quickly advanced the state of general knowledge about these mysterious "macro-molecules."[2] The work in his lab would eventually lead to neoprene and the first truly synthetic fiber, which was provisionally called "fiber 66."[3]

Unfortunately for the scientists at Purity Hall, Stine was promoted in June 1930, and Elmer Bolton, a Harvard-trained organic chemist, took over the chemical department. Unlike Stine, Bolton thought research was valuable only insofar as it led to commercial results. In 1920, he had written a position paper titled "Research Efficiency," which insisted that research be managed so that it did not result in "a loss of time and expenditure of money out of proportion to the return that might be expected."[4]

Despite Bolton's emphasis on applied research, Carothers continued to pursue his own interests. When Bolton insisted he turn his focus to synthetic fibers in the early 1930s, Carothers tapped into the considerable knowledge of polymers he had developed under Stine's freewheeling reign. In 1935, after years of frustration and experimentation with different combinations of polyamides, amides, and esters, he was able to say, "Here is your synthetic textile fiber."[5] The fiber was developed rapidly after that, and a patent application was filed in 1937. Sadly, Carothers committed suicide just a few weeks later, and the Purity Hall experiment soon ended.[6]

But his creation — nylon, as DuPont began calling it — quickly developed a momentum all its own. Some eight hundred thousand pairs of nylon panty hose were bought on the day they were first sold to the public. By December 1941, nylon hose had captured 30 percent of the American market, one of the greatest consumer product success stories of all time.[7]

Disobedience, especially in crucial realms like problem solving, often pays greater dividends than compliance. Innovation requires creativity, and creativity — to the great frustration of well-meaning (and not so well-meaning) managers — often requires freedom from constraints. We can actually go further. As Thomas Kuhn showed in his landmark book *The Structure of Scientific Revolutions*, new paradigms almost invariably come into being because some scientist *didn't* embrace the dominant idea.[8] In other words, the rule about great scientific advances is that to make them you have to break the rules. Nobody has ever won a Nobel Prize by doing what they're told, or even by following someone else's blueprints.

In the early 1920s, Dick Drew, a researcher at 3M, turned his focus from the sandpaper the company was known for to a new kind of tape. He had been inspired by a group of autoworkers cursing the tape they were using to mask part of a car body for a two-tone paint job — it often peeled the paint off the metal. The new research wasn't so different from his usual duties—finding better ways to glue abrasives to paper—but it was different enough that William McKnight, the president of the company, told him to knock it off and get back to work.

Drew agreed that he would, but went right on trying to develop a better kind of masking tape for the automotive industry. When McKnight walked into the lab and caught Drew at it, he didn't say a thing. He did, however, refuse to fund the purchase of the paper-making machine Drew needed to manufacture marketable quantities of his new tape. Undaunted, Drew bent the rules nearly in half; he used his authority to make purchases of up to $100 without permission, to write enough $99 purchase orders to buy his new machine. He eventually confessed the scheme to McKnight, who was so impressed, he created a new corporate policy: "If you have the right person on the right project, and they are absolutely dedicated to finding a solution—leave them alone. Tolerate their initiative and trust them."[9]

By 1925, Drew's work had resulted in the first masking tape with a pressure-sensitive adhesive. Soon after, he created transparent cellophane tape, best known as Scotch tape, and forever changed the course of 3M's business from being a local manufacturer of sandpaper and abrasives to being a widely diversified corporation that still embraces unexpected research, such as the serendipitous accident that created the Post-it Note (a failed attempt to develop a super-strong adhesive that resulted in a reusable, sticky notepad).[10]

What Carothers and Drew had in common was a passion for undirected, free-flowing research, regardless of what their bosses wanted them to do. This was rare in the 1920s and '30s, and may be even more rare now. Our companies, our siloed jobs, even our educational system discourage interest-based learning and exploration, instead teaching students to follow the rules and refrain from asking questions. This is one of the reasons why many people feel less creative as they get older — Joi often asks his audiences how many of them thought they were great painters when they were in kindergarten, and how many of them still think they are. Their answers are depressingly predictable.

This approach to work and to learning — probing, questioning, disobedient — helped create the Internet, and it is also changing industries from manufacturing to security. None of the pioneers of the Internet had business plans, and none of them asked for permission. They simply did what they needed and wanted to do. When Joi helped found the first Internet service provider in Japan, attorneys for the telecom industry wrote letters telling him he couldn't. He did it anyway. So did the innovators who built Silicon Valley, and it still holds a special place as a hub for agile, scrappy, permissionless innovation.

The culture of creative disobedience that draws innovators to Silicon Valley and the Media Lab is deeply threatening to hierarchical managers and many traditional organizations. However, those are the ones who most need to embrace it if they are to support their most creative workers and survive the coming age of disruption. Innovators who embody the principle of disobedience over compliance do not only increase their own creativity — they also inspire others to excellence. Since the 1970s, social scientists have recognized the positive impact of "positive deviants," people whose unorthodox behavior improves their lives and has the potential to improve their communities if it's adopted more widely.[11]

Over the past two and half decades, positive deviance has been used to combat malnutrition, hospital-acquired infections, female genital mutilation, and other health and social problems worldwide.[12] It's also been used by corporations to implement successful change programs that draw on the talents of positive deviants who are already in the company, rather than attempting to impose a new discipline from above — essentially allowing others to adopt the productive disobedience of their positive-deviant colleagues, rather than requiring them to comply with an outsiders' rules, and enabling greater creativity and innovation in the process.[13]

In the industrialized, mass-production society of the nineteenth and twentieth centuries, only a small number of people were supposed to be creative — the rest were simply expected to do as they were told. However, automation, 3-D printing, and other technologies are rapidly creating a new job landscape that requires more creativity from everybody. The people who will be most successful in this environment will be the ones who ask questions, trust their instincts, and refuse to follow the rules when the rules get in their way.

● ● ●

Like a lot of people enmeshed in the overlapping worlds of computer security and digital currencies, Austin Hill has sometimes approached his entrepreneurial efforts with a flexible interpretation of things like standard business ethics. Born in Calgary on June 18, 1973,[14] the second of seven children, Hill has immersed himself in computers and entrepreneurship since he was a child.[15] By the age of eleven he was running an Internet bulletin board, and he founded his first company when he was sixteen. That company was, he admits now, a scam — he and a group of friends, calling themselves "Nelson

Communications," took out ads in newspapers across Canada offering "$400–600 week watching TV." Everyone who responded was of course "selected to review" their favorite shows, pending completion of a $49 training program. Nelson Communications made $100,000 in three months by peddling this training program, and might have made even more had another friend not called Hill out. As he remembers it, she said, "You're one of the smartest people I've ever met in my entire life and I'm really, really sad that that's all you amount to." He realized she was right. "Every company since," he says, "I've made tons of mistakes, but I had a vision for how I could make the world a better place....I've never had to apologize since that day."[16]

Hill ended his formal education in tenth grade, after being suspended for "lipping off" to one of his teachers. It was a bit of a family tradition, really. His older brother Hamnett left school even earlier, in ninth grade. Hamnett later enrolled at the University of Montana (and followed the Grateful Dead on tour), and Austin took a job in a computer store. In 1994, Hill visited his father, Hammie, whose company had temporarily transferred him to Montreal, and convinced Hamnett to join him there. Soon afterward, the brothers founded Infobahn Online Services — one of Montreal's first ISPs — with a $50,000 investment from Hammie and Austin's former boss. The company merged into Total.net in January 1996, and in 1997 the Hills sold their stake for about $180 per share, compared to its original $2.85 asking price.[17]

The money from the sale funded the Hills' next venture, an online privacy company that proved to be years ahead of its time. Its first product, Freedom, used public key cryptography to create secure, pseudonymous (as opposed to anonymous) digital identities for its users. But Zero-Knowledge Systems, as the company was known, was controversial. While a number of reporters framed Freedom's appeal in terms of consumer protection, others focused on the potential for cyber-criminals to hide their nefarious deeds behind a pseudonymous veil. In December 1999, David E. Kalish of the Associated Press described Zero-Knowledge Systems as "a peddler of cyberspace disguises," and said,

"While the service is intended to give Internet users greater privacy to communicate ideas or shop online, critics worry it could also allow the unscrupulous to fearlessly send abusive e-mail and exchange illegal goods such as child pornography and pirated software."[18]

While Hill admits that some Freedom users abused the system—threats against the president of the United States were depressingly common—he says, "We saw thousands of more positive uses of our technology than ever negative." In fact, Freedom was designed from the ground up to discourage abuse, from the monetary cost of the service to its implementation of pseudonymous, not anonymous, identities. As Hill puts it, "Conversations, communities, relationships, and strong emotional bonds are formed through a social form of iterated prisoner's dilemma.[19] When a participant in iterative prisoner's dilemma has no identity or feels free from the responsibility of his or her actions in social interactions, communities quickly degenerate into a race to the bottom."[20]

● ● ●

It is difficult, maybe impossible, to understand the diligently private (read: paranoid), persnickety (read: misanthropic) world from which Bitcoin has emerged without some understanding of a much older milieu—the cloak-and-dagger realm of cryptography. In western Asia and Europe, literacy, and even much of our mathematical knowledge, have been inextricable linked with cryptography since their earliest incarnations.

In the late 1960s, Denise Schmandt-Besserat, a French archaeologist studying the Neolithic use of clay, began investigating the origins and purpose of thousands of tiny clay artifacts scattered across sites from Turkey to Pakistan. Although they had previously been identified as toys, amulets, or game pieces, Schmandt-Besserat came to recognize them as tokens for "correspondence-counting"—a way of tracking the quantities of goods by tallying them against other goods, from bread and oil to cloth and sheep.

Some five thousand years after the first tokens were sculpted out of clay, an innovative group of temple scribes in Sumeria, a wealthy Mesopotamian culture nestled between the Tigris and Euphrates in what is now southern Iraq, developed a precursor to written language by pressing the tokens into clay bullae, or envelopes, recording the shape and surface decoration of each one before sealing the containers. Before long, someone realized that the same marks could be made with a sharpened reed or a piece of bone, rendering the tokens obsolete.[21]

Freed of the necessity to physically count tokens, the scribes of Sumeria were also free to invent new characters that represented numbers, allowing them to write "three loaves of bread" rather than "bread bread bread." As Felix Martin notes in *Money: The Unauthorized Biography*, "When one considers that on a single tablet the receipt of 140,000 litres of grain is recorded it is obvious that the practical advantages were considerable."[22] More relevant to the eventual development of modern cryptography, however, is that this new method of bookkeeping required record-keepers to understand numbers in the abstract, which was vital to the emergence of another Sumerian technology—accounting.

It took nearly three thousand years for Sumerian writing and mathematics to make their way to Greece, probably through trade with Phoenicia, but once they did, they became the wellspring for an outpouring of literary and scientific innovation that shaped the modern world. Greek poets and playwrights created works that are still read and performed today; Greek philosophers developed a materialistic, rational worldview that provided a map for the Enlightenment two millennia later; and Greek merchants synthesized the Sumerian concept of abstract numbers into a new, world-changing idea—that of economic value.[23]

As written communication spread across the ancient Aegean, so did the need to conceal its contents. Then, as now, there were two primary methods of doing so. The first, steganography, hides a plaintext message inside another container. If you've ever written a secret message in lemon juice, or watched a movie with a digital water-mark, you've dabbled in steganography. According to the fifth-century BCE historian Herodotus, contemporary methods of steganography included tattooing a message on a slave's scalp and waiting for his hair to regrow, or writing on a wooden tablet and then coating it with wax (which was probably more expedient, if less dramatic).[24]

The advantage of steganography is that, by definition, it does not draw attention to itself. However, if someone other than the intended recipient discovers the hidden message—say the tattooed slave falls ill on the road, and a well-meaning physician shaves his head to relieve his fever—there is nothing to prevent that person from reading it. Cryptography, on the other hand, encodes information so that only the intended recipient (or a particularly clever or persistent adversary) can decipher it. The trouble is that the resulting messages are obviously encrypted, unless they've been further concealed with steganographic techniques.

One of the earliest methods of encryption was the Spartan *scytale*, a wooden cylinder with a strip of parchment wound around it. The message could be written in plaintext, but once the parchment was unwound, the letters would be an unreadable jumble for anyone without a similarly sized scytale.[25] Another Greek historian, Polybius, developed a grid that allowed written messages to be coded into numbers, which made it possible to pass encrypted communications across long distances by raising and lowering torches—an early form of telegraphy.[26] Julius Caesar also relied on a simple substitution cipher, in which each letter is swapped with one a set distance away from it in the alphabet. In this system, familiar to many schoolchildren, A might become C, while C becomes E and E becomes G.[27]

While all of these ciphers were relatively unsophisticated and crude, so were the means of breaking them. That began to change in the ninth century CE, when the Arab Muslim philosopher Abu Yūsuf Ya'qūb ibn 'Isḥāq aṣ-Ṣabbāḥ al-Kindī published *A Manuscript on Deciphering Cryptographic Messages*. Drawing on advances in mathematics, linguistics, and statistics, all of which were flourishing in Abbasid Baghdad, where he lived and worked, Al-Kindī developed an early approach to frequency analysis. He wrote, "One way to solve an encrypted message, if we know its language, is to find a different plaintext of the same language long enough to fill one sheet or so, and then we count the occurrences of each letter. We call the most frequently occurring letter the 'first,' the next most occurring letter the 'second,' the following most occurring letter the 'third,' and so on, until we account for all the different letters in the plaintext sample. Then we look at the cipher text we want to solve and we also classify its symbols. We find the most occurring symbol and change it to the form of the 'first' letter of the plaintext sample, the next most common symbol is changed to the form of the 'second' letter, and so on, until we account for all symbols of the cryptogram we want to solve."[28]

The first polyalphabetic ciphers in Europe were created by Leon Battista Alberti, who also published the first Western treatise on frequency analysis in the fifteenth century. Alberti was far from the only Renaissance scholar fascinated by cryptography — the growing sophistication of European mathematics; the search for hidden patterns in nature, which might illuminate religious mysteries or reveal secret knowledge; the unprecedented spread of information enabled by the printing press; and the tangled diplomatic environment of Renaissance Europe all provided fertile ground for the development of ever more complex methods of cryptography and cryptanalysis. In the sixteenth century, Johannes Trithemius and Giovan Battista Bellasso created their own polyalphabetic ciphers, while Gerolamo Cardano and Blaise de Vigenère pioneered autokey ciphers, in which the message itself is incorporated into the key.[29]

All of these cryptographic innovations were matched by innovations in cryptanalysis — a Renaissance version of the same escalation that drives advances in both cybersecurity and cyber attacks today. The relatively primitive mechanical devices of early cryptography, like the cipher disk Alberti used to track his shifting alphabets, grew increasingly complex, culminating in advanced cryptographic machines like the German Enigma machine of World War II, whose theoretically unbreakable ciphers were betrayed by a simple design flaw — no letter encoded by an Enigma would ever be encoded as itself. Alan Turing and Gordon Welchman led a team at Bletchley Park, England, that created an electromechanical device to help discover the shifting keys to the Enigma codes. Called the Bombe, the device could eliminate thousands of possible combinations, leaving a much smaller number of potential ciphers for the human cryptographers at Bletchley to try.[30]

When the Nazis replaced Enigma with Lorenz — a secure means of encoding teleprinter messages for radio transmission, which the British knew as "Tunny" — Tommy Flowers, a British engineer, countered with Colossus, the first programmable electronic digital computer. Although the project remained secret until the 1970s, and all of the records associated with it were destroyed, several of the people who had worked on the project went on to build the next generation of digital computers.[31] Much of their work was informed by two papers published by Claude Shannon in the late 1940s, "A Mathematical Theory of Communication"[32] and "Communication Theory of Secrecy Systems,"[33] which established the field of information theory and proved that any theoretically unbreakable cipher must share the characteristics of the one-time pad.

Originally developed in the late nineteenth century, and rediscovered near the end of the First World War, the one-time pad requires that both the sender and the receiver have a key made up of a string of random digits at least the length of the message. Each digit indicates the required shift — the number of places in the alphabet that the letter should be moved up or down. This makes it impossible for a cryptanalyst to decode the message using frequency distribution. However, it also requires that the key be entirely random. In the United Kingdom, the Government Communication Headquarters (GCHQ) adapted circuitry from the Colossus project to generate one-time cryptographic pads from random noise, allowing them to avoid both the pitfalls of mechanical key generators like Enigma and Tunny and the foibles of human operators who might reuse their one-time pads.[34] Other one-time pad generators have used radioactive decay or the blobs of wax that churn inside a lava lamp.[35] Whatever the method of key generation, however, the one-time pad is so expensive in practice that it has been used for only the most extraordinary communications, such as those between world leaders.

If the machinations of princes helped drive cryptographic innovation in the Renaissance, computers and the Cold War served the same purpose for the generation of cryptographers who came of age during and after the Second World War. Until the 1970s, cryptography was the preserve of military and intelligence agencies, which invested in increasingly powerful computers and sophisticated software for both cryptography and cryptanalysis.

Three innovations in the 1970s opened the doors of modern cryptography to curious civilians. The first was the publication, in 1976, of the Data Encryption Standard (DES), a symmetric-key algorithm designed by IBM, the National Standards Bureau (now known as the National Institute of Standards and Technology, or NIST), and the NSA, which had insisted that the algorithm contain no more than 56 bits, or 100,000,000,000,000,000 keys—a number it believed civilian computers would be unable to break, while its own computers could decode it with relative ease.[36] According to security technologist Bruce Schneier, "DES did more to galvanize the field of cryptanalysis than anything else. Now there was an algorithm to study."[37]

In the same year, Whitfield Diffie and Martin Hellman, who had criticized the NSA-hobbled DES algorithm on the grounds that even if contemporary computers could not crack it, that would change within a few years, published "New Directions in Cryptography,"[38] which introduced asymmetric public key cryptography, the first publicly accessible cryptographic technology on a par with governmental systems. As Stephen Levy wrote in the *New York Times Magazine* in 1994, "From the moment Diffie and Hellman published their findings in 1976, the National Security Agency's crypto monopoly was effectively terminated."[39]

While "New Directions in Cryptography" proposed a "public-key cryptosystem," it did not specify a method for implementing it. A year later, MIT mathematicians Ronald L. Rivest, Adi Shamir, and Leonard M. Adleman developed the RSA asymmetric encryption algorithm to do just that.[40] All of the pieces were now in place for the birth of the cypherpunk movement, which came to life in the 1980s.

●●●

Unsurprisingly, concerns about Austin Hill's Freedom system intensified in the wake of the terrorist attacks of September 11, 2001. Its critics needn't have worried. Zero-Knowledge Systems had already made the decision to remove the pseudonymous features from Freedom and turn its focus to corporate security. At the time, Hill explained that Freedom "pushed the boundaries and the envelope in the science of privacy, but at this point it's ahead of its time in terms of market acceptance." Or as the president of Junkbusters Corp. said, "Their network was always a Rolls-Royce design, and there just aren't enough people who want to pay a premium for that."[41]

The loss of its flagship program and the implosion of the tech bubble hurt, but Zero-Knowledge Systems survived. In 2005, it changed its name to Radialpoint, and Hamnett was selected as a finalist for the Ernst & Young Entrepreneur of the Year award. This time, the older brother was following his younger brother's example — Austin was EY's Emerging Entrepreneur for Québec in 2000.[42]

In 2006, Hill transitioned into venture capital with an early-stage angel investment firm, Brudder Ventures, which at the time was one of only a few investment firms in Montreal focusing on new companies. He also began developing Akoha, a game that wove together his interests in technology, entrepreneurship, philanthropy, and social change. Each player received a deck of mission cards printed with suggestions for making someone's day, or life, better. After completing the mission, the player would give the card to the person who had received the suggested kindness, and encourage him or her to play it forward. The most successful missions were played multiple times, with the players' online logs providing a valuable resource for determining which missions and approaches worked best.[43] Although Akoha developed a strong player community, it was never able to meet its revenue goals. The game ended in 2011, a year after Hill left the company.[44]

In late 2013, Hill reconnected with Adam Back, who had been part of the original team at Zero-Knowledge Systems. Dr. Back, whom Reid Hoffman describes as "second only to Satoshi in bitcoin," recruited him for his new start-up, Blockstream.[45] By building side chains and other innovations onto the core Bitcoin blockchain, Blockstream promises to transform Bitcoin technology into a platform for stock trades, self-executing smart contracts, and other Bitcoin 2.0 applications that would normally require a trusted middleman to mediate between the parties. It will also enable developers with innovative ideas to build their applications directly onto Bitcoin, without touching the core Bitcoin code or forking over their own cryptocurrencies.

Blockstream's potential attracted interest—and funding—from Google chairman Eric Schmidt's Innovation Endeavors, Yahoo! cofounder Jerry Yang's AME Cloud Ventures, Reid Hoffman, and other tech-industry giants. It also attracted controversy—because several of the core Bitcoin developers will also be working with Blockstream, some Bitcoin enthusiasts worry that Bitcoin Core will suffer, either because the developers will be unable to manage the demands on their time or because they will face conflicts of interest between the two. Blockstream's for-profit status is a particular concern—as redditor historian1111 put it, "I've spoken with austin hill in the past and have not got along well with him and suspicious of his profit model and ultimate goals to create a monopoly on bitcoin development. I also think he's a snake taking you developers for a ride."[46]

Hill doesn't appear to have responded to the controversies publicly, but there's no reason he should. Disputes like this are common in the open-source community, and this one seems unlikely to affect either Bitcoin's or Blockstream's future development.

• • •

Most systems break when they are attacked or stressed. Some systems—like the immune system or the Internet—get stronger when they are attacked; there is some pain, but the system adapts and becomes stronger. The only way to manage the kind of people and work that flourish at the Media Lab—the complexity and the fact that they're trying to look for things that may not even exist—is to create a system that is self-adaptive.

In order to maximize the creative output of each person in the Lab, people often have to be deprogrammed from needing to know what the "right" answer is, what is being asked of them, what they need to comply with in order to "pass." Sure, there are guidelines, and as part of a large institution, there are some rules that people must follow. The point is that these rules are not the focus. It's the freedom to act without asking permission and, as Timothy Leary said, to "think for yourself and question authority" that will generate breakthroughs.[47]

An institution that measures success through impact and breakthroughs every year requires a culture and a system that encourages and embraces disobedience and views outliers and criticism as not only necessary but essential to the ecosystem.

MIT as part of its 150th anniversary published a book called *Nightwork* documenting and celebrating its "hacks."[48] As an institute, MIT celebrates the fact that students can and do figure out a way to get a campus police car on top of the dome of the central building on campus. At the Media Lab, the favorite opener of any story is, "It turns out that...," which basically means, "We were wrong in this cool way."

It's also important to note that disobedience is different from criticism. There is, for example, a very important design movement called critical design—a perspective that provides a critique of modern techno-utopianism that we technologists often find ourselves espousing. However, criticism is *about* our work, where disobedience *is* the work.

Computer security would not improve without computer network hackers, and we wouldn't exist without our gut microbes—good and bad—although apparently most are somewhere in between.[49]

PS:
Disobedience
with a Conscience

I often have the nine principles displayed on one of the screens in my primary meeting room at the Media Lab. One day, when I was meeting with Mark DiVincenzo, MIT's general counsel, he raised an eyebrow when he saw "Disobedience over Compliance" on the display. In the context of a university, "disobedience" clearly sounds like something that you don't want to promote, especially when it would be at the cost of "compliance." I realized quickly that I needed to explain myself.

I started with my favorite line that we use in this chapter: "You don't win a Nobel Prize by doing as you're told." I continued to explain that the American civil rights movement wouldn't have happened without civil disobedience. India would not have achieved independence without the pacifist but firm disobedience of Gandhi and his followers. The Boston Tea Party, which we celebrate here in New England, was also quite disobedient.

There is a difficult line—sometimes obvious only in retrospect—between disobedience that helps society and disobedience that doesn't. I'm not encouraging people to break the law or be disobedient just for the sake of being disobedient, but sometimes we have to go to first principles and consider whether the laws or rules are fair, and whether we should question them.

Society and institutions in general tend to lean toward order and away from chaos. In the process this stifles disobedience. It can also stifle creativity, flexibility, and productive change, and in the long run, society's health and sustainability. This is true across the board, from academia, to corporations, to governments, to our communities.

I like to think of the Media Lab as "disobedience robust." The robustness of the model of the Lab is in part due to the way disobedience and disagreement exist and are manifested here in a healthy, creative, and respectful way. I believe that being "disobedience robust" is an essential element of any healthy democracy and of any open society that continues to self-correct and innovate.

In July of 2016, we organized a conference at the Media Lab called Forbidden Research. We had academic conversations about end-to-end cryptography that the government couldn't crack, and the importance of scientific research into the personal and societal impact of robot sex. We discussed releasing genetically modified organisms with gene drive technology into the wild and extreme geological engineering, for example, throwing diamond dust into the stratosphere to reflect the sun's rays to cool the earth. We had what I believe to be the first public talk about a campus hack (what MIT calls a particular category of pranks), where students put a fire truck on the MIT dome in the middle of the night. We had Edward Snowden video conference in to give a talk about technologies to protect journalists in war zones. We had Alexandra Elbakyan, the controversial creator of Sci-Hub, the website that illegally hosts almost all of the academic papers available online for free, to the dismay and anger of academic publishers.

At the conference we also announced the formation of a $250,000 Disobedience Prize, funded by Reid Hoffman, to be awarded to a person or group engaged in what we believe is excellent disobedience for the benefit of society.

A few of the senior MIT faculty members told me that the conference made them feel uncomfortable, but that they were happy that the presentations were rigorous and serious. They felt, as I did, that MIT is one of the few places in the world where this list of topics could have been discussed in an academic way with a straight face, and that it was the role of disobedience-robust institutions like MIT to make the space for these kinds of discussions and this kind of research.

—Joi Ito

6   **Practice over Theory**

In theory there is no difference between theory and practice. In practice there is.

— Yogi Berra[1]

The Bayard Rustin Educational Complex looks like an old factory, which in a sense it is. The New York City public school was built in 1931 as the Textile High School. The basement contained a real textile mill. The school yearbook was called *The Loom.*[2] The facility has been repurposed several times since then, and the enormous building currently hosts six separate public schools. Only one of them, however, puts video games at the core of every subject.

Quest to Learn,[3] as PS 422 is called, occupies two floors of the old Textile High building. Students do not take science class, but "The Way Things Work." English — or "English language arts," in the argot of professional educators—is taught during "Code-worlds" and "Being, Space, and Place." Phys ed? You won't find it on these students' schedules. Try "Wellness" instead. Neither do teachers organize the curriculum into "units" on, say, rocks and landforms. Instead there are "quests" and "missions" that culminate in a "boss level," a term well known to any gamer. The goal, school administrators insist, is not to produce a generation of game designers. "We're teaching twenty-first-century competencies," says Arana Shapiro, Quest to Learn codirector.

That might come as news to Dominic, an eleven-year-old fidgeting his way through a "crit," an educational ritual normally endured by would-be artists and poets. His peers, the twenty-three other sixth graders enrolled in "Sports for the Mind," are providing feedback on Dominic's video game. "I'm just saying, the enemies all do one damage except for the boss rhino, but every time it shoots at you it does damage, but if the T-Rex knocks into you, you lose all your health."

"Okay, Cyrus, okay. Those are all good points," says Michael DeMinico, the energetic teacher leading the session. Dominic isn't so sure. He's looking at Cyrus skeptically and writhing in his seat, his hand in the air. He starts to speak but stops when DeMinico puts up his hand. "You'll get your turn, Dominic."

DeMinico turns toward Molly, a blond-haired girl sitting straight in her seat at the front of the classroom, and lays down the ground rules for the second time since the beginning of class. "What's really important is that this person is sharing their game with us and you're going to help them make it better. So be honest. But be nice. You want to think of this person who is showing their game as you would think of yourself."

This goes on for another five minutes, and the kids display all the subtle verbal and gestural cues you might see in a corporate boardroom. At the end Dominic addresses his critics. Defensiveness gives way to conciliation. It's a bit like watching children performing a very adult play, but that's the point. "We listened closely to what universities and companies were saying graduates lacked," says Shapiro, "and the ability to collaborate topped the list."

Quest to Learn is a public school and, as such, must do more than teach students to design video games and construct Rube Goldberg devices. New York City has not been immune to our country's mania for standardized testing. So far, says Shapiro, Quest to Learn has performed just above average on those tests. It's hardly a ringing endorsement for an unconventional educational methodology, and indeed, when I ask a parent waiting in the school office what she thinks of Quest to Learn, she shrugs. "It's okay, I guess. My son does like playing the video games."

But by another measure Quest to Learn may be achieving its aims. Shapiro notes that the school has been cleaning up at the Math Olympiad for four years running. "It's a competition that requires kids to collaboratively solve these math problems, and the fact they do so much collaboration in their normal classes makes it very natural for them."

● ● ●

Putting practice over theory means recognizing that in a faster future, in which change has become a new constant, there is often a higher cost to waiting and planning than there is to doing and then improvising. In the good, old, slow days planning—of almost any endeavor, but certainly one that required capital investment—was an essential step in avoiding a failure that might bring on financial woe and social stigma. In the network era however, well-led companies have embraced, even encouraged failure. Now, launching anything from a new line of shoes to your own consulting practice has dropped dramatically in price, and businesses commonly regard "failure" as a bargain-priced learning opportunity.

While that may sound frightening, it can be an incredibly powerful tool. When you emphasize practice over theory, you don't need to wait for permission, or explain yourself before you begin. And once you've started, if your circumstances change or your development process takes an unexpected turn, you don't always need to stop and figure out what happened before you go on. The level to which you can exercise practice over theory depends on the "layer" you are working on—infrastructure and other capital-intensive projects, obviously, offer fewer opportunities for iteration and relatively painless risk-taking. This stands in contrast to higher, softer layers such as software or marketing, which have radical new cost structures, and should be approached accordingly.

Agile software development, for instance, takes advantage of the decreased cost of innovation. Agile development quickly gained cultural currency for its emphasis on adaptive planning (think: shoot, ready, aim, shoot again), early delivery to clients, and ability to improvise in response to unexpected challenges.

This stands in contrast to traditional approaches to product development, which required detailed plans before any kind of production could start. Because a product launch might require extensive capital outlay in the tooling of new machines and changes to existing factories, the price of failure was high.

Another example: When DuPont's engineers were designing the B Reactor in Hanford, Washington—the world's first full-scale plutonium production reactor—the physicists working with them couldn't understand why they insisted on so many blueprints, or why they wanted to build so much room for error into the design. Enrico Fermi told Crawford "Greenie" Greenewalt, one of DuPont's chemical engineers, "What you should do is to build a pile just as quickly as you can, cut corners, do anything possible to get it done quickly. Then you will run it, and it won't work. Then you'll find out why it doesn't work and you will build another one that does."[4]

Nobody wants to cut corners when it comes to nuclear reactors. But what Fermi was suggesting was the application of practice over theory, even when it comes to a critical, and dangerous, piece of infrastructure. In this case, though, the engineers didn't have the money or the materials necessary for this kind of rapid iteration. You can compare this to much of the work that comes out of the Media Lab, where students regularly build prototypes inspired by casual conversations with their peers. In many cases, the timeline from idea to prototype is measured in hours, and the first iterations may occur within a day. They can do that because technologies like advanced fabrication methods and open-source software have lowered the cost of innovation so far that it's often less expensive to try something than it would be to talk about it. Even so, some organizations will still spend more time studying a proposal and deciding not to fund it than it would have cost to build it.

When a manager or leader allows practice to trump theory (a strategy hardly unique to our digital era), goals from some of the other principles laid out in this book become far easier to achieve. Experimentation and collaboration across disciplines becomes less of a radical notion and something closer to a best practice. This in turn provides a given group of people (whether they're employees or contractors or students collaborating on a school project) a chance to explore new fields—to learn by doing—in a way that doesn't require them to make long-term commitments. This, too, lowers the cost of innovation, as it allows talented people to contribute their time to projects outside their usual areas of expertise. Google famously allows its employees to devote 20 percent of their time to a project of their choice; from the perspective of the command-and-control school of management, this is, at best, an expensive ploy to increase morale. But from Google's perspective, it's an inexpensive method of generating new product ideas. And indeed, a lot of innovation has emerged from the program, eventually contributing tens of millions of dollars to Google's bottom line.[5]

This approach isn't limited to organizations in manufacturing or software development. Synthetic biology applies practice over theory to engineering living cells. Educational systems that allow children to engage in active learning, using tools like Scratch to learn the principles of computer programming by applying them to projects that interest them, are putting this principle to work, as the teachers at Quest to Learn quickly made clear. In fact, the school's fundamental philosophy can be summed up as "Children learn by doing," a notion that can be traced through education pioneers like Maria Montessori and beyond. In this age of increased testing, however, practice is more likely to take a backseat in most schools, just as it does in many organizations across a range of industries.

Old approaches are deeply ingrained. Many nonprofits, for instance, are very metrics-driven. Metrics are important for measuring your progress when you know exactly what you want to do, but they can also stifle innovation. Organizations that rely on grants for much of their funding may become tethered to incrementalism. If each of their grant proposals describes not only the research they intend to carry out but also how it will be measured, they won't be able to explore unexpected paths or pursue an interesting wrong turn.

• • •

In December 2013 a gaggle of teenagers gathered in a small conference room in the offices of Two Sigma, the hedge fund company owned by David Siegel, Mitch Resnick's coconspirator in promoting the children's programming language Scratch.[6] If you look at a map, most of the teenagers at the office that day lived within walking distance of the hedge fund office. But by any other measure, they existed in an alternate universe. These were city kids, mostly black or Latino, a demographic woefully underrepresented in science and technology fields. They took weekly classes at Two Sigma, part of a program Siegel created a few years ago in which some of his best, hotshot programmers are encouraged to take time out from trading to teach kids to code.

It's a testament to Siegel's sincerity that this program started well before his work with Mitch Resnick and the Scratch Foundation. No fanfare is attached to this partnership with local schools; no press releases have been issued. Jeff learned about it only incidentally when he happened to meet Thorin Schriber, the Two Sigma employee who heads up the classes.

On that day the students were joined by a trio of women wearing stylish clothes and heels. They worked for Two Sigma, but were there to participate in the "Hour of Code Challenge," a new initiative held in conjunction with "Computer Science Education Week." The project was the brainchild of Code.org, a nonprofit group that shares some of the same goals as the Scratch Foundation. By week's end some twenty million people had written six hundred million lines of code, the organizers announced.

Code.org boasts deep pockets and a glamorous cast of funders, including Mark Zuckerberg, Bill Gates, and Twitter's Jack Dorsey. Not everyone has been impressed. Shortly after the group launched in February 2013, Dave Winer, a longtime computer industry gadfly and the author of the blog *Scripting News*, wrote that "you should [code] because you love it, because it's fun—because it's wonderful to create machines with your mind. Software is math-in-motion. It's a miracle of the mind. And if you can do it, really well, there's absolutely nothing like it." He took particular exception to Code.org's emphasis on preparing Americans to "compete in a global market." If he were a kid and heard that, he wrote, "I'd run away from that as fast as I can."[7]

Winer's view is representative of a generation of programmers driven more by passion than by pragmatism, who naturally resent seeing an art form reduced to a type of job training.

Whatever the motivation, any effort to integrate programming into a national curriculum faces daunting obstacles. "There's no shortage of very smart people trying to figure out how to get kids to code, to teach them to develop these twenty-first-century skills," Resnick says, "but they're pushing against schools and districts that say this is not a critical path to those high test scores they all want." To make coding a priority, advocates need a two-pronged strategy, persuading not only high-level state officials that set policy but also the teachers on the front lines of America's educational system.

That's easier said than done. A number of studies have shown that visual programming languages like Scratch are effective in teaching kids the basics of programming, and that children exposed to them enjoy the experience enough to say that they're more likely to consider STEM careers.[8] Computational thinking isn't easy to measure, particularly using the kinds of standardized tests on which most American schools rely.

Anecdotally at least, there seems to be a clear causal relationship, and not just between a facility in Scratch and high math scores. One student, Luka, says Scratch has helped him most in his English class because it's "helped me tell stories."

Hearing this, Resnick smiles, but he doesn't look surprised. He's playing the long game, which will be won student by student, teacher by teacher. While he applauds what Code.org has accomplished, he draws a sharp distinction between the two organizations. "There's a growing interest these days in learning to code, but it's because they want to provide a pathway for people to be become programmers and computer scientists. And that's a good ambition. There's a real need for more programmers and computer scientists. But we think that's not the most important mission."

Indeed, as ambitious as Code.org, CodeAcademy, and other groups fighting to get more computer science in our nation's schools are, Resnick and Siegel have an altogether more audacious goal. "We don't have kids learn to write because we want kids to become journalists or novelists," says Resnick. "We teach writing because as you write it helps you learn. The same way we use writing to express ideas, we use coding to express ideas. That's what people don't understand. This isn't just about jobs — though that's a wonderful by-product — this is about teaching people to think." Computer science, in their vision, isn't a subject or discipline. It should be at the root of every subject or discipline.

It's a cruel irony that at present, the very schools most sympathetic to the Scratch Foundation's mission are those least in need of its support. Private schools and wealthy districts have begun enthusiastically integrating robotics and programming into their curricula, a dichotomy that will only reinforce the achievement gap that already exists in our nation's schools.

"We could wind up having two school systems—one for the rich and one for the poor," says James Gee, the linguist, educator, and game designer. The poor one will teach to the tests, adhere to common curricula, and "guarantee you the basics, thus suiting you for a service job." The rich schools, on the other hand, will emphasize problem solving, innovation, and the skills required to produce new knowledge. "Those kids will make out very well in the global system." The latest battleground for civil rights, says Gee, isn't about voter rights or equal employment opportunities. "It's algebra."[9]

On a computer, privilege is synonymous with access. Some users have admin privileges, which grant them the ability to determine who else uses the computer. Others have the privilege to create. Some only have the privilege to consume. It's a telling metaphor in this context, and an implicit question that the nation as a whole must answer. Who gets privileges in an increasingly complex future?

It's a nuanced point: Coding teaches students how to problem-solve and think creatively about the world. But the schools most desperately in need of something like Scratch — in need, occasionally, of the very computers on which it could run — would be overjoyed to have their students join the ranks of programmers and software engineers. "It's not enough that we get Scratch taught in some schools," says Siegel. "We need it taught in *every* school."

Making that happen could be quite a trick. Scratch Day 2013 — an annual festival that attracts families and others interested in the program — featured an educator session titled "What's so great about Scratch?" that was led by Sean Justice, an art education specialist from Columbia University. Seven teachers had gathered around a conference table, and the discussion was lively, reflecting the winking skepticism of the title.

"Teachers ask me about digital tools and I say, 'Have you heard of Scratch?'" says Justice. "'What, no, what's that?' It's a programming language for kids; it's also a social network; it's about sharing and community." Their brows knit in confusion, says Justice, and by the time he's done explaining Scratch, "it's like, why bother?...I have a hard time convincing anybody to even give the program a try, much less bringing it into their curriculum."

Other teachers around the table nodded in commiseration. They represented, without exception, the choir: people like Keledy Kenkel, the computer teacher at Brooklyn's Packer Collegiate Institute, one of New York's most elite private schools, and Maureen Reilly, a fourth-grade teacher and "technology enquirer" at Blue School, an "independent" school founded by members of Blue Man Group. These were some of the most tech-savvy instructors at some of the best institutions in the country. And they were not having an easy time bringing this kind of thinking into their schools.

A few weeks after Scratch Day 2013 ended, a long-time educator with deep ties to educational policymakers noted that Scratch has a wide spectrum of critics. "Some people in Silicon Valley say it's not a real programming language, and so kids are just going to have to unlearn all those bad lessons so you can teach them to really program." But a far more daunting challenge to the Scratch Foundation's mission, Shapiro says, is the current focus on the Common Core curriculum.

Luka and two of his classmates counter that concern, saying Scratch has helped their grades, and for all the elementary reasons that caused Jean Piaget to cast a new light on the notion of play: "It's like it's teaching me things," says one of the kids, Peter May. "I'm having fun while learning."

So what would happen if every kid in the country learned to code? An answer to that question might come sooner rather than later: Estonia, which provides free Wi-Fi to every nook and cranny of the Baltic state, in 2012 started teaching its first graders to code. No one's studied the impact of the new universal curriculum, but it has strong political backing from the Estonian president, Toomas Hendrik Ilves. "Here in Estonia, we begin foreign language education either in grade one or grade two. If you're learning the rules of grammar at seven or eight, then how's that different from the rules of programming? In fact, programming is far more logical than any language."[10]

The concept is spreading. In September 2014, every elementary and secondary student in a public school in the United Kingdom began studying computer programming.[11] The U.S. government has thus far declined to institute such a blanket policy. But that could be changing. A powerful venture capitalist with ties to educators and Washington policymakers says there have been discussions within the U.S. Department of Education about implementing Scratch across the country. And in 2014, a group of educational experts commissioned by the Massachusetts Business Alliance for Education issued recommendations to the state.[12] "We recommend that coding should be a mandatory part of the curriculum at every level," says Saad Rizvi, a Pearson executive vice president and one of the authors of the report. "We also say that Scratch would be the best way to do that in early childhood."[13]

Resnick remains optimistic. He's always been optimistic. At a conference about ten years ago he was giving a talk and a member of the audience rose to ask a question.

"Wasn't Seymour Papert working on these *same things* twenty years ago?" the man asked. He didn't mean it as a compliment. He implied that Resnick had run out of ideas. But Resnick refused the bait.

"Yes, I am doing the *same thing* Seymour Papert was doing twenty years ago," he replied. "I think they are worthy things to be working on. We're making progress and I'll be happy and proud if I spend the rest of my life working on these things, because they're important enough for me to do that."

● ● ●

When we talk about learning—as opposed to education—we're really talking about replacing the traditional, one-way, top-down model of knowledge transmission with an active, connected system that teaches people how to learn. Education is what other people do to you. Learning is what you do to yourself.

A learning-oriented system values students' interests, and gives them the tools they need to discover and pursue them. In formal educational institutions, these systems can still be guided by evidence-based approaches to pedagogy and sequencing, while allowing students room to construct their own curricula, seek out mentors, and share their knowledge with their peers.

The social aspects of learning-oriented systems are particularly important for engaging students. John Dewey realized this nearly a century ago, when he called for a seamless integration between students' lives and their learning.[14] There's been a great deal of research showing that people learn best when they can connect the things they're learning to their interests, their personal relationships, and the opportunities they'd like to pursue. However, the traditional educational system in the United States and many other countries still employs a disconnected, metrics-driven approach built around an outdated model which assumes that children given twelve years of sufficiently rigorous education will emerge with the skills they need to excel in a rapidly changing social and economic environment.[15]

This model still emphasizes rote learning and isolated test-taking — the equivalent of sitting on a mountaintop with a Number 2 pencil and no Internet access — even though the people who will be most successful in the coming decades will be those who can tap into their networks to learn the things they need to meet new challenges as they arise. This is where learning over education meets pull over push — rather than asking students to stockpile knowledge, it empowers them to pull what they need from the network as they need it. It also helps them develop the necessary skills for growing, cultivating, and navigating the social networks that will help them learn throughout their lives.

Whatever students are interested in, having a diverse range of connections will provide them with more opportunities to explore their interests more deeply and contribute to meaningful projects and discussions. Social media and other communications technologies have made it easier for young people and adults to seek out other people with shared interests, but many students have not been given the chance to engage with online communities—because their institutions are underfunded, or because their school districts have attempted to shield them from interactions outside of their limited social circles, or because the adults in charge of their educations consider the Internet a distraction.

Although recent changes in American educational policy have attempted to modernize the curriculum by bringing more technology into the classroom, merely introducing new technology is not enough. In too many schools, teachers lack the time to learn new technology, or don't have the institutional support to fully integrate it into the curriculum. One way of overcoming these issues is to invite subject-matter experts who are passionate about the technology to share their knowledge with the students, while the instructor oversees assessment and directs the conversation as necessary.

This kind of solution might not have been possible when both the teacher and the subject-matter expert had to be present in the classroom, but social media, streaming video, and other real-time communications technologies allow students and their teachers to connect with inspiring mentors worldwide. Dr. Mizuko Ito, who chairs the MacArthur Foundation's Connected Learning Research Network (and who happens to be Joi's sister), refers to this as the "unbundling" of functions that have historically resided in the same person: subject-matter expertise, pedagogical mastery, and assessment. Unbundling can allow teachers to focus on their areas of expertise— pedagogy and assessment — while outside experts fuel students' enthusiasm and help them discover their interests.

While not all of the students in every classroom will become interested in the same things, allowing them to engage in interest-driven learning (practice) often helps them grapple with the more tedious but necessary aspects of the curriculum (theory), and leads them to a fully rounded educational experience. Joi, who famously ran away from both kindergarten and university, loves diving and tropical fish. Fully exploring those interests meant learning to teach diving students about the mathematics underlying Boyle's law, water chemistry, marine ecosystems, and scientific naming conventions. More recently, he revisited linear algebra and learned Markov models, because he wanted to understand what one of the students at the Media Lab was trying to teach him about machine learning—the foundation for artificial intelligence. None of these things were directly related to his formal academic career, which began with computer science and ended with physics, but they were important to his continual quest for knowledge.[16]

This leads us to another reason to focus on learning over education—curriculum changes are typically driven by the current and anticipated needs of the marketplace, as are students' choices regarding their academic concentrations. As the pace of technological and social change continues to accelerate, students who merely absorb the education offered to them, without also developing the capacity for interest-driven, self-directed, lifelong learning, will be at a perpetual disadvantage. Students with a passion for learning will always be able to teach themselves the things they need to know, long after their formal education ends.

Forward-thinking, innovative companies can help schools change their focus to learning over education by developing new selection criteria that emphasize creativity and skills, rather than privileging certain degrees, certain universities, or certain programs. A flexible approach to this problem might combine technical and social tools to cast the widest possible net. For example, a company seeking programmers could invite applicants to an open competition, then analyze their entries algorithmically. From there, it could ask the best candidates whom else it should talk to, potentially expanding its networks well beyond the few schools where it holds on-campus interviews, and providing opportunities to nontraditional candidates whom it might otherwise have missed.

The Media Lab is focused on interest-driven, passion-driven learning through doing. It is also trying to understand and deploy this form of creative learning into a society that will increasingly need more creative learners and fewer human beings who can solve problems better tackled by robots and computers.

Jerome Wiesner was president of MIT from 1971 to 1980. In addition to being brilliant and bold, he had a unique background in both arts and sciences. Nicholas Negroponte, a young professor in the architecture department at the time, happened to have his office very close to where Professor Wiesner's driver would wait for him and became acquainted with Wiesner because he passed Negroponte's desk every day.

As Wiesner was preparing to retire from the presidency, it was clear that he wasn't ready to really do so. One day he asked Negroponte: If you could design a bold new lab or department, what would you do? Negroponte, seizing the moment, said: I have *just* the idea.

Sitting on the back of MIT alum and longtime Media Lab Advisory Council member Alex Dreyfoos's boat, Negroponte had concocted an idea for a new department that would be about both arts *and* sciences, a department to pick up some of the best professors at MIT, like MIT Press art director Muriel Cooper, artificial intelligence pioneer Marvin Minsky, and the computer scientist and educational theorist behind Logo, Seymour Papert.

Could they build a department that was also a lab so that the research itself could be the learning? Could the program be called "Arts and Sciences"?

Negroponte often recalls this period as being similar to driving with a gorilla sitting in the passenger's seat. Every time the Institute pulled him over for breaking the rules, they'd see Wiesner beside him and tell them to just move on. The combination of forward-looking ex-president of MIT and radical genius Nicholas Negroponte was a magical mix that paved the way for the experiment that is the Media Lab.

When the Lab was created, Negroponte and Wiesner were able to "hack" the system and give the Lab its own academic program—a graduate program that would have a degree program for a master's degree and a PhD in Media Arts and Sciences under the School of Architecture + Planning. This was a critical innovation. Although MIT is exceedingly hands-on and its motto is *mens et manus*—"mind and hand"—the Media Lab ventured even further in the direction of learning through doing. When the Lab was set up, the MAS program eliminated almost all classes and created a system where research projects became the way that students and faculty learned—learning through construction rather than instruction.

More than a decade of pedagogical research shows that learning out of context is very difficult, yet we teach our students using textbooks and abstract problem sets. We demand "no cheating" on tests where students are required to give the "correct" answer to an abstract problem, even though there's evidence that allowing them to collaborate on exams can improve learning outcomes.[17] We teach kids (and adults) to be punctual, obedient, predictable, and orderly. We discourage play, or relegate it to recess periods. We treat math and science as "serious work," then wring our collective hands when students fail to pursue careers in science, technology, engineering, and math. And yet when employers are asked what attributes they desire most in a new hire, they reliably list items such as creativity, sociability, inventiveness, passion, and playfulness.

In fact, we are now almost always connected, we are collaborative as a default setting, and as robots and AIs get better and repetitive jobs move offshore and then into data centers, creativity is becoming an exceedingly important part of our lives.

It turns out that financial rewards and pressures can increase the speed at which people solve incremental or linear problems, but these pressures actually slow people down when they have to imagine creative solutions or nonlinear futures.[18] For these sorts of questions, play has a much more important role—when the problem is not to provide an "answer" but rather to imagine something completely new.[19]

In the future, we will grow up with and be continuously connected to AIs and robots that will augment our minds and our bodies. Why continue an educational system that tries to turn human beings into meat-based robots programmed to succeed in factories, not in our post-industrial, pre-AI society? Why not amplify the sloppy, emotional, creative, and organic nature of human beings that together with the AIs and robots of the future will create the workforce of the future?

PS:
When Theory Fails

Too much theory can be fatal: In the early fall of 1347 an unremarkable vessel slipped into the busy harbor of Messina in Sicily. Genoese merchants could be found in every port of the Mediterranean, but these sailors carried an unwelcome cargo——Yersina pestis, the bacteria responsible for the bubonic plague. Within the space of a year the epidemic had ravaged Europe, wiping out half the population of many cities and towns. Then as now, a panicked people looked to the experts for answers. In the fourteenth century the closest equivalent to the World Health Organization was the faculty of the medical school at the University of Paris. Throughout the terrible summer of 1348 these medical luminaries engaged in research and debate, issuing, the following October, the university's "Scientific Account of the Plague."[20]

The first half of the treatise examines the etiology of "this great mortality," as it was called in its day. "In 1345, at one hour after noon on 20 March, there was a major conjunction of three planets in Aquarius." This conjunction of Mars and Jupiter "caused a deadly corruption of the air" that spread up from Sicily to infect the rest of Europe. Those most at risk, the authors write, include those "bodies... which are hot and moist," as well as "those following a bad life style, with too much exercise, sex, and bathing."

It's easy, with nearly seven centuries of hindsight, to regard these solemn pronouncements with amazement. But what's far more amazing is that, considered on its own terms, the University of Paris report is a careful and thoughtful piece of scholarship, an excellent representative of human knowledge in thrall to a doctrine of theory. Consider that between 1348 and 1350 there were twenty-four scientific tracts written about the plague, many by the leading intellectuals of the day. None came any closer to identifying a bacterial infection as the cause; the first microscope wouldn't appear for another three hundred years. None identified the rat or the flea as the cause of the disease's rapid spread.

They do, however, make careful use of precedent by citing the writings of Aristotle, Hippocrates, and the great medieval philosopher, Albertus Magnus. Largely dependent on theories over one thousand years old, contemporary theories of pathology combined astrology and the notion of the "four humors" to create a coherent system. Within this system, the authors of the plague treatise are right. They're just right in a very wrong way. Direct observation—the lifeblood of modern science—was not encouraged by an academy still nearly inseparable from the strictures of the Catholic faith. In lieu of any empirical basis, it could be difficult to tell whether these castles in the sky were tethered to any kind of provable truth.

It would be easy to believe that our enlightened age is immune from such follies, but much evidence points to the contrary. In 1996 a physicist named Alan Sokal submitted a paper to *Social Text*, a highly respected academic journal in the burgeoning field of cultural studies. The paper, "Transgressing the Boundaries: Towards a Transformative Hermeneutics of Quantum Gravity," proposed that quantum physics was in fact a social and linguistic construct. Evidently impressed by Sokal's argument, the editors published the paper in its spring/summer edition.

The problem is that, according to Sokal, there was no argument. It was an experiment to see "if a leading North American journal would publish an article liberally salted with nonsense if (a) it sounded good and (b) it flattered the editors' ideological preconceptions?" The answer turned out to be yes. Sokal's paper, in his own words, was nothing more than a "pastiche" of quotes from postmodern rock stars like Jacques Derrida and Jacques Lacan, "held together by vague references to 'nonlinearity,' 'flux,' and 'interconnectedness.'" Nowhere in all of this, Sokal wrote in an article revealing the hoax, "is there anything resembling a logical sequence of thought; one finds only citations of authority, plays on words, strained analogies, and bald assertions." The irony is that, as with the astrological explanation of the black plague, Sokal's paper isn't exactly wrong; it's just right within a coherent and uselessly recondite system of understanding, like a winning argument in a language spoken only on some remote island.

None of this is to dispute the central role theory has played in the effusion of knowledge that occurred over the last century and a half. But theory on its own can be as seductive as it is dangerous. Practice must inform theory just as theory must inform practice; in a world of rapid change, this is more important than ever. In the coming years some scientific discoveries are sure to test some of our most cherished beliefs. We need to make sure we don't assume the role of the Vatican when confronted by evidence that we're just another planet revolving around a star.

—Jeff Howe

7   Diversity over Ability

In the fall of 2011 the journal *Nature Structural and Molecular Biology* published a paper revealing that after more than a decade of effort, researchers had succeeded in mapping the structure of an enzyme used by retroviruses similar to HIV.[1] The achievement was widely viewed as a breakthrough, but there was something else astonishing about the article. Listed among the international group of scientists that had contributed to the discovery was something called the "Foldit Void Crushers Group." It was the name for a collective of video gamers.

Foldit,[2] a novel experiment created by a group of scientists and game designers at the University of Washington, had asked the gamers—some still in middle school and few with a background in the sciences, much less microbiology—to determine how proteins would fold in the enzyme. Within hours, thousands of people were competing against (and collaborating with) one another. After three weeks, they had succeeded where the microbiologists and the computers had failed. "This is the first example I know of game players solving a long-standing scientific problem," David Baker, a Foldit cocreator, said at the time.[3]

It wasn't to be the last. Foldit has continued to successfully produce accurate models for other highly complex enzymes. Other research projects have similarly tapped the crowd to perform tasks ranging from the simple collection of data to advanced problem solving. Another of Foldit's cocreators, Adrien Treuille, has gone on to develop a similar game, Eterna, in which gamers create designs for synthetic RNA.[4] Eterna's tagline neatly sums up the project's central premise: "Solve puzzles. Invent Medicine." The designs created by Eterna's top citizen-scientists are then synthesized at Stanford.

Foldit and some of the other efforts discussed in this chapter may well revolutionize how we treat disease. But they're holding out another promise as well: a realization that conventional management practice is often dead wrong about who is best suited for a task. The best way to match talent to task, at least in the world of nanobiotechnology, isn't to assign the fanciest degrees to the toughest jobs, but rather to observe the behavior of thousands of people and identify those who show the greatest aptitude for the cognitive skills that the task requires.

"You'd think a PhD in biochemistry would be very good at designing protein molecules," says Zoran Popović, the University of Washington game designer behind Foldit. Not so. "Biochemists are good at other things. But Foldit requires a narrow, deeper expertise."

Some gamers have a preternatural ability to recognize patterns, an innate form of spatial reasoning most of us lack. Others—often "grandmothers without a high school education," says Popović—exercise a particular social skill. "They're good at getting people unstuck. They get them to approach the problem differently." What big pharmaceutical company would have anticipated the need to hire uneducated grandmothers? (We know a few seniors in need of work, if Eli Lilly HR is thinking of rejiggering its recruitment strategy.)

Treuille noted that he and his colleagues at Eterna were able to "filter through hundreds of thousands of people who are experts at very esoteric tasks." They are able, in other words, to match talent to task with exceptional efficiency—not based on someone's CV, and not based on the magic of "self-selection," but rather through the thousands of data points generated by the game.[5] Eterna represents a radical rethinking of one of capitalism's central assumptions, that labor is best allocated through a command-and-control style of management. Eterna instead relies on an attribute—diversity—that has traditionally been underestimated. Indeed, before the Internet, it often seemed difficult to achieve.

In June 2006, Jeff wrote an article for *Wired* magazine entitled "The Rise of Crowdsourcing."[6] Drawing evidence from industries like stock photography and customer support, the article proposed that a radical new form of economic production had sprung from the fertile soil of open-source software, Wikipedia, and the dramatic decline in the price of technological tools ranging from digital cameras to benchtop laboratory equipment. "Hobbyists, part-timers, and dabblers suddenly have a market for their efforts, as smart companies... discover ways to tap the latent talent of the crowd," Jeff wrote. "The labor isn't always free, but it costs a lot less than paying traditional employees. It's not outsourcing; it's crowdsourcing."

The term, originally coined in a joking conversation between Jeff and his *Wired* editor Mark Robinson, was quickly adopted, initially by people in vocations like advertising and journalism in which crowdsourcing had taken root, and then by the public at large. (The word first appeared in the *Oxford English Dictionary* in 2013.)[7] As a business practice crowdsourcing has become standard operating procedure in fields ranging from technology and media to urban planning, academia, and beyond.

When it works—and contrary to the initial hype, it's hardly a digital age panacea—crowdsourcing exhibits an almost magical efficacy. Institutions and companies like NASA, the LEGO Group, and Samsung have integrated public contributions into the core of how they do business. In the process they've remade the boundary that has traditionally separated the producers of a thing from the consumers of that thing. It is now a permeable layer, in which ideas and creativity and even control over such crucial aspects as determining long-term strategy are a collaborative effort.

The theoretical underpinnings for this approach lie in the nascent discipline of complex systems; the potency of the pixie dust in crowdsourcing is largely a function of the diversity that naturally occurs in any large group of people.

The sciences have long utilized various distributed knowledge networks that were able to effectively marshal the diversity that exists across a wide range of disciplines. One of the best-known examples is the Longitude Prize. In 1714 the English Parliament offered a £10,000 prize to anyone who could figure out a method to determine longitude. Some of the leading scientific minds focused their considerable talents on this problem, but the purse was eventually claimed by the self-taught clockmaker John Harrison.[8]

Of course, amateurs have always made contributions to disciplines like astronomy and meteorology that thrive on large numbers of observations. But before the Internet, the public had little opportunity to contribute to the creation of other types of scientific knowledge. In recent years a wide range of companies, individuals, and academic fields have utilized this global communications network to increase the sheer brainpower brought to bear on any individual problem and, more important, facilitate a cognitive diversity that is often lacking in the rarefied climes of the corporate or academic laboratory.

Founded in 2000 by the pharmaceutical company Eli Lilly, InnoCentive built its business model on being able to deliver that kind of highly diversified intellectual muscle to its clients. InnoCentive takes difficult problems from major companies, commercial R&D labs, and medical research initiatives and posts them to an online bulletin board. These are frequented by nearly four hundred thousand professional and amateur scientists from some two hundred countries, with more than half living outside of the Americas.[9] These are not your run-of-the-mill scientific pickles. If the thousands of chemists at a multinational pharmaceutical company like Merck can't solve a chemistry problem, you wouldn't think it's going to fall to some first-year electrical engineering student at the University of Texas.

And yet...anyone can post a solution. If it works, the individual receives a reward, generally between $10,000 and $40,000. InnoCentive says about 85 percent of the problems are eventually solved, which is quite a batting average given the scale of the challenges. But what's interesting is who solves the problems, and how. According to research out of Harvard Business School, there's a positive correlation between successful solutions and what the researcher, Karim Lakhani, calls "distance from field." In plain language, the less exposed a given solver is to the discipline in which the problem resides, the more likely he or she is to solve it.[10]

What's more remarkable than the fact that more than 60 percent of InnoCentive's "solvers," as they're known, boast a master's degree or PhD is the fact that nearly 40 percent don't. In fact, one of the most prolific solvers was a Canadian handyman who had dropped out of his PhD program in particle physics in order to care for his parents.

This isn't as astonishing as it sounds. Recall that InnoCentive's challenges are generally filled with problems that smart minds have already failed to solve. If a large consumer products company faces a challenge in economically producing a chemical compound, it's likely to assign its best chemists to the challenge. We're inclined to believe that the smartest, best-trained people in a given discipline — the experts — are the best qualified to solve a problem in their specialty. And indeed, they often are. When they fail, as they will from time to time, our unquestioning faith in the principle of "ability" leads us to imagine that we need to find a *better* solver: other experts with similarly high levels of training. But it is in the nature of high ability to reproduce itself — the new team of experts, it turns out, trained at the same amazing schools, institutes, and companies as the previous experts. Similarly brilliant, our two sets of experts can be relied on to apply the same methods to the problem, and share as well the same biases, blind spots, and unconscious tendencies. "Ability matters," says Scott E. Page, author of *The Difference: How the Power of Diversity Creates Better Groups, Firms, Schools, and Societies.*[11] "But in the aggregate it offers diminishing returns."

All this seems a little heady, but it has actionable implications for how we allocate intellectual capital, or as we may increasingly find, how we allow it to allocate itself, à la projects like InnoCentive or Eterna. Due to an increasing body of research demonstrating that diverse groups are more productive in a wide range of applications,[12] diversity is becoming a strategic imperative for schools, firms, and other types of institutions. It may be good politics and good PR and depending on an individual's commitment to racial and gender equity, good for the soul. But in an era in which your challenges are likely to feature maximum complexity as well, it's simply good management, which marks a striking departure from an age when diversity was presumed to come at the expense of ability.

Race, gender, socioeconomic background, and disciplinary training are all important, but only inasmuch as they are ciphers for the kinds of life experiences that produce cognitive diversity. Further, because we can't know in advance which of those diverse backgrounds, educational experiences, or intellectual tendencies might produce a breakthrough, said Page in an e-mail to the authors, "we should think of our differences as forms of talent. To leverage that talent requires patience and practice." This poses its own challenge, because whatever its advantages, diversity is a quality we often struggle to produce, and the consequences go well beyond the realms of business.

On April 20, 2015, the *New York Times* revealed an unsettling demographic mystery. A large number of African American males seemed to have disappeared. Many more than you could, say, fit on a missing poster. Census data isn't generally a source of shocking headlines, but this one couldn't help but catch the most casual reader's attention: "1.5 Million Missing Black Men." The piece was the work of the paper's data journalism team, Upshot, but you didn't need to be an investigative journalist to spot the glaring statistical anomaly at the heart of the 2010 census. At that time there were barely seven million black men between the ages of twenty-four and fifty-four living outside an institution and over eight and a half million black women between the same ages.

The use of the term "missing" was provocative, but telling. Clearly, a million and a half Americans had not suddenly been abducted by aliens. But they are no less missed. They aren't in church; you won't find them in the kitchen or helping their kids with their homework or running some errands before dinner. You'll find some of them—about six hundred thousand—in jail. And the other nine hundred thousand? Some small portion may have been homeless at the time, and some were serving military tours overseas. But the largest chunk, by far, would seem to be dead, victims of heart disease and diabetes and the worst epidemic of all, homicide, which may have accounted for a sobering two hundred thousand dead black men in the age bracket demographers rightly call "prime age."

The median black woman in America is likely to live in a community in which there are only forty-three men for every sixty-seven women. The gender gap is worst, the *Times* discovered, in Ferguson, Missouri — the same community that became the locus of the Black Lives Matter movement after a police officer killed an unarmed black teenager in 2014. The gap is also greater in North Charleston, where the police killed an African American suspect, Walter Scott, also unarmed, as he tried to run away.

Taking so many people out of circulation cripples communities that are often already facing challenges to their schools, businesses, and social structure. Recent research by two University of Chicago economists[13] suggests that the disparity discourages long-term commitments and family formation by men who don't have to compete for wives or partners. This in turn exacerbates the factors contributing to the absence of black men, ranging from an increase in gang violence, to unprotected sex, to suicide. A vicious cycle in which loss on a vast scale turns communities into the municipal equivalent of the walking wounded.

It's hard not to become desensitized to these negative feedback loops. The problems that beset our most troubled communities, from failing schools to teen pregnancy to poor nutrition, have stubbornly persisted through generations of well-intentioned reform movements and policy prescriptions. The headlines can bleed into one another until it's easy to forget every victim, assailant, and bystander is someone's brother or sister or child.

But then, the forces that encourage our apathy have generally seemed stronger than those that inspire our action. In 1938, not long after Kristallnacht (the pogrom in which at least ninety-one Jews were murdered and more than a thousand synagogues destroyed), a psychologist interviewed forty-one Nazi Party members and found that only 5 percent approved of racial persecution.[14] The Germans have wrestled with questions of guilt and complicity ever since. One argument holds that the Nazi rise to power and the crimes that ensued were the unrepeatable product of circumstances entirely unique to a time and a place. A militaristic nation had been shamed and impoverished by the Treaty of Versailles, leading to riots and chaos and despair. From this wreckage emerged Hitler, an authoritarian figure who offered order and national redemption. Hitler delivered on these promises, and by the time his dark and nihilistic intent was clear, it was too late to oppose him. This story offers many comforts. It has enough truth to be persuasive; it absolves all those who kept their heads down and prayed someone would kill the madman; and it tells the rest of us that it couldn't happen to us.

Unless it is happening here. We imagine we'll hear history when it calls. When it doesn't, we return to our daily lives, our moral mettle still intact. But maybe history doesn't call, or maybe you have to be listening closely to hear it. To prioritize diversity over perceived merit—the colorblind assessment of ability that has never really been colorblind at all—is to recognize that strategic imperatives can't be the sole benchmark by which we distribute society's prizes. There's an increasing sense—among the millennials who fill our lecture halls, but out in the rougher world of cubicles and delivery vans and hospital waiting rooms as well—that it's not enough to be right, or profitable, or talented. You must also be just.

It's no small matter to charge anyone as complicit in the disappearance of over a million people, and doing so risks depriving the individuality of brothers and fathers and sons that make up that abstract figure. We all exercise agency over our lives, but agency isn't an evenly distributed good in our society. It's well beyond the scope of our book to limn the causes and consequences of racism. Two statistics suffice: Between 1934 and 1962, the federal government backed $120 billion in home mortgages. It was, as Melvin L. Oliver and Thomas M. Shapiro write in their 1995 book, *Black Wealth/White Wealth*, "the greatest mass-based opportunity for wealth accumulation in American history," and it generated trillions of dollars in equity that would eventually be converted into choices: the choice to go to a better college, or to take an unpaid internship, or to hire a better lawyer to keep a promising-but-occasionally-foolish adolescent out of prison. Ninety-eight percent of those loans went to white families. By 1984 the median white family in the United States had a net worth of over ninety thousand dollars. The median black family had less than six thousand dollars. Real estate continued to appreciate in the subsequent decades, causing the wealth gap to increase. By 2009 the median white family held two hundred sixty-five thousand dollars in assets. The median black family? Twenty-eight thousand five hundred dollars, almost an exact order of magnitude less than their white counterparts.

Writing for the majority in *Obergefell v. Hodges*, the case that struck down restrictions against same-sex marriage, Justice Anthony Kennedy wrote that "the nature of injustice is that we may not always see it in our own times."[15] But in 2016, it must be acknowledged, we see better than ever before. With the previous century's genocides fresh in our collective consciousness, and the fruits of systemic racism arrayed across our front pages every day, we can neither claim innocence nor ignorance.

Far more than at any previous point in history, we also understand how history will judge us. A few years before the Civil War the American theologian and abolitionist Theodore Parker delivered these words from his pulpit:

I do not pretend to understand the moral universe; the arc is a long one, my eye reaches but little ways; I cannot calculate the curve and complete the figure by the experience of sight; I can divine it by conscience. And from what I see I am sure it bends towards justice.

One hundred years later Martin Luther King Jr. would paraphrase Parker, and irrevocably insert into our collective consciousness the notion of a moral arc, the idea that justice-for-all has a slow and halting gait, but is sure of its destination.

In his magisterial study of violence throughout human history, the Harvard psychologist Stephen Pinker discovered that the moral arc is long indeed, but that as with the pace of change generally, it has recently picked up speed. In his book *The Better Angels of Our Nature* Pinker marshals centuries of crime and war data to show that since the end of the Middle Ages our species has grown remarkably more peaceful; in Scandinavia, to list just one example, murders have declined from one hundred homicides per one hundred thousand people to *one* per one hundred thousand. Pinker credits this pacification, in part, to what he calls the "expanding circle of sympathy." We once reserved our love and concern for our kin, then we learned to expand it to cover our tribe. From there we embraced the village and by the 1800s the general run of humanity would grudgingly grant their regard to those of similar race, religion, creed, and most of all, nationality. Then came World War II, *Homo sapiens'* terrible object lesson in national sympathy run amok. In the wake of that collective trauma this circle of communitarian regard began its greatest period of expansion. This impulse found its classic formulation in the poem "First they came..." by the German Lutheran pastor and Nazi concentration camp survivor, Pastor Martin Niemöller:

First they came for the Socialists, and I did not speak out —

Because I was not a Socialist.

Then they came for the Trade Unionists, and I did not speak out —

Because I was not a Trade Unionist.

**Then they came for the Jews,
and I did not speak out —**

Because I was not a Jew.

**Then they came for me —
and there was no one left to speak
for me.**

It's no great gamble, in other words, to bet that we will be held accountable for the injustices of our day. The 2016 election season has already occasioned a reassessment of our government's reactive criminal justice policies, which led to the incarceration of over two million American men, 37 percent of them African American. It's not hard to imagine future historians concluding that our country's policymakers created a federally mandated system by which a race would remain impoverished for generations to come, criminalized the symptoms of dysfunction that resulted, then fought, tooth and claw, the modest initiatives intended to bring some relief to those whose only sin was to be born poor and nonwhite at a time when their fellow citizens were still unsure how far the circle of sympathy should extend.

Of course, many people, many institutions, even many states have similarly concluded that diversification of our universities and our workplaces is both the right thing and the smart thing to do. Minorities make up 37 percent of the population in the United States. The fact that few organizations have achieved anything like parity with that figure should not be equated with a lack of effort. The technology and media fields currently have made some of the least headway in diversifying their workforces and, more damning still, their respective boardrooms and executive suites. As of late

2014 Google, Yahoo, and Facebook combined employed only 758 African Americans. Fewer than 3 percent of all leadership positions in the U.S. tech industry were black. The gender gap is at least as bad. Twitter has a particularly poor record, with women holding only 10 percent of the technical roles at the company. Twitter's senior executives were so (un)concerned about the image this conveyed that in the middle of a high-profile gender bias case in July 2015 they hosted a staff "frat party."

To their credit, the big tech firms have made genuine efforts to bring more minorities and women into their ranks. Their limited success, they claim, has more to do with "the pipeline"—the available pool of applicants with reasonable qualifications for the job—than any lack of initiative on their part. But to hear many of the women and minority coders who have broken into the business tell it, an unconscious bias about what a "techie should look like" is a more likely obstacle.

The Media Lab has had its own struggles in this regard—it has not been immune to the same social dynamics and unconscious biases that have beset the efforts to create diversity at firms like Twitter or Facebook. The application process, like everything else at the Media Lab, is idiosyncratic. Prospective graduate students (the Media Lab doesn't grant undergraduate degrees) apply to three of the Lab's twenty-five research groups. At that point the decision is largely left up to the faculty in charge of those groups. Until recently, there was very little central oversight over the final numbers of female and minority applicants getting offers.

During Joi's first few years as the director of the Media Lab, this passivity had a predictable consequence. One hundred-thirty-six students enrolled for the 2012–2013 academic year. Thirty-four of these were women; five were underrepresented minorities. The following year saw a small improvement—twenty women and seven minority students out of a class of fifty-five. Joi had touted diversity as one of his central missions for his tenure at the helm of the Lab, and was anxious to turn the numbers around. As a first step he created a new position—assistant director for diversity and student support—and encouraged efforts to strengthen the Lab's Diversity Committee.

Over the next few years the Lab instituted a range of programs to address the imbalance. First, they took far more proactive steps to both identify prospective applicants and pair them with current students who can help them develop their application materials. Additionally, they have started several initiatives to introduce the culture and excitement of the Media Lab to prospective students. In this, the Media Lab reflects a broader effort on the part of higher education to overcome a culture gap in which high-achieving students from economically disadvantaged communities fail to apply to elite colleges for the simple reason that either there is no one who knows that their grades and test scores give them an excellent chance of admission, or no one who can tell them why the school's programs would be a good match for their ambitions.

In the Media Lab's case, the efforts paid off—in part. While still short of the target, the number of women and underrepresented minorities enrolled in the Lab's programs have noticeably improved, even though the numbers still vary greatly by research group. While the percentage of underrepresented minority applicants has remained constant at approximately 6 percent, minorities represented 16 percent of the incoming master's students for the 2016–17 academic year, while women represented 43 percent of the 2016 master's cohort, and 53 percent of the PhD cohort.

There is a sense, among not just the new class of students, but faculty and staff as well, of a culture change, a feeling that the Lab has become a more interesting place to be, with a wider range of possibilities, even within an institution famed for encouraging eclectic research interests. It's not just the Media Lab, either. This impression, however difficult to quantify, is not out of line with some of the most recent research into diversity's effects. A few years ago Team Bettencourt, the same group of young synthetic biologists whose tuberculosis detection kit we profiled in chapter one, conducted a study of the effects of gender diversity on synthetic biology projects. Their first discovery was hardly encouraging—only 37 percent of synthetic biologists were women, a number consistent with related scientific disciplines. But when they drilled down into their data the picture became a lot rosier. The number of women participating in iGEM—the annual competition that serves as both contest and cultural touchstone for SynBio's rapidly growing ranks—had increased dramatically over the previous four years. Further, teams with greater gender parity were outperforming the ones with fewer women. It's the kind of result we're beginning to see more and more of.

A bigger circle benefits us all.

PS:
The Difference
Difference Makes

I spent much of 2007 and 2008 writing a book about crowdsourcing. I had no trouble identifying fascinating case studies; a burst of ambitious, if often ill-conceived, start-ups had sprung up in the years since *Wired* published my original article on the subject. But there were very few serious researchers studying the kinds of group behaviors that either made crowdsourcing click, or insured that it didn't. Discovering Scott E. Page's work on the mechanics of diversity represented a turning point—diversity was more than a policy plank or an indifferent bullet point on some HR presentation. It was smart strategy.

Page and other researchers and scholars were showing that diversity produced benefits all around the table, for the employer and the employee, the manager and the workforce. Organizations with cognitively diverse workforces seemed to show advantages in problem solving. This seemed like especially valuable information in the years following the mortgage crisis and the resulting recession. Many industries saw a reversal of fortune, but unlike construction—housing demand always returns—the media business was beset by what economists (and the more observant journalists) would call "cyclical" as well as "secular" headwinds, which is to say that journalism was in trouble even before the Great Recession hit, and barring a burst of innovative, alternative business models, was hardly poised for a robust recovery.

It seemed like the kind of problem you'd want your best — meaning, your most diverse — group of problem solvers attacking. Unfortunately that was no longer possible. Diversity hit its high-water mark in 2006, when fewer than 14 percent of journalists were members of racial or ethnic minorities (compared to 37 percent of the American population).[16] Unsurprisingly, this did little to increase minority readership. And diversity was one of the worst victims of our most recent recession—"last hired, first fired" means that the very people recruited to diversify, and thereby improve, the newsroom were the first to go when the money ran out. Minorities are much more likely to read news online, but no more likely to find themselves or their communities accurately represented. And with organizations like the Online News Association (ONA) and digital news in general the problem's become much worse, marrying the media's historical monoculture with the overwhelmingly white, male culture of Silicon Valley.

When times were good, the industry did its level best to recruit women and minorities from the end of the pipeline, but we failed to probe further when that only succeeded in increasing diversity by single-digit percentages. That may be where the greatest moral failure—or at the very least, the greatest failure of imagination—has occurred. And it's where we should concentrate our efforts now. Instead of bemoaning the contents of the pipeline from the vantage of its exit point, go to the origin of the pipeline—recruit in the headwaters. One of the future goals of Northeastern University's Media Innovation program is to create a footprint in a neighborhood like Dudley Square (an African American district near the university) and launch an eight-year mentorship in nonfiction storytelling across a range of media. That vision is very much inspired by OneGoal, a Chicago program whose tagline says it all: "College Graduation. Period."

If the program succeeds, Media Innovation could one day be a stool with three legs: first, undergraduates and graduate students from Northeastern; second, the journalism faculty, with a fellowship program built in that would trade office space and stipends for professionals willing to come teach for a semester or two; third, a mentorship program based out of some Dudley Square storefront, with a foot in area middle schools. Kids with an interest in nonfiction storytelling (documentary video, investigative reporting, podcasts, comic book journalism, whatever) would be invited into an eight-year mentorship program based on OneGoal.

Ideally, Gannett or Advance or some other behemoth would have created a whole series of such programs back when they were still posting healthy growth figures. Now it's more likely that someone like Google would need to foot the bill. It seems like a moon shot, of course, but then Google sells plenty of advertising on the backs of our content, and Silicon Valley and American newsrooms would both benefit mightily from an experientially richer, more diverse pipeline of talent—coders and journalists alike.

—Jeff Howe

8 Resilience over Strength

Steel isn't strong, boy. Flesh is stronger!

—Thulsa Doom,
Conan the Barbarian

The classic illustration of resilience over strength is the story of the reed and the oak tree. When hurricane winds blow, the steel-strong oak shatters, while the supple, resilient reed bows low and springs up again when the storm has passed. In trying to resist failure, the oak has instead guaranteed it.

Traditionally, large companies have, like the oak, hardened themselves against failure. They have stockpiled resources and implemented hierarchical management structures, rigid processes, and detailed five-year plans meant to insulate them from the forces of chaos. In other words, they have valued safety over risk, push over pull, authority over emergence, compliance over obedience, maps over compasses, and objects over systems.

The software companies that grew up in the age of the Internet, however, have taken a different approach. Their field was so new and changing so rapidly that the measured risk aversion of their predecessors would have left them stranded in the middle of the course while their competitors surged ahead. As a result, they often failed — but their initial investments were low enough to let them learn from their failures and move on.

YouTube provides an excellent example of this approach. In its earliest iteration, YouTube was a video dating site called "Tune In Hook Up." It failed, but its ghost lives on at Archive. org, where the earliest capture of YouTube.com includes the menu

options "I'm a Male/Female seeking Males/Females/Everyone between 18 and 99."[1]

The YouTube founders, however, had already real-
ized that what the Internet needed was not another dating site but an
easy way to share video content. They were inspired in part by two
events that occurred in 2004. One was Janet Jackson's "wardrobe mal-
function" at the Super Bowl; the other was the Indian Ocean tsunami.
There were thousands of videos of both events, but it was difficult
to find the sites that hosted them, and they were too large to send as
email attachments.[2]

Chad Hurley, Steve Chen, and Jawed Karim registered
YouTube.com on February 14, 2005, and the site launched in April
of that year. Karim starred in the first video uploaded to the site —
a twenty-three-second clip of him standing in front of the elephant
enclosure at the San Diego Zoo.[3] In October 2006, the trio sold their
creation to Google for $1.7 billion.

From a traditional perspective, YouTube did not begin in a place of strength. It had only three members, one of whom
went back to school before the site launched, rather than taking on
management responsibilities. Its initial funding came from the bo-
nuses its founders received when eBay bought their former employer,
PayPal. It had no business plan, no patents, and no outside capital, but
that left it free to change its focus when its original idea failed.

Even an organization whose basic mission never
changes can embrace resilience over strength by keeping its costs low,
so that it can bounce back from failure. In 1993, Joi's bathroom in Tokyo
was transformed into the Japanese office of IIKK (later PSINet Japan), the
first commercial Internet service provider in Japan. Most of the equipment was old, and much of it was broken. When the server overheated,
they had to blow on it until they could have a new fan delivered.

An established telecommunications company, with
entrenched standards and high overhead, would never have implemented this kind of makeshift setup, but the traditional company's
strength came at a high cost. What PSINet Japan had built for thou-

sands of dollars would have cost the telephone company millions—but when its equipment failed, PSINet Japan recovered, and when demand increased, it scaled up quickly. Within a year, it had moved out of Joi's bathroom into a real office, and it continued to be profitable even as its parent company, in Virginia, overextended itself and fell into bankruptcy.[4] Bill Schrader, who founded PSINet in 1989, later said, "We moved a little too fast. We didn't need to enter three countries at once. We could've just entered one. We would've been behind but we would still be in business now."[5]

PSINet, in short, had traded much of its early resilience for rapid growth. As a publicly traded company with billions of dollars in debt, it no longer had the agility it needed to bounce back from the collapse of the dot-com bubble in 2001.

Organizations resilient enough to successfully recover from failures also benefit from an immune-system effect. Just as a healthy immune system responds to infection by developing new defenses against pathogens, a resilient organization learns from its mistakes and adapts to its environment. This approach has helped shape the Internet as it exists today; rather than planning for every possible attack or failure, the Internet has developed an immune system by responding to and learning from attacks and security breaches as they occur. In its early days, when the price of failure was low, this gave it the resilience it needed to survive without increasing costs. However, even as the cost of malicious attacks and accidental failures rises, this kind of flexible immune response will continue to improve the resilience of the network.[6]

Over time, focusing on resilience over strength may also help organizations develop more vibrant, robust, dynamic systems, which are more resistant to catastrophic failure. Because they do not squander resources anticipating distant eventualities, or expend excessive quantities of time or energy on unnecessary formalities and procedures, they can build up a baseline of organizational health that will help them weather unexpected storms. This is just as true for hardware companies, civic organizations, and nonprofits as it has been for Internet start-ups and software companies. In all of these fields, the cost of innovation—and therefore the cost of failure—is declining so rapidly that an emphasis on strength over resilience may no longer make sense.

Of course, none of this is to say that innovators and their organizations should never plan for the future or anticipate potential sources of trouble. It simply recognizes that at some point there will be failures, and that the most functional systems will be able to regenerate rapidly. The key is to recognize when resisting failure costs more than yielding to it, and to maintain your resilience even as your organization grows.

● ● ●

Fewer fields show the importance of resilience over strength better than cybersecurity. During the summer of 2010 a new malware sample (a small file that contains the offending code to allow researchers to analyze and defeat it) grabbed the attention of security professionals around the world. For those active in the field, some new piece of malicious code is hardly big news; by some estimates the security industry sees around 225,000 malware strains every day. But Stuxnet, as this particular sample was called, was a different animal. It was the first time anyone had seen malware that targeted the customized software that is used to control industrial machineries such as turbines and presses.

After months of relentless analysis it became apparent that the code targeting these supervisory control and data acquisition (SCADA) systems had a very specific purpose: to disrupt the process of uranium enrichment in nuclear facilities. When the centrifuges connected to the system met certain conditions, the malware would forcibly alter the rotation speed of the motors, ultimately causing the centrifuges to break years before their normal life span. More importantly, the centrifuges would fail to properly enrich the uranium samples. The malware would also cleverly alter the information sent back on the computer screens so that its sabotage of the turbine would remain undetected for a long time. Stuxnet's two great accomplishments—the ability to infiltrate a highly secure industrial system and the ability to stay hidden for many years—made it the object of sustained fascination among cybersecurity professionals.

It also, however, demonstrates why resilience is always preferable to strength: There is no Fort Knox in a digital age. Everything that can be hacked will, at some point, be hacked. To convey just how stunned security experts were when Stuxnet became public, consider this: The SCADA systems in use at a nuclear plant are "air-gapped." That means that they have absolutely no connection to the outside world. When technicians *do* need to transfer data in or out of these systems, they do so by protected USB sticks. Stuxnet had either managed to get onto a plant employee's jump drive, or it was an inside job. This feat gained considerably more stature once analysts determined that the virus had targeted five nuclear facilities in Iran— thought to be of the securest sites anywhere in the world.

Stuxnet's second great coup lay in avoiding detection until it had already destroyed nearly one thousand of Iran's centrifuges and put the country's nuclear program back years. What's telling is that these systems turned out to have virtually no security at all. Once Stuxnet got past a first, supposedly impervious line of defense, it became a fox in a hen house. The farmer—Iran's nuclear establishment—spent years wondering why it kept losing so many chickens.

The flaws of opting for strength at the expense of flexibility and resilience do not begin with computer systems. After the first World War, the French were understandably paranoid about the prospect of Germans with guns showing up without an invitation. So from 1930 to 1939 they built a series of massive fortifications along the country's 450-mile long border with Germany. The Maginot Line was billed as utterly impervious, the perfect fortification. And so it would have been—for the previous war. As just about any schoolchild might tell you, in the event the Germans simply shrugged and went *around* the wall. Embedded in that wall along with all that steel and concrete were certain assumptions. The first was that Germany would not violate Belgian or Dutch neutrality in the case of a war between the two West European superpowers. The second was that airplanes—and bombers in particular—would continue to play only a minor role in modern warfare. The third was that there was no need to build cannons that could rotate to fire in any direction, because the Germans couldn't possibly outflank France's entrenched fortifications and attack from the French side of the line. The irony is that the Maginot Line never physically failed. To this day it remains an impenetrable fence. The failure occurred in the imagination of the men who built it, the inability to imagine how to lose in a way that allows you to continue fighting, which is as neat a definition of resilience as you can find.

Deception played an equally important role in Stuxnet's success. The PLCs, programmable logic controllers, that controlled the turbines not only lacked a mechanism to detect malicious code designed to alter the behavior of the motors, but also had no means of detecting attempts to avoid detection by faking the data displayed to the system. Once Stuxnet bypassed the walls used to maintain security at the nuclear facilities, it never encountered another defensive measure.

This failure of imagination, this inability to resist the allure of the impervious defense, is hardly limited to Iran or even nuclear plants. The information security field is littered with Maginot Lines, despite their repeated failures to keep the bad guys at bay.

Today when we think about cybersecurity we immediately think about computers and their vulnerabilities, but cybersecurity evolved from the basic need of protecting information—a need that dates back to the earliest days of written language. For centuries people have relied on more or less scientific forms of cryptography to exchange sensitive information.

Up until the 1970s, cryptography had largely been a game for military intelligence and the occasional educated nerd. In the latter category, we have men like Johannes Trithemius, the German abbot who wrote the three-volume *Steganographia* in 1499—a cryptographic treatise disguised as a book of magical spells and incantations. It circulated in manuscript form until 1606, when a publisher in Frankfurt dared to print it, along with the decryption key for the first two volumes. John Dee tracked down a copy in 1562, and apparently believed it to be a manual for instantaneous long-distance communication enabled by astrology and angels. (Imagine the fun either man would have had on the Internet!)

Another German, Wolfgang Ernst Heidel, broke Trithemius's code in 1676—but since he re-encoded the result using his own code, no one else read it until Dr. Jim Reeds, a mathematician in the mathematics and cryptography department of AT&T Labs, and Dr. Thomas Ernst, a German professor at La Roche College in Pittsburgh, independently solved the puzzle in the 1990s. According to Dr. Reeds, the most difficult thing about decoding the manuscript was transcribing the old monk's numerical tables into his computer—"after all," he told the *New York Times*, "there has been some progress in the last 500 years."

That progress—the increasing sophistication of cryptographic techniques, combined with the increasing speed, processing power, and ubiquity of networked computers—has transformed cryptography, and with it, long-distance communications, monetary transactions, and innumerable other aspects of modern life.

As it had been since the dawn of cryptography, key exchange was the most severe of the inconveniences. Existing cryptographic solutions, from the Caesar cipher to Enigma to the one-time pad, all required that both the sender and the receiver have a copy of the key. However, given that transmitting an unencrypted key would allow an eavesdropper to decrypt any subsequent messages encrypted with it, even electronic messages required a physical exchange of keys. This was problematic even for well-funded governments and military agencies.

This was the problem that consumed Whitfield Diffie's attention in the early 1970s, but he didn't find anyone to share his interest until a cryptographer at IBM's Thomas J. Watson Research Center in New York recommended that he talk to Martin Hellman, a professor at Stanford. After an initial meeting, Hellman found Diffie a place as a graduate student in his research lab, and with a third collaborator, Ralph Merkle, they focused their efforts on solving the key distribution problem.

They soon realized that the solution lay in one-way functions, which are mathematical functions that cannot be easily undone. Think of them like mixing different shades of paint, or cracking eggs—in fact, they're sometimes called Humpty Dumpty functions.[7]

Diffie, meanwhile, had had a breakthrough of his own—a flash of inspiration that led to the first asymmetric cipher. Unlike any previously known code, asymmetric ciphers do not require the sender and receiver to have the same key. Instead, the sender (Alice) gives her public key to Bob, and Bob uses it to encrypt a message to Alice. She decrypts it using her private key. It no longer matters if Eve (who's eavesdropping on their conversation) also has Alice's public key, because the only thing she'll be able to do with it is encrypt a message that only Alice can read.

The following year, MIT mathematicians Ronald L. Rivest, Adi Shamir, and Leonard M. Adleman developed RSA, a method for implementing Diffie's asymmetric cipher that is still used today.[8] Like Diffie-Hellman-Merkle key exchange, RSA relies on a one-way modular function. In this case, the function requires Alice to choose two very large prime numbers and multiply them to get N. With another number, e, N will be Alice's public key. It's reasonably secure, because cracking N is enormously complex. Specifically, the best-known algorithms used today are practically infeasible for very large numbers, hence the bigger the number the less likely a computer is to factorize it in a reasonable time frame.

The first public message encrypted with RSA used a relatively small value of N—only 129 digits. It still took seventeen years before a team of six hundred volunteers donating their spare processor cycles, in the way of SETI@Home, cracked the code. Of course, a day may come when mathematicians discover an easier way to factor large numbers, and the day will come when RSA cannot produce a large enough key to make it secure against the world's most powerful computer networks.

We have come a long way from Caesar's cipher, but even today we rely on the dubious notion that the key, the secret that allows us to decrypt a message, can be kept secure and private—that we have the strength to protect our secrets. In contrast, the history of system security is relatively new. It wasn't until 1988, when Robert Tappan Morris (son of the legendary cryptographer and National Security Agency director Robert Morris) used a buffer overflow to spread the first malware, that people understood that computers were indeed vulnerable to attacks. We have, thus, built a castle in the sand. More troubling yet is that instead of changing our strategy—instead of embracing the inevitable defeats and learning how to contain and limit the damage they cause—we just add more sand to the castle, falling prey again to the illusion of the wall so strong that nothing, not even our blinkered adherence to outdated presumptions, can defeat it

● ● ●

In July 2014 Wall Street sent an ominous document to lawmakers in Washington. The financial service industry's largest trade group asked the government to form a "cyber war council" due to the imminent danger of a cyber attack that could destroy vast amounts of data and drain untold millions from bank accounts. "The systemic consequences could well be devastating for the economy as the resulting loss of confidence in the security of individual and corporate savings and assets could trigger widespread runs on financial institutions that likely would extend well beyond the directly impacted banks, securities firms, and asset managers."

Compounding the danger, the document noted, was the banks' reliance on an electrical grid that faces its own set of security vulnerabilities. That very month the security firm CrowdStrike revealed that a group of Russian hackers known as "Energetic Bear" had been attacking energy companies in the United States and Europe, ostensibly in response to the West's opposition to Russian aggression in Ukraine. According to one security expert who had tracked the group for years, they had a level of organization and wherewithal that suggested government support. They first emerged in 2012, targeting electricity generation firms, grid operators, and petroleum pipeline operators. At the time, Energetic Bear appeared to be on an espionage mission, but the malware in current use gives them access to the industrial control systems utilized by the energy companies themselves. A researcher from Symantec, a Fortune 500 Internet security company, told Bloomberg News "We're very concerned about sabotage."[9]

During the latter part of 2012 U.S. banks suffered from waves of distributed denial of service (DDOS) attacks, in which bad guys flood a targeted server with messages, overwhelming a company's IT infrastructure and forcing normal operations to grind to a halt. And that, the trade group said, was just a warm-up for far more sophisticated attacks to come, likely in the "near-medium term." At present, the trade group admitted, the industry is ill-prepared to defend itself against such attacks.

Big banks and infrastructure companies aren't the only targets. In the perpetual game of cyber offense vs. cyber defense, offense has been winning, but lately it's become a rout. Some eight hundred million credit card numbers were stolen in 2013, three times the number taken in 2012.[10] This gargantuan figure — representing over 10 percent of the world's population—still does sparse justice to the breadth and severity of the problem. Try this, from the chief information security officer of a Fortune 500 company: "Our operating assumption is that within ten minutes of booting up a new server it's been 'owned,'" industry parlance for successfully infiltrating a device.

The unifying theme in the cryptography example, Stuxnet, and the current state of cyber security is not that we are bad at creating strong systems, but rather that we aren't always quick enough to adopt new defensive strategies as our attackers adapt.

In 2012 Ron Rivest and his collaborators wrote a paper taking a game theoretic approach to cybersecurity. The goal of the paper was to find the optimal strategies for both players so that they would each maintain control over the system with the lowest cost. They started from the assumption that however strong your system is it will be compromised. They then proceeded to show that whenever an attacker is adaptive, the best defensive strategy is to play "exponentially"—to make a defensive move (such as resetting a password or destroying and rebuilding a server) at the same average time but at different and hard-to-predict intervals for each instance.

A key factor in playing a defensive game, then, becomes the ability to move faster than attackers and become unpredictable. Resilience over strength. Today malware, computer viruses, and other forms of cyber attacks can respond with blazing speed, circumventing defenses as quickly as they can be mounted. The only way defense might catch up, then, is to appreciate that the modern Internet bears a closer resemblance to the complexity found in a host of other networks composed of heterogeneous actors. "Malicious elements are ubiquitous in complex systems," says cybersecurity expert and Santa Fe Institute fellow Stephanie Forrest. "That's true of biological systems, ecologies, markets, political systems, and of course the Internet." [11]

In fact, the Internet has become so overrun with nefarious actors—Ukrainian cyber mafiosi, Chinese cyber spooks, bored American script kiddies, you name it—that their greatest obstacles are no longer the security regimes on any given network, but each other. And increasingly, the first line for both offense and defense is an automated system. In August 2016, the Defense Advanced Research Projects Agency (DARPA) hosted its first "All-Machine Hacking Tournament," the Cyber Grand Challenge. [12] Over the course of a twelve-hour competition, the machines tested each other's defenses, patched the systems they were programmed to protect against vulnerabilities, and "validated the concept of automated cyber defense."

Aggravating the problem is that a cyber attack has the deck stacked in its favor. Unlike in a police investigation, hackers don't have to worry about national borders or jurisdictional niceties. And to be successful, an attack need only pierce the castle in one place. The king, on the other hand, has to protect every inch of the wall around his kingdom. And none of this reckons with the sheer speed and agility with which hackers work.

"The mismatch between speed-of-light electronic communications and the time required for human institutions to respond to data security and privacy concerns is large and growing," noted a blog post on the *Harvard Business Review*, coauthored by Forrest. To even begin to correct for that lag, the authors wrote, we'd need to stop conceiving of cybersecurity as a technical problem and recognize its political and social dimensions.[13]

Institutions move at the speed of any large group of humans attempting to navigate a complex new landscape. With so much at stake, each will have his or her own brilliant plan and, if you scratch the surface, a hidden agenda. But computer viruses don't only move at the speed of light, they also *adapt* at the speed of evolution—which for a biological virus happens to be very, very fast. One of the most common viruses, *influenza A* or *B*, or the common flu virus, can produce one thousand to ten thousand copies of itself within ten-hours.[14] Sooner or later a virus will emerge with a mutation rendering it resistant to whatever vaccine is in its host's body. Within months, or even weeks, that mutation—or successful adaptation, from the virus's point of view—can spread like, well, a virus.

Likewise, malware, computer viruses, and other forms of cyber attacks can respond with blistering speed, circumventing defenses as quickly as they can be mounted.

The emerging field of complex systems has begun to illuminate the hidden dynamics and patterns that underlie the seeming chaos of, say, the ecosystem of a Florida swamp, or the dark markets in mortgage derivatives. Increasingly, Forrest believes, it will help us mimic those systems as well. To catch a mouse, think like a mouse. And to catch a virus, it might help, say a rising chorus of security experts, to think like an antibody, or an immune system.

"Biological systems have evolved to cope with a multitude of threats such as proliferating pathogens, autoimmunity, escalating arms races, deception, and mimicry," says Forrest. "One design strategy that helps biological systems achieve robustness to these threats is *diversity*—genetic diversity in a species, species diversity in an ecosystem, and molecular diversity in an immune system."[15]

By contrast, the computer industry specializes in homogeneity: churning out near-infinite quantities of identical pieces of hardware and software. The result is that an agent that can wreak havoc in one host—read: computer, or increasingly, any number of the objects joining the Internet of Things—can as easily infect any number of those copies.

The product of hundreds of millions of years of evolution, our immune system is characterized by byzantine complexity, but at its root essence it plays a complicated game of Us vs. Them. Anything that's foreign to the host body is Them; anything that's not is on our team. Forrest and her colleagues employ "agent-based modeling," a kind of war gaming that plays out over powerful computers and pits innumerable individual agents against one another in order to mimic a complex system. Unlike other computer modeling systems used by climate scientists, for instance, agent-based modeling allows individual actors to act selfishly and, most important, to learn and adapt from their mistakes, just like individual participants in an ecosystem or the perpetual intracellular warfare within the human body.[16]

"It allows us to see how a tipping point is reached in an epidemic," Forrest says. "And by imputing 'selfish' behavior to each agent, we get a view of what happens in a complex system five, ten, or fifteen moves into the chess game." Some cyber defense policies, in other words, make a great deal of sense in the short term, but prove disastrous in the long run. One of the smartest immunological strategies to mimic is the ability to operate at full capacity *even during the heat of battle*. This resilience involves a level of humility and acceptance unusual for the military mind-set common to cybersecurity outfits. But as Forrest's research indicates, it may be the only safe way forward, short of following In-Q-Tel executive Dan Geer's example and simply staying as far off the grid as possible.[17]

PS:
Making Peace with Chaos, or Expecting the Unexpected

I have a personal relationship with this principle because I was raised to value strength, but the circumstances of my adult life have required a unique degree of resilience. In January 2008 my son was diagnosed with "global developmental delays." Finn was four months old at the time, but his neck muscles couldn't support the weight of his head and he couldn't seem to gain weight. What truly worried the doctors, though, was his stony, expressionless demeanor. Eventually Finn would not only laugh, but develop a vocabulary of cackles and giggles and shrieks that has become one of his most winning qualities, standing in as they often do for verbal communication. As I write this Finn is nearing his ninth birthday. He faces an array of physical and intellectual challenges that include, but are not limited to, autism. None of this is meant to garner sympathy. My wife and I are incredibly lucky to possess the resources, financial and otherwise, to provide Finn and his neuro-typical sister a good life.

This story is meant to illustrate that many of these principles have profound personal implications. Finn excels at many things—he does a mean headstand, and is a cunning strategist in a water fight—but his greatest talent may lie in disrupting our own humble status quo. I never really know when we might need to leave the house—it could be for the emergency room, or to sate an urgent need to run up and down the aisles of our local grocery store—or return to it. Every day our son—a complex, chaotic system if ever there was one—offers us the opportunity to learn a valuable lesson with applicability far beyond the domestic realm: My instincts are to dig in my heels—my dad wasn't the Marlboro Man, but he'd spent his summers shooting coyote on a wheat ranch, and could set a stern example. I want to put up a courageous front, exercise my will, test my endurance, and try to win.

But that never works. I've caught wise the last few years and have accepted that all my expectations about parenting or, hell, free will, created a false dichotomy: By trying to win, I'll always lose. Only when I accept that there will be no winning or losing, just events unfolding and the way I chose to react to them, do I succeed.

What could all this possibly have to do with the world of business and rapid technological change? Quite a lot, by my lights. I covered the music and the newspaper industry for *Wired* magazine during the very disruptive 2000s. Resilience doesn't necessarily mean anticipating failure; it means anticipating that you can't anticipate what's next, and working instead on a sort of situational awareness. With Finn, that means understanding that a panicked gesture of fist rubbed against cheek means "Home Now!" not "Let's go home once you've finished paying for your new headphones, Dad!" For the music industry it meant acknowledging that the Internet was an opportunity to exploit, not a threat to be neutralized. Print media outlets closely covered the carnage that was music industry in rapid decline, then proceeded to make stunningly similar mistakes. They failed to invest meaningfully in innovative news products during the long years of milk and honey, which meant many great companies withered and shrank when profits grew lean.

Both the music and news industries are small enough to be considered canaries in the coal mine; what happens when sweeping technological change threatens to disrupt the law and medicine and energy—as it already shows signs of doing? If this book is written for anyone, it's the individual determined to make the hard call and chart a new strategy predicated less on winning and power than on thriving in an unpredictable world. As Finn has helped me understand, acceptance is its own brand of courage.

—Jeff Howe

9   Systems over Objects

The Media Lab gathers some of the most accomplished artists and thinkers and engineers in the world, but that's also true of MIT in general, or, for that matter, the academic institution on the *other* end of Massachusetts Ave.—Harvard. What makes the Lab unique is that while ability and talent are respected attributes, the most prized characteristics are original thinking, bold experimentation, and extreme ambition, qualities that can quickly lead to trouble in most academic departments. The Lab prides itself on being an "island for misfit toys" (a winking reference to the animated Christmas special *Rudolph the Red-Nosed Reindeer*). In truth, it's something closer to the Legion of Super-Heroes.

And yet even here Ed Boyden, a neuroscientist whose work spans multiple disciplines, stands out. There's a story people like to tell about the time Boyden went to the World Economic Forum, an annual conference for the world's most powerful CEOs, politicians, and tastemakers. The real action — mergers, treaties, billion-dollar trade deals—occurs away from the official events, at the dinners and private parties that might find Bono exchanging gardening tips with Canadian prime minister Justin Trudeau. Thus Boyden found himself at the storied "Nerds Dinner" held on the final night of the conference. At the beginning of the meal, the guests, who that night included CNN's Fareed Zakaria and the National Institutes of Health's Francis Collins, offered brief summaries of their accomplishments and goals. Finally it came around to Boyden. Slight, bearded, vaguely unkempt, he stood and surveyed the celebrated company before speaking. "My name is Ed Boyden." he said. "I'm solving the brain." Then he sat back down.[1]

The story would be less impressive if Boyden were given to hyperbole or self-promotion, but he's not. Boyden is a classic scientist, with all the caution and skepticism that help define that vocation. He says he's solving the brain because the balance of evidence points in this direction. The brain, our most enigmatic organ, has proven highly resistant to our best efforts to understand it. But we've made great strides in the past decade, in no small part because of the breakthroughs in which Boyden, thirty-six, played a prominent role.

Until very recently, science approached the study of the brain the same way it tackled the study of the kidney. In other words, researchers treated the organ as an *object* of study, and devoted entire careers to specializing in its anatomy, its cellular makeup, and its function within the body. But Boyden didn't come from this academic tradition. The synthetic neurobiology group, as his lab within the Media Lab is known, tends to regard the brain as more verb than noun, less discrete organ than locus of overlapping systems that can only be understood in the context of the ever-changing stimuli that determine their function.

Small surprise then that Boyden's group is a pragmatic bunch, tending to prize practice over theory. "The premise I put to people who start in my group is: Assume the brain is solved in fifty years, and that we'll need to invent lots of new tools to get there. What are those tools, and which one should we work on now?" he says.[2] In his laboratory, power tools and soldering boards share space with beakers and pipettes. And because systems don't respect neat disciplinary boundaries, Boyden consciously recruits people with diverse — if highly accomplished — backgrounds; his team of more than forty crack researchers, affiliates, postdocs, and grad students have included a former concert violinist, a venture capitalist, a comparative literature scholar, and several college dropouts.

● ● ●

Solving the brain is not a "hard problem." A hard problem would involve attempting to simply express the quantity and quality of interrelated challenges that have frustrated our attempts to understand the organ we use for understanding. For one, the sheer scale is overwhelming; There are one hundred billion neurons in the

average human brain. If neurons were people, a square millimeter—
think of a poppy seed—of brain tissue could contain the city of Bur-
bank, California. And that's not even counting the one trillion glia—
the cells that surround and tend to the neurons, as a pit crew tends to
an Indy driver.[3]

      But what awes—and confounds—the neuroscien-
tist isn't the number of cells in the brain, but what lies between them.
Love cannot be traced to a set of neurons; there is no neatly defined
cerebral district responsible for various forms of anger. Consciousness is the ultimate example of emergence; it emanates, as best we can
tell, out of the countless chemical signals hurtling through our brain
every second we draw breath. A single neuron can have thousands
of connections, a.k.a. synapses, to other neurons. That those hundred
trillion connections are equivalent to the number of stars in a thousand Milky Way galaxies speaks to why the brain rivals the cosmos as
a vast, unknown frontier in human understanding.

      The computing power produced by these connections
should be enough to restore anyone's self-esteem. Your brain can hold
2.5 petabytes of data,[4] which means it would take just ten people—
and their accompanying gray matter—to exceed the storage space
of every hard drive manufactured in 1995.[5] And while it's true that
mankind has managed to build a supercomputer capable of the brain's
2.2-billion-megaflop processing speed, there are only four of them,
they take up entire warehouses, and each one uses enough energy to
power ten thousand homes. The brain, considerably more compact,
uses the same amount of energy as a dim lightbulb.[6] So no, solving
the brain is not a hard problem; it is a historical quandary without
precedent or comparison.

      And it's not just understanding the brain that defies
traditional approaches. So do many of the thorny problems touched
on in the preceding pages. Building weather forecasts for a radically
changed climate? Building financial markets that are global, robust,
yet resilient enough to bounce back from inevitable failure? Both, says
Boyden, fall into a class of problem unique to the twenty-first century.

"People talk a lot about moon shots," he says. "But the original moon shot was achieved using well-established principles from one scientific discipline—physics. The fundamental science, the building blocks, were already known."

These new problems, whether we're talking about curing Alzheimer's or learning to predict volatile weather systems, seem to be fundamentally different, in that they seem to require the discovery of all the building blocks in a complex system. "We're going to have to enter realms the human brain has a hard time comprehending," says Boyden. "But it doesn't mean we should stop trying to confront reality on its own terms." These realms, in brief, are those that by their nature involve complex systems.

Solving a problem involving complex systems highlights the subtle but incredibly important distinction between an *interdisciplinary* approach and an *antidisciplinary* approach. The former might involve bringing physicists and cellular biologists together in an interdisciplinary field commonly known as cellular physiology. But Boyden is posing a far more profound question: What if solving these "intractable" problems requires reconstructing the sciences entirely—the creation of entirely new disciplines, or even pioneering an approach that eschews disciplines altogether? He's come to prefer the term "omnidisciplinary."

At the age of fifteen Boyden left high school for MIT—classes started two weeks after his sixteenth birthday. He emerged four years later with two bachelor's degrees and one master's degree. His intellectual preoccupations ranged from lasers to quantum computing, but he combined two attributes once seen as mutually exclusive: He was driven, but he was also—as E. B. White once described those with insatiable, open minds—"willing to be lucky."[7] Or to put it another way, Boyden didn't draw strict boundaries around an object of study—he didn't have *objects* of study at all. Instead, he was fascinated by life itself, in all its vibrant complexity—the process by which different compounds create a chemical reaction, say, or how cells reproduce or become cancerous.

In Boyden's final year at MIT he spent a few weeks at Bell Labs in New Jersey. There he discovered a team of scientists from disparate backgrounds pursuing a common goal: Hack the brain. Specifically, they were trying to understand how a bird's neural circuits generated birdsong. Hacking the brain, Boyden discovered, was something particularly suited to a young scientist as interested in soldering circuit boards as in understanding the complex algorithms they would eventually employ, and before the year was out he was at Stanford pursuing a PhD in neuroscience.

Stanford played host to its own crew of brain hackers, and Boyden soon fell in with a medical student named Karl Deisseroth. The two spent long hours brainstorming ways they could trigger specific neurons that, unlike the current state of brain science, were actually embedded in living brains. They considered an approach that would have used magnetic beads to open ion channels within individual neurons. Soon, however, Boyden discovered research that would lead him down a very different path to the same goal—using light-sensitive proteins called opsins to "pump ions into or out of neurons in response to light."[8]

Side projects being what they are, some years passed before Deisseroth and Boyden revisited their original idea to activate individual neurons. By 2004, Deisseroth was a postdoc, and he and Boyden decided to obtain a sample of an opsin and begin research. That August, Boyden went into the lab, put a dish of cultured neurons into the microscope, and triggered the program he had written to pulse blue light at the neurons. "To my amazement, the very first neuron I patched fired precise action potentials in response to blue light. That night I collected data that demonstrated all the core principles we would publish a year later in *Nature Neuroscience*, announcing that ChR2 could be used to depolarize neurons."[9]

This was a significant breakthrough—and in 2015 it would be recognized as exactly that when Deisseroth and Boyden received $3 million each as part of the Breakthrough Prize awards organized by Mark Zuckerberg and other tech-industry philanthropists.[10]

Previously neuroscientists were simply spectators at brain events, watching vast swaths of neurons react to this or that stimulus, and attempting to infer causality. But with "optogenetics," as Deisseroth and another colleague called the new technique, researchers could stimulate individual neural circuits and observe how they behaved.

Boyden is quick to share credit for optogenetics — with his collaborators, but also with other scientists who were hot on the trail in 2005 when he and Deisseroth first went public with their method. But it seems far from accidental that the two people who "thought of what no one thought of before,"[11] in the words of one prominent neuroscientist, were both outsiders who tended to view the brain as an entity within a larger system. As Boyden has noted, creating a "light switch for the brain" required employing molecular biology, genetic engineering, surgery, fiber optics, and lasers.[12] Just one of these would find its way onto the standard neurology curriculum.

Optogenetics has revolutionized the study of the brain, and since the original discovery Boyden and other researchers have refined the technique so that neurons can be genetically modified to recognize different colors of light. Clinical applications are years in the future, though the first test in a human patient was approved in 2016.[13] A few years ago, Boyden and a team of other researchers used it to cure blindness in mice. While it's impossible to say exactly what the blind mice with the light-sensitive cells "saw," the researchers determined that they were able to navigate a six-armed maze in which the exit was marked by a bright light just as well as sighted mice, and much more easily than their untreated blind cousins. The effect lasted for the full ten months of the study.[14]

The promise of optogenetics is not limited to neurology, or to the treatment of certain forms of blindness.[15] In the decade since Boyden, Deisseroth, and Feng Zhang developed the technique, it has been used to study brain function; control neurons involved in narcolepsy,[16] Parkinson's, and other neurological disorders[17]; and investigated for applications such as cardiac pacing[18] — imagine a pacemaker that's truly part of the heart it regulates, or a cure for epilepsy.

As new opsins are discovered—in microbes and algae—the possibilities multiply, as they react to different types of light and work differently in mammalian cells, allowing multichannel control over mixed groups of cells, or the use of, say, red light instead of blue. Additionally, optogenetics research is helping to stimulate further development of complementary tools, such as neural recording and imaging technologies.[19]

"There are more than a billion people on this planet that suffer from some kind of brain disorder," says Boyden. "A great many of those diseases—from Parkinson's to epilepsy to PTSD—might eventually be treated using insights that arose from optogenetics."

● ● ●

Not long after Joi first joined the Media Lab, he orchestrated a trip to Detroit. He had recently launched a program called the Innovator's Guild, which was intended to bring new ideas into the often rarefied environment of a prestigious academic institution, as well as to help the Lab connect to the larger world. Launched in conjunction with the Knight Foundation and the design consulting firm IDEO, the trio had the goal of bringing Media Lab ingenuity to bear on some of inner-city Detroit's most pressing problems, like access to fresh produce.

But as the team discovered after arriving, the community had its own notion of what a difficult problem was. Because the wiring in many streetlights had been stripped and sold for salvage, many of Detroit's streets were dangerously dark after sunset. Some of the Lab's designers began working on a potential solution, using photovoltaic systems with plastic components. However, after talking to more people in the community, they again realized that their initial theory was wrong. It wasn't the lack of lighting that was the real problem. It was that without any street lighting, people couldn't be sure where the other members of their community were, and that made them feel unsafe. By working with them and listening to people in a way they wouldn't have been able to if they hadn't been willing to discard their original theory, the engineering and design students helped their Detroit counterparts develop a solution that drew on the community's resources and empowered them to create their own street lighting.

When the students and designers sat down with members of the community, they found that the only retail businesses in the area were liquor stores, which didn't seem promising until they realized that liquor stores sell flashlights, and flashlights can be taken apart. They spent several days teaching the children to solder, and the kids built wearables that not only provided light, but also let them find each other in the dark. They didn't theorize about it; they just helped the kids build it. And most of the ideas came from the kids themselves, which was tremendously exciting. And a lesson for the Media Lab team: Intervening responsibly meant understanding the role any innovation would play in a much larger system. Anything the Lab designs on its own would have been, by contrast, an object. Could the photovoltaic light have been integrated into the particular needs and circumstances and complexity of Detroit's overlapping communities? Possibly, but it would have been more by accident than intent.

Systems over objects recognizes that responsible innovation requires more than speed and efficiency. It also requires a constant focus on the overall impact of new technologies, and an understanding of the connections between people, their communities, and their environments.

Previous generations of innovation have largely been driven by questions of individual or corporate profit—questions like "What does this thing do for me? How do I use it to make money?" However, the era in which innovators could develop new products and technological interventions without considering their ecological, social, and network effects has passed. In the future, the drive toward innovation must be tempered with a deep consideration of its potential systemic effects. By fully embracing this principle, we can help to ensure that future innovations have either a positive or, at worst, neutral impact on the various natural systems in which we exist.

In order to reach this goal, we must develop a fuller understanding of the communities in which we work. At the Media Lab, this has meant shifting the emphasis from creating objects to building relationships—to making the Media Lab a node in a network. In the past, the Lab has been something of a container for innovative people, products, and ideas. That isn't to say that the Media Lab hasn't always worked on improving interfaces, empowering individuals, and expanding the potential of digital devices to enable social networking and communications. Some of its projects have involved building the network itself—like DonkeyNet (yes, literally using donkeys to provide "drive-by" Wi-Fi for remote communities) followed by DakNet, a collaboration that served as a "'electronic postman for India." Other past efforts have focused on mobile diagnostics or tools for rural health workers, or on hardware, including the One Laptop per Child (OLPC) project, which designed a low-cost laptop and later a tablet to provide computers to children all over the world.[20]

In the past several years, the Media Lab has attempted to move closer to a model that envisions the Lab as more of a platform that uses extensive networks—one that is connected to the global community and welcomes ever-more diverse inputs. The Lab is expanding its work with charitable foundations, individual philanthropists, and local communities around the globe through efforts such as the Director's Fellows program, which has created a network of fellows across geographies and fields from Libya to Detroit, from chess grandmasters to Buddhist monks. While past projects like DakNet and OLPC provided avenues for much-needed connectivity, the Director's Fellows are part of an expanding network of human knowledge and initiative.

Embracing a systems-over-objects approach helps us encode the principle that every scientific or technological intervention must consider its effect on the entire global network.

Contrast this with traditional industrial design, which has been informed by price and engineering concerns. A popular story that illustrates this approach is that Henry Ford mandated black paint for the Model T because it dried faster. While recent research by Professor Trent E. Boggess at Plymouth State College has called this anecdote into question, his alternative explanation also suggests that Ford took an object-based view of the Model T. Boggess says, "The Model T was a most practical car. No doubt Henry Ford was convinced that black was simply the most practical color for the job. Model Ts were not painted black because black dried faster. Black was chosen because it was cheap and very durable."[21]

Although cheap, durable paint jobs may have been an admirable quality in cars intended for "the great multitude" and "so low in price that no man making a good salary will be unable to own one — and enjoy with his family the blessing of hours of pleasure in God's great open spaces"[22] — they were not, as it turned out, the only thing that car buyers wanted. In 1927, the cheap, durable Model T gave way to the Model A, which incorporated many of the stylish aesthetic elements and advanced technologies that Ford had previously rejected.[23]

While these changes were made in response to public demand, it was not until the 1980s that social science research was applied to design in a systematic way. The result was human-centered design, which attempts to respond to the needs of the user.[24] As Steve Jobs once put it, "You've got to start with the customer experience and work backwards to the technology."[25] By the late 1990s, this had evolved into participatory design, in which users are asked to contribute their ideas. Codesign takes this a step further by inviting users to become designers themselves.[26]

By its very nature, codesign empowers users to develop solutions that are embedded in and responsive to the systems in which they live. Many of these solutions will be highly idiosyncratic — perfectly suited to the people who created them, but not intended for a mass audience. In Henry Ford's industrial age, this might have been fatal, but modern digital and manufacturing technology has made it increasingly affordable to customize products and software for small numbers of users.

One of the advantages of this approach is that it creates highly resilient systems, which can respond quickly when their users need change. Rather than completely retooling, as Ford needed to do when it replaced the Model T with the Model A, an engaged community can redesign its solutions in real time, or something close to it.

Of course, codesign is not the only way of creating systems-oriented solutions, nor is the Media Lab the only organization working toward incorporating this principle into its work. In describing its self-driving car, Google has emphasized that the car itself is merely an object—the artificial intelligence that drives it is the system, and it must mesh seamlessly into the other systems it touches. As such, its sensors and software are being designed to work with existing road infrastructure and to solve common problems such as drunk driving and transport for people with mobility challenges. An object-based approach to driverless vehicles might have resulted in nothing more than expensive toys or cargo vehicles designed to maximize corporate profits. By utilizing a systems-based approach, however, Google is positioned to make a real difference in people's lives.

PS:
Working in the
White Space

In March of 2016, the Media Lab, together with the MIT Press, launched the *Journal of Design and Science* (JoDS) in an attempt to bring design and science closer.

This connection includes both the examination of the science of design and the design of science, as well as the dynamic relationship between the two. The idea is to foster a rigorous but flexible approach in the Media Lab's signature antidisciplinary fashion.

When I think about the "space" we've created, I like to think about a huge piece of paper that represents "all science." The disciplines are represented by a line of widely spaced little black dots. The massive amounts of white space between the dots represent antidisciplinary space. Many people would like to play in this white space, but there is very little funding for it, and it's even harder to get a tenured position without some sort of disciplinary anchor in one of the black dots.

Additionally, it appears increasingly difficult to tackle many of the interesting problems—as well as the wicked, or intractable, problems—through a traditional disciplinary approach. Unraveling the complexities of the human body is the perfect example. Our best chance for rapid breakthroughs should come through a collaborative "one science." But instead, we seem unable to move beyond "many sciences"—a complex mosaic of so many different disciplines that often we don't recognize when we are looking at the same problem, because our language is so specialized and our microscopes are set so differently.

With funding and academic prestige so focused on the disciplines, it takes greater and greater effort and many more resources to make a unique contribution. While the space between and beyond the disciplines can be academically risky, it often has less competition; requires fewer resources to try promising, unorthodox approaches; and provides the potential to have tremendous impact by unlocking connections between existing disciplines that are not well connected. The Internet and the diminishing costs of computing, prototyping, and manufacturing have also lowered many of the costs of doing research.

Design has become what many of us call a suitcase word. It means so many different things that it almost doesn't mean anything. On the other hand, design encompasses many important ideas and practices, and thinking about the future of science in the context of design—as well as design in the context of science—is an interesting and fruitful endeavor.

Design has also evolved from the design of objects both physical and immaterial, to the design of systems, to the design of complex adaptive systems. This evolution is shifting the role of designers; they are no longer the central planners, but rather participants within the systems in which they work. This is a fundamental shift—one that requires a new set of values.

Today, many designers work for companies or governments developing products and systems focused primarily on making sure that society works efficiently. However, the scope of these efforts is not designed to include—nor care about—systems beyond our corporate or governmental needs. These underrepresented systems, such as the microbial system, have suffered, and still present significant challenges for designers.

MIT faculty members Neri Oxman and Meejin Yoon teach a popular course called Design Across Scales, in which they discuss design at scales ranging from the microbial to the astrophysical. While it is impossible for designers and scientists to predict the outcome of complex self-adaptive systems, especially at all scales, it is possible for us to perceive, understand, and take responsibility for our intervention within each of these systems. This would be much more of a design whose outcome we cannot fully control—more like giving birth to a child and influencing his or her development than designing a robot or a car.

An example of this kind of design is the work of Media Lab Assistant Professor Kevin Esvelt, who describes himself as an evolutionary sculptor. He is working on ways of editing the genes of populations of organisms such as the rodent that carries Lyme disease and the mosquito that carries malaria to make them resistant to the pathogens. The specific technology—CRISPR gene drive — is a type of gene edit such that when carrier organisms are released into the wild, all of their offspring, and their offspring's offspring, will inherit the same alteration, allowing us potentially to eliminate malaria, Lyme disease, and other vector-borne and parasitic diseases. His focus is not on the gene editing or the particular organism, but the whole ecosystem—including our health system, the biosphere, our society, and its ability to think about these sorts of interventions.

As participant designers, we focus on changing ourselves and the way we do things in order to change the world. With this new perspective, we will be able to more effectively tackle extremely important problems that don't fit neatly into the current academic system: in essence, we are seeking to redesign our very way of thinking to impact the world by impacting ourselves.

—Joi Ito

Conclusion

Once you learn to see a certain pattern you can begin to recognize it everywhere you look. If all living things, for instance, evolve in fits and starts—the pattern of long periods of stability interrupted by brief intervals of explosive change usually called "punctuated equilibrium"—is it any wonder the games humans play would do the same? Basketball fans, for example, might point to Julius Irving's reverse layup during the 1980 NBA playoffs as a defining moment in the evolution of the game. Hockey fans might argue that by demonstrating that the greatest acts of athleticism were in what you did when you *didn't* have the puck, Wayne Gretsky turned hockey into a true team sport.

Serious students of the board game Go can point to similar instances when a single player resets the table; they just draw on considerably more history in doing so. There was the famous "dual ladder breaker," move first performed during the Tang dynasty when a Chinese master scored an upset against a prince visiting from Japan, or the legendary "ear reddening game" from 1846, in which a single risky move changed the way people played the game for generations to come.[1] Decades might pass between the appearances of these "myoshu"— moves so "surprising and startling in [their] insight" they achieve a kind of legendary status.[2] It's all the more remarkable, then, that not one but two moves that may come to be seen as myoshu were performed in a high profile match in early March 2016.

Go is often mentioned in the same breath as chess, but outside of their being strategy games played by two people facing each other across a table, Go is both simpler, in that it only has two rules, and far more complex, in that there are more possible moves, by orders of magnitude, than there are atoms in the universe.[301] High-level Go players position small, black and white stones on a grid composed of nineteen lines in both directions, while beginners may opt for a simpler game—nine by nine, or thirteen by thirteen. Whatever the size of the board, the goal is to capture as much territory, and as many of your opponent's stones, as possible.

"Chess," the German master Richard Teichmann once said, "is 99 percent tactics," and success requires seeing the long-term consequences of any given move. But no earthly intelligence could compute the possible outcomes from the 361 moves that greet a competitor when facing an empty Go board. Go prodigies tend to possess uncanny pattern-recognition skills and rely on their intuition. In fMRI studies the right hemisphere of the brain—the side that governs visual awareness and holistic awareness—lights up more strongly in Go players than the left.[4] In fact, with its nearly infinite possibilities, a Go board has more in common with the painter's blank canvas than it does with the game of chess. The Chinese, who probably invented the game around the time the Old Testament was being written, must have thought so. Go was considered, along with painting, calligraphy, and playing the lute, one of the "four arts" that every gentleman was expected to master.

Until recently these characteristics — near-infinite possibilities, more intuitive than logical—made programming a computer to play Go what's known, in mathematics, as a "hard problem," which is a euphemism for impossible. Nor was it a problem that could be solved in the same way that the superficially similar problem of chess had been. A team of computer scientists at IBM spent twelve years building Deep Blue, a computer capable of defeating a chess grandmaster. It succeeded in 1997, beating Garry Kasparov in a six-game series. Capable of analyzing two hundred million positions per second, Deep Blue relied on a "brute force" algorithm, simply evaluating every possible consequence of a move up to a depth of twenty steps.

Two hundred million calculations a second sounds like a large number, but Deep Blue couldn't have challenged a moderately talented eighth-grader at Go. The sheer scale of possibilities contained within those 360 black and white stones is dizzying. Whole new fields of game theory and mathematics were created so our humble brains could even ponder such questions. For a brute-force kind of machine intelligence like Deep Blue to play Go would require more processing time than the one-thousand-trillion-year life expectancy of our universe.

Then in 2006 a French computer scientist named Rémi Coulom published a paper[5] that hinted at a new line of attack. In the 1950s researchers had developed a search algorithm, named for the grand casino in Monte Carlo, to model the effects of a nuclear explosion. Unable to explore every possible outcome, Monte Carlo searched a statistical sampling of the whole. On its own the algorithm didn't work for Go, but Coulom refined it so that the software recognized that some moves deserved more scrutiny than others. Some were nodes that branched out to many more possibilities. Coulom programmed his Monte Carlo Tree Search algorithm to identify which move in any given sequence held the most promise, then focus on outcomes emanating from that particular node. This allowed the software to "learn" successful patterns of play that human competitors internalized subconsciously from countless hours of play.

In the next few years Coulom's program, Crazy Stone, began racking up impressive wins against other software products, and in 2013 it bested one of the world's leading professionals, but only after receiving a four-move head start—the sort of handicap a professional might extend to a talented amateur. In fact, at the time the common consensus within both the Go and machine-learning communities was that it would be many years before artificial intelligence reached a point at which it could compete against the best human players without the benefit of a handicap. A machine simply couldn't replicate the improvisational, creative kind of genius that animated the highest level of play.

That was before the scientific journal *Nature* published a bombshell article in January 2016 reporting that Google's artificial intelligence project, DeepMind, had entered the race.[6] Its program, called AlphaGo, first learned from a huge history of past Go matches, but then, through an innovative form of reinforcement learning, played itself over and over again until it got better and better. The previous November, the article revealed, Google had orchestrated a five-game match between European Go champion Fan Hui and AlphaGo. The final score? The Machine: 5, the Human: 0. It was a watershed moment in the field of machine learning—the first time a computer had beaten a professional Go player without a head start. The article quoted Rémi Coulom saying he'd expected it to take another ten years for a machine to show true mastery of the game. Another AI researcher, Jonathan Schaeffer, noted that Deep Blue was regularly beating chess grandmasters by 1989, but it had taken another eight years for it to become good enough to beat Garry Kasparov.

AlphaGo was about to receive its Kasparov moment. In March, *Nature* revealed, the software would play Lee Sedol, commonly regarded as the greatest living master, or sensei, of the game. "No offence to the AlphaGo team, but I would put my money on the human," Schaeffer told *Nature News*. "Think of AlphaGo as a child prodigy. All of a sudden it has learned to play really good Go, very quickly. But it doesn't have a lot of experience. What we saw in chess and checkers is that experience counts for a lot."[7]

Not everyone has cheered on the machine's inexorable invasion of all aspects of our lives. On the day the *Nature* article was published, Mark Zuckerberg wrote a post announcing that Facebook had its own AI capable of beating humans at Go. "Why don't you leave that ancient game alone and let it be without any artificial players? Do we really need an AI in everything?"[8] By June the comment had received more than eighty-five thousand reactions and four thousand comments.

● ● ●

Fan Hui, the European champion, had played his five matches against AlphaGo in front of an audience of two: a referee and an editor from *Nature*. Lee Sedol opened the first match at the Seoul Four Seasons Hotel against a backdrop of television cameras that had come from around the globe to watch our last, great hope try to redeem our flawed, unpredictable humanity. Sedol made a series of risky, unorthodox moves that might have been expected to throw a machine — with its vast catalog of textbook games — off guard. But AlphaGo never blinked, and punished Sedol's aggression by gradually taking command of the board until it had secured the win. What was immediately evident, according to other professional players, was that AlphaGo had become a much more accomplished player in the few months since it had beat Fan Hui in London.

In beating Sedol once, the DeepMind team had already accomplished the hard problem of mastering a game long regarded as a mirror of the human thought process. Suddenly the prospect of winning the entire series seemed within reach.

In the second match Sedol displayed his newfound respect for AlphaGo by playing careful, flawless Go. It wasn't designed to wow the 280 million people who would eventually watch the series, but from someone of Sedol's rank, it constituted nearly unbeatable play, and Sedol exuded a quiet but unmistakeable confidence. Then, as the game began to enter its middle phase, AlphaGo did something unusual: it instructed its human attendant to place a black stone in a largely unoccupied area to the right of the board. This might have made sense in another context, but on that board at that moment AlphaGo seemed to be abandoning the developing play in the lower half of the board. This historic move was something that no human would have feasibly played — AlphaGo calculated the probability that a human would play that move at 1 in 10,000.[9] It produced instant shock and confusion among the spectators. Lee Sedol paled, excused himself, and left the room for a full fifteen minutes before returning.

The English-language commentators went silent before one said, with great understatement: "That's a very surprising move."

At first Fan Hui, who was watching the game with Cade Metz, a writer for *Wired* magazine, was as befuddled as anyone else. "It's not a human move," he told Metz. "I've never seen a human play this move." As Metz would later note,[10] nothing in the 2,500 years of collected Go knowledge and understanding prepared anyone for move

37 of the second game in the series. Except Hui. Since losing to AlphaGo the previous fall Hui had spent hours helping the Google DeepMind team train the software for the match with Sedol, an experience that allowed him to understand how the move connected the black stones at the bottom of the board with the strategy AlphaGo was about to pursue. "Beautiful," he said, then repeated the word several more times. This was not mere "tesuji"—a clever play that can put an opponent off guard. This was a work of aesthetic as well as strategic brilliance, possibly even a my-oshu. Sedol continued to play nearly flawless Go, but it wasn't enough to counter the striking creativity the DeepMind software displayed, even after move 37. By the end of the day the big news wasn't that AlphaGo had won a second game, but that it had displayed such deeply human qualities—improvisation, creativity, even a kind of grace—in doing so. The machine, we learned, had a soul.

● ● ●

A few weeks after the conclusion of the Humans vs. Machines Showdown, Demis Hassabis — one of the artificial intelligence researchers behind Google's DeepMind—gave a talk at MIT to discuss the match, and how his team had developed AlphaGo. Held in one of the university's largest lecture halls, the DeepMind event drew a standing-room-only crowd—students were all but hanging off the walls to hear Hassabis describe how their approach to machine learning had allowed their team to prove the experts who had predicted it would take ten years for a computer to beat a virtuoso like Sedol wrong.

The key was a clever combination of deep learning—a kind of pattern recognition, similar to how a human brain (or Google) can recognize a cat or a fire truck after seeing many images—and "learning" so that it could guess statistically what something was likely to be, or in the case of Go, what a human player, considering all of the games of the past, was likely to play in a particular situation. This created a very rudimentary model of a Go player that guessed moves based on patterns it learned from historical matches. Then, they added a kind of reinforcement learning, which allows the computer to try new things. Just as the brain learns by being rewarded with dopamine when it does something that succeeds, which reinforces the neural pathway that "got it right," reinforcement learning allows a computer to try things and rewards successful experimentation, thus reinforcing those strategies. AlphaGo started with a basic version of itself, then created slightly different versions to try multiple strategies millions of times, rewarding the winning strategies until it got stronger and stronger by playing against successively better versions of itself. Then, later, after playing an expert human, it made both the human and itself stronger as it continued to learn.

In his talk Hassabis revealed breakthrough after breakthrough — some things researchers in the room had previously said they thought might be impossible. The excitement was palpable. He also showed images and videos from the rest of the match between AlphaGo and Lee Sedol. As it turned out, move 37 wasn't the last dramatic moment of the match. After the second game Sedol had done his homework, developing a strategy based on known weaknesses of the Monte Carlo Tree Search algorithm. Sedol opened the third game by forcing a "ko fight," in which one side removes its opponent's stone, forcing him or her to retaliate or relinquish the initiative. Such an aggressive opening in the hands of someone at Sedol's level of play would have annihilated most opponents. AlphaGo, however, seemed to effortlessly counter every brilliant stroke. One commentator wondered if the audience wasn't watching a "third revolution" in the way Go is played. After move 176, Sedol conceded the game, the match, and the $1 million prize that went with it. During a post-game press conference Sedol, looking as though the burden of representing an entire species weighed heavily on his shoulders, apologized to the global audience. Humans, he noted, have to contend with the psychological game as well as the one played out in wood and stone. "I was," he said sadly, "incapable of overcoming the pressure."

Small wonder that game four opened against a somber backdrop. Having so handily defeated Sedol at his ingenious best,

AlphaGo seemed fated to execute a clean sweep in the last two games. And nothing during the first half of game four seemed to indicate the contrary. But then Sedol did something radical and unexpected— he played a "wedge" move in the middle of the board. AlphaGo, it suddenly became clear to millions of people around the world, had no idea how to respond. It made several clumsy plays and then conceded. Sedol, commentators noted, had created a masterpiece—a potential myoshu all his own.

AlphaGo ended up winning four out of the five matches. One could imagine that a computer beating a historically legendary Go champion might diminish interest in Go for humans or make it less interesting to play. In fact, more people watched the video online than watched the Super Bowl,[11] Go board sales increased dramatically,[12] and a student from the MIT Go club announced that the size of the club had doubled. In his talk at MIT, Hassabis said that the interaction with AlphaGo had renewed Sedol's excitement about Go.

Clearly, AlphaGo didn't make Go less interesting, but rather injected a burst of creativity and energy into the game and the community of players and scholars. The positive response and strong ongoing relationship between the machine and the Go community— they gave AlphaGo an honorary rank of 9th dan (the highest rank for Go players)—strengthened Joi's belief that the future doesn't have to hold Terminator-like intelligences that will decide that humans are a bad idea and eliminate them. It could, rather, contain a society in which humans and machines work together, inspiring each other and augmenting a growing collective intelligence.

• • •

Ray Kurzweil, a futurist and familiar presence on the lecture circuit, popularized the idea of exponential change in his 2005 book, *The Singularity Is Near*. Kurzweil predicts that a computer will read as well as a human by 2029, and that the singularity—the point at which machines become more intelligent than humans—will arrive by 2045. At that point, according to the theory of singularity, we will witness an "intelligence explosion" in which the machines will rapidly design ever more intelligent versions of themselves, not unlike the scenario depicted in the 2013 movie *Her*.

Most experts in machine learning believe AI will progress to that point someday, though most would sooner address the Nobel Prize committee in their skivvies than offer so specific a date as Kurzweil. A singularity, technically speaking, is the point at which a function takes an infinite value, such as what happens to space and time at the center of a black hole. What happens after a technological singularity? According to Kurzweil we enter a period of blissful transhumanism, in which the line between human and machine becomes indistinguishable, and the superintelligences that roam the planet solve all of mankind's problems. Others — Elon Musk, Paypal alum and the inventor behind Tesla Motors, for one — believe the machines will rightly see humans as a kind of metastasizing cancer infecting the planet, and zap *Homo sapiens* out of existence.

We encourage a broader view: Maybe AI's good, maybe it's bad. Or just maybe that's beside the point when measured against the other threats and positive outcomes that might develop in the coming century. A climate process in the Arctic called a positive feedback is currently accelerating the melting of the Arctic's sea ice — if it moves faster than forecast, we could be facing a global calamity that sends us back into a dark age. Or a nihilist group of hackers could wipe out our global financial markets in one fell swoop, causing panic, then widespread conflict. Or there might be a pandemic on the scale of the fourteenth century's bubonic plague.

An extinction event isn't so unlikely as it seems. It's almost happened before, after all. A volcanic eruption some seventy thousand years ago is estimated to have reduced the global population of humans to a one-taxi town. And yet, we would encourage a less pessimistic view: we no more understand what ultimate uses our new technologies will serve than the "animated pictures" audiences of 1896 could have predicted *Citizen Kane*. The point of this book isn't to scare you with dread visions of the future. It's as useful to entertain visions of life on Kepler-62e.

Because "Artificial Intelligence" is used as a label for everything from Siri to Tesla automobiles, we now describe this kind of problem-solving AI as "narrow" or "specialized" AI, to differentiate it from AGI—artificial general intelligence. Artificial intelligence expert Ben Goertzel suggests that an AGI would be a machine that could apply to college, be admitted, and then get a degree.

There are many differences between a specialized AI and an AGI but neither is programmed. They are "trained" or they "learn." Specialized AIs are carefully trained by engineers who tweak the data and algorithms, and keep testing them until they do the specific things that are required of them. These AIs are not creative—they are instead heavily supervised, and their applications are narrow.

There are dozens of advances in machine learning and other fields still standing between us and an AGI, but AlphaGo has already realized several of them. It appears to be creative; it appears to be capable of deriving some sort of symbolic logic through a statistical system. It's hard to overstate the significance of this accomplishment— many people didn't believe you could get to symbolic reasoning from deep learning.

However, while AlphaGo is very smart and very creative, it can only beat you at Go—not at checkers. Its entire universe of expression and vision is a grid of nineteen lines and black and white stones. It will take many more technological breakthroughs before AlphaGo will be interested in going to nightclubs or running for office. In fact, we may *never* have a machine that goes to nightclubs or runs for office. However, it might not be too long before something like AlphaGo will be determining parole, setting bail, flying airplanes, or teaching our children.

As artificial intelligence progresses, machines may well become an integrated part of our bodies, our homes or vehicles, our markets, our court systems, our creative endeavors, and our politics. As a society, we are already more intelligent than we are as individuals.

We are part of a collective intelligence. As our machines continue to integrate into our networks and our society, they become an extension of our intelligence—bringing us into an extended intelligence.

Some of the Singularitarians (Worst. Cult. Name. Ever.) believe that it won't be long before AI is good enough to put many humans out of work. This may be true, especially in the short run. However, others argue that the increase in productivity will allow us to create a universal basic income to support the people made redundant by the machines. At the same time, many worry that our jobs give us dignity, social status, and structure—that we need to be more concerned with how we will entertain ourselves and what we'll create, possibly through academic or creative endeavors, than with merely providing income.

We should also ask ourselves how humans and machines will work together, and how we'll ensure that people feel as if the artificial intelligences they live with share their values and reflect their ethics, even as they evolve. One promising approach is what Iyad Rahwan, head of the Scalable Cooperation group at the Media Lab, calls "society in the loop" machine learning, which uses social norms to train and control AIs, possibly leading to a system of co-evolution between humans and machines.[13]

This year, the United States Department of Defense budgeted $3.6 billion for artificial intelligence. And yet, AI researchers both in academia and industry have called for a world in which the machines and the people who train them are part of an open discussion with the public. The question is, are we seeing a race between open society's attempt to create an AGI and a more secretive, military-controlled effort to develop one, or will this golden age of open research in AI slowly close down as private companies become more competitive and get closer to "the answer"?

These events will unfold over the next decade or so and may well affect the world more than anything else discussed in this book. Whatever happens, though, the Singularitarians are right about one thing. It's not just technology that's moving at an exponential pace, but change itself. That is a product of technology, but of other developments as well. In the past twenty-five years we have moved from a world dominated by simple systems to a world beset and baffled by complex systems. In the introduction we explain the factors behind this shift. They are, namely, complexity, asymmetry, and finally, unpredictability. We will summarize our goal, which is no less ambitious than to provide a user's manual to the twenty-first century: Create organizations built around resilience, agility, and educational failure.

● ● ●

We first met to work on this book on a blustery spring day in 2012. It was a Sunday afternoon, and the streets around the MIT Media Lab were virtually empty. The previous fall Joi had been appointed director of the Media Lab, which occupies a storied position as ground zero for many of the technological innovations driving the information economy. Joi had biked in from his temporary apartment in Boston's South End. (He eventually bought a house in Cambridge, but rarely stays anywhere for more than two or three days.) Our literary agent, John Brockman, had recommended that we meet. We shook hands a little awkwardly, then went upstairs to one of the Media Lab's many glass conference rooms to see if we wanted to write a book together.

By the end of the day a few themes had emerged. We were both broadly curious about the world, and neither one of us had come to academia through the usual route, which meant we were spared the kind of disciplinary tunnel vision that can afflict the lifelong academic. Joi was a college dropout who established his intellectual bona fides as an entrepreneur and blogger. Jeff had been a longtime writer for *Wired* magazine before a Harvard fellowship led to a tenure track post at Northeastern University.

Both of us had spent the past several years speaking to large audiences of decision makers, from Fortune 500 managers to FBI agents to foreign leaders. And both of us had emerged from the experience deeply concerned about the ability of large institutions to weather a crucial juncture in human history, which is to say, our own historical moment, a worry exacerbated by a shared belief that the future holds far more radical, tumultuous change than the average executive understood.

What also emerged that first day was a mutual skepticism toward the field of futurism. Humans have an appalling record at predicting future events, and the prophecy racket is only going to get tougher in the years to come.

Most importantly perhaps, we discovered that we both actually *care*. It often seems books wrestling with new ideas swing between clinical, detached treatments on one hand, and rather dubious vehicles for speaking engagements on the other. We wanted to write something new that would combine the rigor of scholarship with the passion of a much more personal work

Because the ideas we discussed that first day, and that have come to be the organizing principles for this book, matter in a very concrete way. People's livelihoods are at stake. Whole industries are in danger. Observing institutions of immense economic and social value stumble blithely into a buzzsaw struck us as less dinner party conversation and more four-alarm fire.

We're not trying to sell you a way to organize your workdays or an exercise regimen, and we're definitely not trying to make you believe in our vision of the future, because we don't have one, other than a firm belief it will be very, very different from the world we inhabit right now. We do have an argument to make: Innovation isn't about learning how to use social media to generate sales leads. And modifying a business for a networked globe will require more than buying fancy teleconferencing gear for your management team. Instead, we think it requires a deeper, more fundamental shift: an entirely new mode of thinking—a cognitive evolution on the scale of a quadruped learning to stand on its hind two feet.

● ● ●

One way of thinking of these principles is that they're observations of how two simple but profound developments initiated a powerful change in how humans interact with the world. The first, obviously, is the development of the Internet, which unlike any previous communication technology provided connections from many-to-many as well as one-to-many. The British economist Ronald Coase famously described how the firm could allocate and manage resources better than independent agents in an open market—in "Coase's Penguin, or Linux and the Nature of the Firm," Yochai Benkler shows that when collaboration costs are reduced, as in projects like Linux and Wikipedia, allowing people to allocate themselves to projects can create assets and organizations more effectively than top-down and structured companies. He calls this "commons based peer production."[14] This off-the-balance-sheet, below-the-radar, not-part-of-our-GDP explosion of creativity is taking over more and more of our world. Everyone involved in it is at the same time a producer and a consumer, a worker and a manager. Money is just one of the many currencies you need to thrive and be happy in a world that requires and rewards attention, reputation, networks, learning, creativity, and tenacity. Suddenly we are all broadcasters, publishers, or would-be demagogues.

Progress in most academic disciplines now seems to move at the speed of "instantaneous," with discoveries building atop one another at a dizzying pace. Yet that's nothing compared to the private sector; the most valuable start-up of the last ten years began as Silicon Valley's equivalent of a bar bet. Six years later Uber is valued at $62.5 billion—more than Hertz and all the other major car rental companies combined. Unlike most companies with market valuations greater than most island nations, however, Uber seems to get by on something of a skeletal staff, with only one thousand employees. That's the same number as Walmart employs—in its Lehigh Valley, Pennsylvania, distribution center, anyway.

All of this is a testament to what happened when the Internet and Moore's law got together. They turned a few quantitative measures (speed, cost, size) into qualitative facts. When a few engineers in Shenzhen, say, can prototype, focus-group, and distribute a new product at great scale and little cost, that's no mere change in degree. That doesn't represent a "new revenue model" for the bank that might have provided them with a small business loan a few years before. They've also managed to sidestep the regulation that would hamstring a larger company. Now the bank and the government are cut out of the loop entirely. That's a qualitative, not quantitative, change.

What's next? You don't know? Guess what. Neither does anyone else. No one can predict the future. In fact, experts and so-called futurists have some of the worst records of all—underperforming that perennial contender, Random Guess.

And that's good, because maintaining a healthy relationship with uncertainty is one of the big themes that run through the principles. Mankind has been humbled during the last few years, but that's nothing compared to what's headed our way. Successful organizations will not, for instance, bet the house on quarterly sales predictions, knowing that a black swan could be just over the next pass. Instead they might not bet big at all, choosing to adopt a portfolio strategy in which small bets are made on a variety of products or markets or ideas.

If the industrial era was about command-and-control management systems, hierarchies and facts, Network Age logic reflects decades in which we—Americans, but all humans as well—have reevaluated our place in the world. We've learned that we can't command or control the weather, and in fact we've had limited success controlling complex systems of our own making, be that protecting sensitive networks from cyber attacks or using monetary policy to influence the markets. If there is one thing on which the otherwise disparate researchers, scientists, and thinkers throughout this book might agree, it's that we are only now learning enough to discover just how little we know. It's difficult to believe that in 1894 the Nobel Prize–winning physicist Albert Michelson could say that "it seems probable that most of the grand underlying [scientific] principles have been firmly established."[15] All that remained, he seemed to believe, would be to tie up a few loose ends. Within thirty years the theory of relativity would render all such statements absurd displays of hubris.

The world is in the midst of a fundamental structural change. We have to be able to hardwire an ability to adapt and see things that we'd otherwise ignore because they don't fit our old conditioning. We are going through a phase where the world is completely changing and in our lifetimes may change completely again with AI.

Human beings are fundamentally adaptable. We created a society that was more focused on our productivity than our adaptability. These principles will help you prepare to be flexible and able to learn the new roles and discard them when they don't work anymore. If society can survive the initial whiplash when we trade our running shoes for a supersonic jet, we may yet find that the view from the jet is just what we've been looking for.

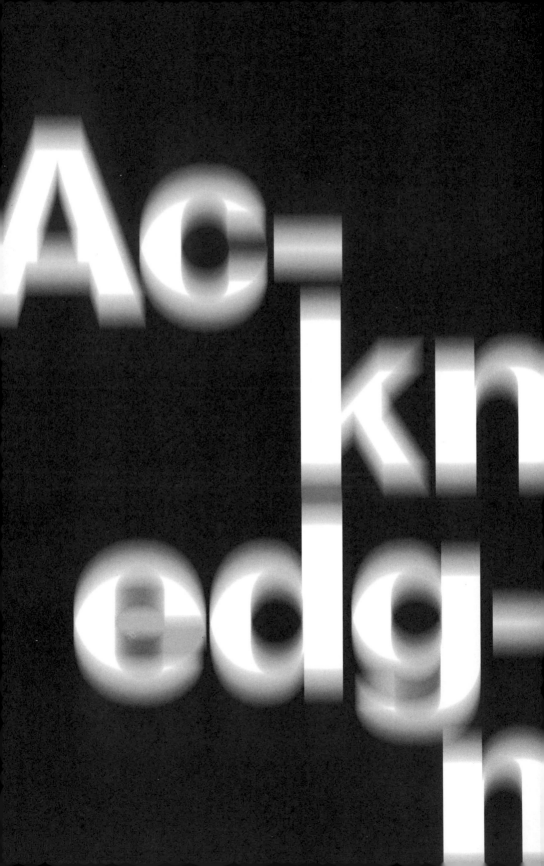

Acknowledgments

From Joi:

This book is the result of years of tireless work from Jeff Howe, my coauthor, and our researcher, Chia Evers, without whom none of this would exist. This book grew from an amazing collaboration between three people contributing different skills, backgrounds, and points of view. I believe the collaboration produced a final manuscript that is far greater than the sum of its parts.

I met John Brockman and his wife, Katinka Matson, in a café in Tokyo in 1997. They told me that I should write a book and that they would represent me. Ever since then, John has been my agent. Fifteen years later, Max Brockman, John's son, introduced me to Jeff Howe, with whom he was working, and suggested we meet and discuss coauthorship. Thanks to the Brockmans for having faith, and to Max for the brilliant insight of connecting me with Jeff. Many thanks as well to our editor, Gretchen Young, at Grand Central Publishing for her invaluable editorial input and to Gretchen and Katherine Stopa for their deep commitment to putting out the best book possible.

Thanks to Megan Smith, who turned to me on a bus trundling from Oxford to Cambridge and asked if I'd be interested in becoming the director of the Media Lab.

Thanks to Nicholas Negroponte for being an amazing mentor and always pushing me to think bigger. Nicholas's adherence to his principles and his relentless struggle against incrementalism and mediocrity has made the Media Lab what it is and sets the standard to which I strive.

Thanks to the faculty of the Media Lab, who have expanded my curiosity and understanding of everything, as well as my interest in academia. The faculty has also played a critical role in the development of these principles, arguing and discussing them at faculty retreats and through endless e-mail threads.

In many ways the Media Lab — its students, staff, and faculty—has become my extended family over the past five years. And while there are too many people to call out individually, I would like to acknowledge all of them for their boundless creativity, energy, and enthusiasm; endless hours of help; and the way they constantly challenge my thinking. Likewise, MIT's central administration has been amazingly supportive of my unconventional background and the Media Lab's unconventional approach. In particular, I'd like to thank Rafael Reif, now MIT president, who was provost when he gave me the final interview and approved a college dropout to become the director of the Lab. Also Professor Bob Langer, who has been an incredible mentor, helping me navigate the loving but sometimes complex ecosystem that is MIT; Provost Marty Schmidt; Vice President of Finance Israel Ruiz; Dean Hashim Sarkis; and Vice President for Research Maria Zuber.

No book can be written about the Media Lab without acknowledging the late Jerry Wiesner, who convinced MIT that it made sense to create a "department of none of the above," and also the late Marvin Minsky and Seymour Papert (both of whom died this year) and Muriel Cooper — the Lab's "three pioneers" — who along with Jerry and Nicholas created the original DNA of the Lab.

George Church, of Harvard, offered witty and thoughtful advice and inspiration, continuing to remind us that "if what you're doing has competition, you're doing something uninteresting." Reid Hoffman has been my "thought partner" for just about everything, and a continuing source of encouragement and support in thinking about the Media Lab and the principles. Thanks to John Seely Brown and John Hagel for *The Power of Pull*, and to my late adopted godfather, Timothy Leary, for being a "performing philosopher," showing me how to be disobedient with style, and for "question authority and think for yourself." Also Barack Obama for helping me with my messaging around "deploy."

Thanks to Seth Godin, J. J. Abrams, Walter Isaacson, Paola Antonelli, Vincenzo Iozzo, Jeremy Rubin, Ron Rivest, Scott E. Page, Mitch Resnick, Demis Hassabis, Sean Bonner, Colin Raney, Scott Hamilton, Ellen Hoffman, Natalie Saltiel, and many others for helping to review and revise the text.

My executive assistant, Mika Tanaka, and former assistant Heather deManbey, who have had the thankless task of organizing my schedule and workflow throughout this process. Chiaki Hayashi for organizing everything in Tokyo that needs to be organized and being such a tireless and positive force. Wes Neff for wrangling all of my speaking engagements. Mark Stoelting and his team for being the best travel agents in the world; I certainly put their skills to the test.

My sister, Mimi, who is the real academic in our family, and her husband Scott Fisher, who was my original connection to the Media Lab. My father, the first scientist in my life. My late mother for bringing me into this world and giving me the support and the confidence to be myself and pursue my own path. Lastly and most importantly, thanks to my wife, Mizuka, for her love and support through the writing of this book, and for putting up with my crazy life.

From Jeff:

One day in the spring of 2012 my agent called to ask if I would be interested in coauthoring a book. The first thing I said was, "Nope." When writers gather around to tell war stories, some of the most harrowing involve creative partnerships gone wrong. "Who's the other writer?" I asked, just out of curiosity. "Joi Ito," he said. "Oh," I said. "In that case, yes." I'd written a short profile of Joi for *Wired* magazine in 2003. He was one of the handful of people who helped guide the Internet through its infancy, hardwiring it for transparency and democracy, and who has an abundant respect for the wonderful and the weird. More impressive was the devotion he inspired among colleagues and friends. If *Forbes* measured social capital instead of financial capital,

Joi would top the list. Four years on I can easily understand why. Joi possesses all the brilliance you would expect from the leader of one of the world's top research labs, but it's nothing compared to the infectious glee and wonder with which he regards the world. This book was often challenging; thanks to Joi, it was *always* fun.

If humans really do discover a cure for mortality, as we suggest they might, I still will not have time to repay the immense debt I owe Chia Evers. She brings her diligence, intelligence, and serenity to bear on everything she touches. Her contributions to this book are as immense as her boundless curiosity, and it is truly a product of the collaboration between three different but complementary people.

I owe many thanks as well to John Brockman for suggesting that Joi and I write a book together, and Max Brockman for providing priceless counsel and advocacy through the many twists and turns that accompanied work on this book.

It is conventional to thank one's editors in a book's acknowledgments, but as our team at Grand Central can attest, the editorial process on this book was anything but conventional. Thanks to Rick Wolf for acquiring our book, Mitch Hoffman for his enthusiastic encouragement, and most of all Gretchen Young, who took a leap of faith and saw this book through to its completion. Many, many thanks as well to Kyle Pope, whose wisdom, editorial and otherwise, has been illuminating my darkest passages for many years, and to Katherine Stopa, Jeff Holt, Jimmy Franco, Andrew Duncan, and the rest of the fantastic team at Grand Central.

The MIT Media Lab deserves its reputation for attracting some of the most original minds of our time, but this book ultimately benefited most from the profound humanism that has characterized the Media Lab since its inception. The Media Lab staff, faculty, and students continuously demonstrate that the value of technology should be measured by its capacity to improve the lives of its users. Mitch Resnick exercised an influence over this book that extends far beyond the field of education, as did David Kong, whose compassion and commitment to social justice rivals his polymathic intelligence. Time and again the Media Lab staff, faculty, and students freely offered me the most precious resource: their time. Innumerable thanks to Ellen Hoffman, Neri Oxman, Nadya Peek, Deb Roy, Jeremy Rubin, Stacie Slotnick, Philipp Schmidt, Jessica Sousa, and the many others whose fingerprints, in one way or another, found their way into these pages. Thanks as well to the many sources—Tom Knight, Scott Page, and many others—outside the Media Lab who took so much time to translate ideas of great complexity to the language even the most obtuse of journalists might understand.

Books can be beastly things, selfish and unmerciful. Such creatures are never vanquished without the support of friends, family, and colleagues. I owe a tremendous debt to Northeastern University for supporting my work on this book, and to the many individuals there I'm inexpressibly proud to call my colleagues. A lot of life happens in four years, and it's no exaggeration to say this book would never have come into being without Steve Burgard, who hired me to teach journalism at Northeastern before passing away halfway through this book's completion. I owe a great debt as well to our current director, Jonathan Kaufman, and to my colleagues in the Media Innovation program, Dina Kraft and Aleszu Bajak. I was at every step in the process the beneficiary of the wise counsel and unstinting encouragement of my official mentor, Alan Schroeder, as well as my generous unofficial mentors, Mike Beaudet, Susan Conover, Chuck Fountain, Carlene Hempel, Dan Kennedy, Laurel Leff, Gladys and Link McKie, and John Wihbey.

Likewise, when I look back at the previous few years, I see many footprints, but rarely my own. My inexpressible appreciation and love to our community of friends, as full of grace as they are of talent, who helped support me when the light grew dim and my muscles weak. Without Martha Bebinger, Harlan Bosmajian, Gary Knight, Andrea Meyer, Valerie Stivers, Fiona Turner, and Pat Whalen I might have collapsed under the weight of this book somewhere well short of the finish line. The same could easily be said of Dircelene Rodriguez, whose unflagging love and care for our family these past six years have formed the bedrock on which everything else is built.

If this book demonstrates a love of learning and of passing that love to others, that is thanks to my father, Robert Howe, whose long career has been devoted to that project. If it demonstrates a fundamental faith in human nature, that is due to my mother, Alma, who died before this book was completed, but not before deeply influencing one of its authors. And if it demonstrates any art in its construction, that is due to my sister, Jeanine Howe, who has devoted her life to her students and helping them bring the make-believe to life.

As always, the greatest debt of all is owed to my huge-hearted daughter, Annabel, my mischievous son, Finn, and my beautiful and talented wife, Alysia Abbott. No one should have to share a home with a writer writing a book, least of all another working writer. It's one thing to sacrifice one's well-being for an important project. It's something close to unconscionable to inflict sacrifice on the people you love the most. The English language doesn't provide the tools to express the gratitude I feel toward my patient, forgiving, and miraculously good-humored family.

This book is written, at least in part, to the memory of John Melfi. I'll see you in Nymphana, buddy, where the lines are always tight.

Notes

Introduction

1   Emmanuelle Toulet, *Birth of the Motion Picture*, (New York: Harry N. Abrams, 1995), 21.

2   The brothers hired a celebrated painter, Henri Brispot, to illustrate the scene, then turned it into the world's first movie poster.

3   Martin Loiperdinger and Bernd Elzer, "Lumière's Arrival of the Train: Cinema's Founding Myth," *The Moving Image* 4, no. 1 (2004): 89–118, doi:10.1353/mov.2004.0014.

4   Daniel Walker Howe, *What Hath God Wrought* (Oxford: Oxford University Press, 2007), 7.

5   David L. Morton, Jr. *Sound Recording: The Life Story of a Technology* (Baltimore: Johns Hopkins University Press, 2006), 38–39.

6   Paul A. David, "The Dynamo and the Computer, an Historical Perspective on the Modern Productivity Paradox." *American Economic Review*, 80, no. 2 (1990): 355–361.

7   Ashley Lutz, "20 Predictions from Smart People That Were Completely Wrong," *Business Insider*, May 2, 2012, http://www.businessinsider.com/false-predictons-2012-5?op=1#ixzz3QikI1PWu.

8   David Lieberman, "CEO Forum: Microsoft's Ballmer Having a 'Great Time,'" *USA Today*, April 30, 2007, http://usatoday30.usatoday.com/money/companies /management/2007-04-29-ballmer-ceo-forum-usat_N .htm.

9   Michel Foucault, *The Archaeology of Knowledge* (New York: Pantheon, 1972).

10   Thomas S. Kuhn, *The Structure of Scientific Revolutions: 50th Anniversary Edition* (University of Chicago Press, 2012).

11   Ibid.

12   Daniel Šmihula, "The Waves of the Technological Innovations," *Studia Politica Slovaca*, issue 1 (2009): 32–47; Carlota Perez, *Technological Revolutions and Financial Capital: The Dynamics of Bubbles and Golden Ages* (Northampton, MA: Edward Elgar Publishing, 2002).

13   Frank J. Sonleitner, "The Origin of Species by Punctuated Equilibria," *Creation/Evolution Journal* 7, no. 1 (1987): 25–30.

14   Chris Mack, "The Multiple Lives of Moore's Law," *IEEE Spectrum* 52, no. 4 (April 1, 2015): 31–31, doi:10.1109 /MSPEC.2015.7065415.

15   Janet Browne, *Charles Darwin: Voyaging* (New York: Knopf, 1995).

16   Ibid.; Janet Browne, *Charles Darwin: The Power of Place* (New York: Knopf, 1995); Adrian Desmond and James Moore, *Darwin* (London: Michael Joseph, 1991).

17   Dietrich Stoltzenberg, *Fritz Haber: Chemist, Nobel Laureate, German, Jew; A Biography* (Philadelphia: Chemical Heritage Foundation, 2004).

18   Marc Goodman, *Future Crimes: Everything Is Connected, Everyone Is Vulnerable and What We Can Do About It* (New York: Doubleday, 2015).

19   Peter Hayes, *From Cooperation to Complicity: Degussa in the Third Reich* (New York: Cambridge University Press, 2007).

20   "Through Deaf Eyes," PBS, http://www.pbs.org/weta /throughdeafeyes/deaflife/bell_nad.html.

21   We should note that this may be an apocryphal quote.

22   Mark Cousins, *The Story of Film* (London: Pavilion, 2012), Kindle Edition, chapter 1: "Technical Thrill (1895–1903), The sensations of the first movies."

23   Richard Brody, "The Worst Thing About 'Birth of a Nation' Is How Good It Is," *New Yorker*, February 1, 2013, http://www.newyorker.com/culture/richard-brody/the -worst-thing-about-birth-of-a-nation-is-how-good-it-is.

24   This "cosmic calendar" originated with the late Carl Sagan, in *The Dragons of Eden* (New York: Ballantine, 1977). It has since been expanded and revisited in Sagan's PBS series *Cosmos: A Personal Voyage* (1980), as well as National Geographic's 2014 series *Cosmos: A Spacetime Odyssey*, starring Neil DeGrasse Tyson.

25   John Hagel III, John Seely Brown, and Lang Davison,

"The Big Shift: Measuring the Forces of Change,"
Harvard Business Review, July–August 2009,
https://hbr.org/2009/07/the-big-shift-measuring
-the-forces-of-change.

26 Šmihula, "The Waves of the Technological Innovations";
Perez, *Technological Revolutions and Financial Capital.*

27 John Hagel III, John Seely Brown, and Lang Davison,
"The New Reality: Constant Disruption," *Harvard
Business Review*, January 17, 2009, https://hbr.org
/2009/01/the-new-reality-constant-disru.html.

28 For just one recent example, see Devlin Barrett, Danny
Yadron, and Damian Paletta, "U.S. Suspects Hackers
in China Breached About 4 Million People's Records,
Officials Say," *Wall Street Journal*, June 5, 2015,
http://www.wsj.com/articles/u-s-suspects-hackers
-in-china-behind-government-data-breach-sources
-say-1433451888.

29 James O'Shea, *The Deal from Hell: How Moguls and Wall
Street Plundered Great American Newspapers* (New York:
PublicAffairs, 2012).

30 Matt Levine, "Guy Trading at Home Caused the Flash
Crash," *Bloomberg View*, April 21, 2015,
http://www.bloombergview.com/articles/2015-04-21
/guy-trading-at-home-caused-the-flash-crash.

31 Melanie Mitchell, *Complexity: A Guided Tour* (New York:
Oxford University Press, 2009), 10.

32 Ibid., 176

33　Ibid., 13

34　Page is referring to the famous scene in the
mockumentary *This Is Spinal Tap* in which the mentally
addled lead guitarist, Nigel Tufnel, tries to explain the
significance of an amplifier with the capacity to exceed
the conventional 10 on the volume knob. "Well, it's one
louder, isn't it?"

35　Quoted in Joichi Ito and Jeff Howe, "The Future: An
Instruction Manual," *LinkedIn Pulse*, October 2, 2012,
https://www.linkedin.com/pulse/20121002120301-1391
-the-future-an-instruction-manual.

36　Nate Silver, *The Signal and the Noise: Why So Many
Predictions Fail* (New York: Penguin, 2012); Louis Menand,
"Everybody's an Expert," *New Yorker*, December 5, 2005,
http://www.newyorker.com/magazine/2005/12/05/
everybodys-an-expert; Stephen J. Dubner, "The Folly of
Prediction," *Freakonomics* podcast, September 14, 2011,
http://freakonomics.com/2011/09/14/new
-freakonomics-radio-podcast-the-folly-of-prediction/.

37　National Council for Science and the Environment,
*The Climate Solutions Consensus: What We Know and What to
Do About It*, edited by David Blockstein and Leo Wiegman
(Washington, D.C.: Island Press, 2012), 3.

38　*Oxford Advanced Learner's Dictionary*, http://www
.oxforddictionaries.com/us/definition/learner/medium.

39　The Media Lab's website includes a comprehensive
overview of the Lab's funding model, current research,
and history. http://media.mit.edu/about/about-the-lab.

40   Olivia Vanni. "An Ex-Apple CEO on MIT, Marketing
& Why We Can't Stop Talking About Steve Jobs,"
BostInno.com. April 8, 2016. http://bostinno.streetwise
.co/2016/04/08/apples-steve-jobs-and-john-sculley
-fight-over-ceo/.

41   To select just a few biologically inspired projects at the
Media Lab as of May 2016, Kevin Esvelt's Sculpting
Evolution group is studying gene drives and ecological
engineering; Neri Oxman's Mediated Matter group is
experimenting with microfluidics and 3D-printing living
materials; and Hiroshi Ishii's Tangible Media group has
created a fabric with "living nanoactuators" that use
bacteria to open or close vents in the material in response
to the wearer's body temperature.   .

42   Malcolm Gladwell. "Creation Myth: Xerox PARC, Apple,
and the Truth about Innovation." *New Yorker*, May 16,
2011, http://www.newyorker.com/magazine/2011/05/16
/creation-myth.

Chapter 1:
Emergence over Authority

1   Steven Johnson, *Emergence: The Connected Lives of Ants, Brains, Cities, and Software* (New York: Scribner, 2001), 64.

2   Balaji Prabhakar, Katherine N. Dektar, and Deborah M. Gordon, "The Regulation of Ant Colony Foraging Activity without Spatial Information," Edited by Iain D. Couzin, *PLoS Computational Biology* 8, no. 8 (August 23, 2012): e1002670. doi:10.1371/journal.pcbi.1002670. Also see Bjorn Carey, "Stanford Biologist and Computer Scientist Discover the 'Anternet,'" *Stanford Engineering: News and Updates*, August 24, 2012, http://engineering.stanford .edu/news/stanford-biologist-computer-scientist -discover-anternet .

3   F. A. Hayek, "The Use of Knowledge in Society," *American Economic Review* 35, no. 4 (1945): 519–30.

4   As of November 15, 2015, more than 3.2 billion people (40 percent of the world's population) had access to the Internet, http://www.internetlivestats.com/internet-users/.

5   Jim Giles, "Internet encyclopaedias go head to head," *Nature* 438 (December 15, 2005), 900–901.

6   Prabhakar, Dektar, and Gordon, "The Regulation of Ant Colony Foraging Activity without Spatial Information."

7   World Health Organization, "Tuberculosis: Fact Sheet No. 104," reviewed March 2016, http://www.who.int /mediacentre/factsheets/fs104/en/.

8   Thomas M. Daniel, "The History of Tuberculosis,"
          Respiratory Medicine 100, issue 11 (November 2006):
          1862–70, http://www.sciencedirect.com/science/article
          /pii/S095461110600401X.

9   Mark Nicas, William W. Nazaroff, and Alan Hubbard,
          "Toward Understanding the Risk of Secondary Airborne
          Infection: Emission of Respirable Pathogens," *Journal of
          Occupational and Environmental Hygiene* 2, no. 3 (2005):
          143–54, doi:10.1080/15459620590918466, PMID
          15764538.

10   Centers for Disease Control and Prevention (CDC),
          "Tuberculosis Morbidity—United States, 1994,"
          Morbidity and Mortality Weekly Report 44, no. 20 (May 26,
          1995): 387–89, 395, http://www.ncbi.nlm.nih.gov
          /pubmed/7746263.

11   World Health Organization, "What Is Multidrug-Resistant
          Tuberculosis (MDR-TB) and How Do We Control It?"
          updated October 2015, http://www.who.int/features
          /qa/79/en/.

12   World Health Organization, "WHO's First Global Report
          on Antibiotic Resistance Reveals Serious, Worldwide
          Threat to Public Health," press release, April 30, 2014,
          http://www.who.int/mediacentre/news/releases/2014
          /amr-report/en/.

13   Team Bettancourt, "Fight Tuberculosis with
          Modern Weapons," http://2013.igem.org/Team:Paris
          _Bettencourt.

14   Ibid.

15   Interview with Jeff Howe.

16   As this book nears completion, researchers at the Joint
BioEnergy Institute (JBEI) at Lawrence Berkeley National
Laboratory have announced a major advance toward
producing commercially viable biofuels from biomass
and *E. coli*. According to the University of Washington's
Conservation magazine, the new process utilizes *E. coli*
engineered to not only tolerate the molten salts used
to break down the plant materials, but also produce
enzymes that are tolerant of the salts. The eventual goal
is to produce biofuels in a "low-cost, one-pot process."
Aindrila Mukhopadhyay, the vice president of the Fuels
Synthesis Division at the JBEI says, "Being able to put
everything together at one point, walk away, come back,
and then get your fuel, is a necessary step in moving
forward with a biofuel economy." See Prachi Patel, "Green
Jet Fuel in One Easy Step." *Conservation* magazine, May
12, 2016, http://conservationmagazine.org/2016/05
/green-jet-fuel-one-easy-step; Marijke Frederix, Florence
Mingardon, Matthew Hu, Ning Sun, Todd Pray, Seema
Singh, Blake A. Simmons, Jay D. Keasling, and Aindrila
Mukhopadhyay, "Development of an *E. Coli* Strain for
One-Pot Biofuel Production from Ionic Liquid Pretreated
Cellulose and Switchgrass," Green Chemistry, 2016,
doi:10.1039/C6GC00642F.

17   Nathaniel Rich, "The Mammoth Cometh," *New York Times
Magazine*, February 27, 2014, http://www.nytimes.com
/2014/03/02/magazine/the-mammoth-cometh.html.

18   Interview with Jeff Howe.

19   DIYBio, https://diybio.org/.

20   Ryan Mac, "Already Backed with Millions, Startups Turn to Crowdfunding Platforms for the Marketing," *Forbes*, August 6, 2014, http://www.forbes.com/sites /ryanmac/2014/08/06/backed-with-millions-startups -turn-to-crowdfunding-for-marketing/#6cfda89c56a3.

21   For a more extensive discussion of crowdsourcing, Jeff modestly recommends his first book, *Crowdsourcing: Why the Power of the Crowd Is Driving the Future of Business*, (New York: Crown Business, 2009).

22   See, for example, Christina E. Shalley and Lucy L. Gilson, "What Leaders Need to Know: A Review of Social and Contextual Factors That Can Foster or Hinder Creativity," *Leadership Quarterly* 15, no. 1 (2004): 33–53, doi:10.1016/j .leaqua.2003.12.004: "[Researchers] have identified a set of core personality traits that are reasonably stable across fields and result in some individuals being more creative than others....These traits include broad interests, independence of judgment, autonomy, and a firm sense of self as creative. In addition to personality traits, creative performance requires a set of skills specific to creativity...the ability to think creatively, generate alternatives, engage in divergent thinking, or suspend judgment. These skills are necessary because creativity requires a cognitive-perceptual style that involves the collection and application of diverse information, an accurate memory, use of effective heuristics, and the ability and inclination to engage in deep concentration for long periods of time. When individuals access a variety of alternatives, example solutions, or potentially related ideas, they are more likely to make connections that lead them to be creative." (Internal citations omitted).

23 Interview with Jeff Howe.

24 Harold J. Morowitz, "The Understanding of Life: Defining Cellular Function at a Molecular Level and Complete Indexing of the Genome," publication date unknown, but likely 1984, paper provided by Tom Knight.

25 James J. Collins, Timothy S. Gardner, and Charles R. Cantor, "Construction of a Genetic Toggle Switch in Escherichia Coli," *Nature* 403, no. 6767 (January 20, 2000): 339–42, doi:10.1038/35002131.

26 Michael B. Elowitz and Stanislas Leibler, "A Synthetic Oscillatory Network of Transcriptional Regulators," *Nature* 403, no. 6767 (January 20, 2000): 335–38, doi:10.1038/35002125.

27 Tom Knight, Randall Rettberg, Leon Chan, Drew Endy, Reshma Shetty, and Austin Che, "Idempotent Vector Design for the Standard Assembly of Biobricks," http://people.csail.mit.edu/tk/sa3.pdf.

28 Interview with Jeff Howe.

Chapter 2:
Pull over Push

1   "Nuclear Meltdown Disaster," *Nova* (PBS), season 42, episode 22.

2   Nassim Nicholas Taleb, *The Black Swan: The Impact of the Highly Improbable* (London: Penguin UK, 2008).

3   David Nakamura and Chico Harlan, "Japanese Nuclear Plant's Evaluators Cast Aside Threat of Tsunami," *Washington Post*, March 23, 2011, https://www.washingtonpost.com/world/japanese-nuclear-plants-evaluators-cast-aside-threat-of-tsunami/2011/03/22/AB7Rf2KB_story.html.

4   Yuki Sawai, Yuichi Namegaya, Yukinobu Okamura, Kenji Satake, and Masanobu Shishikura, "Challenges of Anticipating the 2011 Tohoku Earthquake and Tsunami Using Coastal Geology," *Geophysical Research Letters* 39, no. 21 (November 2012), doi:10.1029/2012GL053692.

5   Gwyneth Zakaib. "US Government Advises Wider Evacuation Radius around Crippled Nuclear Plant." *Nature News Blog*, March 16, 2011, http://blogs.nature.com/news/2011/03/us_residents_advised_to_evacua_1.html.

6   "In many ways, [the Media Lab] is a business," Moss told *The Tech*, MIT's student newspaper, at the time of his appointment. He suggested the Media Lab should conduct research into projects of interest to its corporate sponsors. "You have to strike a balance between having academic freedom and doing different types of research, and havingthe work sponsored by companies that want to see research commercialized. At the Media Lab, we may have to go a step further than we've done in the past and build prototypes with sponsors."

7   The organization's website is located at http://www .safecast.org.

8   "Nuclear Fears Spark Rush for Radiation Detectors," *Agence France-Presse*, March 29, 2011.

9   Always with the lower-case "b."

10 Andrew "bunnie" Huang, "Hacking the Xbox (An Introduction to Reverse Engineering)," n.d., http://hackingthexbox.com/.

11 The information regarding Safecast comes from published histories of the organization and conversations with the founders.

12 An idea pioneered by Jacob Schmookler, in *Invention and Economic Growth* (Boston: Harvard University Press, 1966). For an overview of Schmookler's work, see F. M. Scherer, "Demand-Pull and Technological Invention: Schmookler Revisited," *The Journal of Industrial Economics* 30, no. 3 (1982): 225–37, http://www.jstor.org/stable /2098216.

13 See https://aws.amazon.com/what-is-cloud-computing/.

14 David Weinberger. *Small Pieces Loosely Joined: A Unified Theory of the Web* (New York: Basic Books, 2003).

15   Dan Pink, "The Puzzle of Motivation," TED Talk, July
2009, https://www.ted.com/talks/dan_pink_on_motivation.

16   IETF, "Mission Statement," https://www.ietf.org/about
/mission.html

17   As of May 2016, more than eighty institutions and
organizations—including Jeff's home university,
Northeastern—were using Experiment.com to raise
funds for research. According to the site, research funded
through its platform had been published in twenty
scientific papers. https://experiment.com/how-it-works.

18   Interview with Jeff Howe.

19   For more information about the case, including court
filings, see "Rubin v. New Jersey (Tidbit)," Electronic
Frontier Foundation (EFF), https://www.eff.org/cases
/rubin-v-new-jersey-tidbit.

20   Now available as a PDF from the Bitcoin Foundation,
https://bitcoin.org/bitcoin.pdf.

21   Erik Franco. "Inside the Chinese Bitcoin Mine That's
Grossing $1.5M a Month," *Motherboard*, February 6, 2015,
http://motherboard.vice.com/read/chinas-biggest
-secret-bitcoin-mine?utm_source=motherboardyoutube.

22   Quoted in Maria Bustillos, "The Bitcoin Boom," *New
Yorker*, April 1, 2013.

23   Joshua Davis. "The Crypto-Currency: Bitcoin and Its
Mysterious Inventor." *The New Yorker*, October 10, 2011.

24   Ethan Zuckerman, "The Death of Tidbit and Why It
      Matters," ...*My Heart's in Accra*, May 28, 2015,
      http://www.ethanzuckerman.com/blog/2015/05/28
      /the-death-of-tidbit-and-why-it-matters/.

25   John Hagel III, John Seely Brown, and Lang Davison,
      *The Power of Pull: How Small Moves, Smartly Made, Can Set
      Big Things in Motion*, (New York: Basic Books, 2012)

26   Mark S. Granovetter, "The Strength of Weak Ties,"
      American Journal of Sociology 78, no. 6 (1973): 1360–80,
      http://www.jstor.org/stable/2776392.

27   Malcolm Gladwell, "Small Change: Why the Revolution
      Will Not Be Tweeted," *New Yorker*, October 4, 2010,
      http://www.newyorker.com/reporting/2010/10/04
      /101004fa_fact_gladwell?printable=true.

28   Yves-Alexandre de Montjoye et al., "The Strength of
      the Strongest Ties in Collaborative Problem Solving,"
      Scientific Reports 4 (June 20, 2014), doi:10.1038/srep05277.

29   Doug McAdam, "Recruitment to High-Risk Activism:
      The Case of Freedom Summer," *American Journal of
      Sociology* 92, no. 1 (1986): 64–90, http://www.jstor.org
      /stable/2779717.

30   "2013 Everett M. Rogers Award Colloquium," YouTube,
      https://www.youtube.com/watch?v=9l9VYXKn6sg.

31   Ramesh Srinivasan and Adam Fish, "Internet Authorship:
      Social and Political Implications within Kyrgyzstan,"
      Journal of Computer-Mediated Communication 14, no. 3 (April
      1, 2009): 559–80, doi:10.1111/j.1083-6101.2009.01453.x.

32   Ethan Zuckerman, *Digital Cosmopolitans: Why We Think the Internet Connects Us, Why It Doesn't, and How to Rewire It* (W. W. Norton & Company, 2013).

33   Like the William Gibson quote that appears in the introduction, the origin of this well-known sentiment is unclear. The Institute for Cultural Studies, which Mead founded in 1944, and which closed its doors in 2009, says, "We have been unable to locate when and where it was first cited....We believe it probably came into circulation through a newspaper report of something said spontaneously and informally. We know, however, that it was firmly rooted in her professional work and that it reflected a conviction that she expressed often, in different contexts and phrasings." http://www.interculturalstudies.org/faq.html.

34   Maria Popova, "Autonomy, Mastery, Purpose: The Science of What Motivates Us, Animated," *Brain Pickings*, http://www.brainpickings.org/index.php/2013/05/09 /daniel-pink-drive-rsa-motivation/.

Chapter 3:
Compasses over Maps

1   Interview with Jeff Howe.

2   James Aley, "Wall Street's King Quant David Shaw's
         Secret Formulas Pile Up Money. Now He Wants a Piece
         of the Net," *Fortune*, 1996, 3–5, http://money.cnn.com
         /magazines/fortune/fortune_archive/1996/02/05
         /207353/index.htm.

3   Rob Copeland, "Two Sigma Readies New Global Equity
         Fund," *Institutional Investor Magazine*, November 1, 2011,
         http://www.institutionalinvestor.com/article/2925681
         /asset-management-equities/two-sigma-readies-new
         -global-equity-fund-magazine-version.html#
         /.VoPhbpMrK34.

4   Reported by HFObserver in 2014. The website has since
         become members-only, and the page is no longer available.

5   "Silk Pavillion Environment | CNC Deposited Silk Fiber
         & Silkworm Construction | MIT Media Lab,"
         accessed May 24, 2016, http://matter.media.mit.edu
         /environments/details/silk-pavillion.

6   "CNSILK—CNC Fiber Deposition Shop-Bot Deposited
         Silk Fibers, MIT Media Lab," accessed May 24, 2016,
         http://matter.media.mit.edu/tools/details/cnsilk.

7   "The Year in Review," *Metropolis*, December 2013, http://
         www.metropolismag.com/December-2013/The-Year-in
         -Review/.

8   Programme for International Student Assessment (PISA), "PISA 2012 Results—OECD," http://www.oecd.org/pisa /keyfindings/pisa-2012-results.htm.

9   Paul E. Peterson et al., "Globally Challenged: Are U.S. Students Ready to Compete?" PEPG Report No. 11-03 (Cambridge, MA: Program on Education Policy and Governance, Harvard University), http://hanushek .stanford.edu/publications/globally-challenged-are-us -students-ready-compete.

10   Christina Clark Tuttle et al., "KIPP Middle Schools: Impacts on Achievement and Other Outcomes" (Washington, D.C.: Mathematica Policy Research, February 27, 2013), https://www.mathematica-mpr.com /our-publications-and-findings/publications /kipp-middle-schools-impacts-on-achievement-and -other-outcomes-full-report.

11   See "Standards in Your State | Common Core State Standards Initiative," accessed May 26, 2016, http://www.corestandards.org/standards-in-your-state/.

12   Anu Partanen, "What Americans Keep Ignoring About Finland's School Success," *Atlantic*, December 29, 2011, http://www.theatlantic.com/national/archive/2011/12 /what-americans-keep-ignoring-about-finlands-school -success/250564/.

13   Interview with Jeff Howe.

14   "The United States Standard Screw Threads," accessed May 26, 2016, https://www.asme.org/about-asme/who

-we-are/engineering-history/landmarks/234-the-united
-states-standard-screw-threads.

15 Tom Knight, "Idempotent Vector Design for Standard
    Assembly of Biobricks," *MIT Libraries*, 2003, 1–11,
    http://dspace.mit.edu/handle/1721.1/45138.

16 "About Me(redith)," http://www.thesmartpolitenerd.com
    /aboutme.html.

17 Interview with Jeff Howe.

18 Nicholas Wade, ed., *The New York Times Book of Genetics*
    (Guilford, CT: Lyons Press, 2002), 250.

19 Human National Human Genome Research
    Institute, "The Human Genome Project Completion:
    Frequently Asked Questions," https://www.genome
    .gov/11006943.

20 "MIT Independent Activities Period (IAP),"
    http://web.mit.edu/iap/.

21 "iGEM 2004—The 2004 Synthetic Biology Competition—
    SBC04," http://2004.igem.org/index.cgi.

22 Anselm Levskaya et al., "Synthetic Biology:
    Engineering Escherichia Coli to See Light," *Nature* 438,
    no. 7067 (November 24, 2005): 441–42, doi:10.1038/
    nature04405.

23 iGEM, "Main Page—Registry of Standard Biological
    Parts," accessed May 26, 2016, http://parts.igem.org
    /Main_Page.

24 "Team:Paris Bettencourt/Acceptance—2015.igem.org,"
    accessed May 26, 2016, http://2015.igem.org/Team:Paris
    _Bettencourt/Acceptance.

25 "Team:NYMU-Taipei—2013.igem.org," accessed May 26,
    2016, http://2013.igem.org/Team:NYMU-Taipei.

26 "Team:EPF Lausanne/Perspectives—2013.igem.org,"
    accessed May 26, 2016, http://2013.igem.org/Team:EPF
    _Lausanne/Perspectives.

27 According to Negroponte, he saw the phrase written on
    a wall clock on the fourth floor of the original Media Lab
    building. Stewart Brand included it in his book about
    the Media Lab, and a motto was born. Joichi Ito, "Deploy:
    How the Media Lab's 'Demo or Die' Evolved to 'Deploy,'"
    PubPub, January 31, 2016, http://www.pubpub.org/pub
    /deploy.

28 Ibid.

29 "Seymour Papert," accessed May 26, 2016,
    http://web.media.mit.edu/~papert/.

30 Seymour Papert, "Papert on Piaget," March 29, 1999,
    http://www.papert.org/articles/Papertonpiaget.html.
    Originally published in *Time* magazine's *The Century's
    Greatest Minds*, March 29, 1999.

31 Seymour A. Papert, *Mindstorms: Children, Computers,
    And Powerful Ideas* (New York: Basic Books, 1993).

32 Ibid., xvi.

33 Eric Hintz, "Remembering Apple's '1984' Super Bowl Ad," *National Museum of American History*, January 22, 2014, http://americanhistory.si.edu/blog/2014/01 /remembering-apples-1984-super-bowl-ad.html.

34 From an interview with Mitch Resnick.

35 "About Us," *Scratch Foundation*, accessed May 27, 2016, http://www.scratchfoundation.org/about-us/.

Chapter 4:
Risk over Safety

1   There are, of course, more Apple stores now—over 400 of them worldwide, at last count. "Apple Retail Store—Store List," Apple, http://www.apple.com/retail/storelist/.

2   Liam Casey, interview with Jeff Howe, April 3, 2012.

3   Since then, Hu has moved away from hardware to focus solely on the software side. Lyndsey Gilpin, "Julia Hu: Lark Founder. Digital Health Maven. Hip-Hop Dancer," *TechRepublic*, July 27, 2015, http://www.techrepublic.com /article/julia-hu-lark-founder-digital-health-maven -hip-hop-dancer/.

4   And expected to increase in value to $3 trillion by 2020. Michael De Waal-Montgomery, "China and India Driving $3T Consumer Electronics Boom, Smart Home Devices Growing Fastest," *VentureBeat*, n.d., http://venturebeat .com/2015/11/05/china-and-india-driving-3t-consumer -electronics-boom-smart-home-devices-growing-fastest/.

5   Steven Levy, "Google's Larry Page on Why Moon Shots Matter," *WIRED*, January 17, 2013, http://www.wired.com /2013/01/ff-qa-larry-page/.

6   David Rowan, "Chinese Pirates Are Tech's New Innovators," *Wired UK*, June 1, 2010.

7   David Barboza, "In China, Knockoff Cellphones Are a Hit," *New York Times*, April 27, 2009, http://www.nytimes .com/2009/04/28/technology/28cell.html.

8   Robert Neuwirth, "The Shadow Superpower," *Foreign Policy*, accessed May 29, 2016, https://foreignpolicy .com/2011/10/28/the-shadow-superpower/.

9   Douglas S. Robertson et al., "K-Pg Extinction: Reevaluation of the Heat-Fire Hypothesis," *Journal of Geophysical Research: Biogeosciences* 118, no. 1 (March 1, 2013): 329–36, doi:10.1002/jgrg.20018.

10   Bjorn Carey, "The Perils of Being Huge: Why Large Creatures Go Extinct," Live Science, July 18, 2006, http://www.livescience.com/4162-perils-huge-large -creatures-extinct.html.

11   "MLTalks: Bitcoin Developers Gavin Andresen, Cory Fields, and Wladimir van Der Laan" (MIT Media Lab, November 17, 2015), http://www.media.mit.edu /events/2015/11/17/mltalks-bitcoin-developers-gavin -andresen-cory-fields-and-wladimir-van-der-laan.

12   The immediate justification for revoking Andresen's commit access was a blog post he wrote stating that he believed Australian programmer Craig Wright's claim to be Satoshi Nakamoto, and which other core developers took as evidence that Andresen had been hacked. For an overview of the controversy, see Maria Bustillos, "Craig Wright's 'Proof' He Invented Bitcoin Is the 'Canadian Girlfriend of Cryptographic Signatures'," *New York*, May 3, 2016, http://nymag.com/selectall/2016/05/craig-wright-s-proof -he-invented-bitcoin-is-basically-a-canadian-girlfriend.html.

13   "2009 Exchange Rate—New Liberty Standard," February 5, 2010, http://newlibertystandard.wikifoundry.com /page/2009+Exchange+Rate.

14   John Biggs, "Happy Bitcoin Pizza Day!," *TechCrunch*,
May 22, 2015, http://social.techcrunch.com/2015/05/22
/happy-bitcoin-pizza-day/.

15   Robert McMillan, "The Inside Story of Mt. Gox,
Bitcoin's $460 Million Disaster," *WIRED*, March 3, 2014,
http://www.wired.com/2014/03/bitcoin-exchange/.

16   Cade Metz, "The Rise and Fall of the World's Largest
Bitcoin Exchange," *WIRED*, November 6, 2013,
http://www.wired.com/2013/11/mtgox/.

17   Ibid.

18   AP, "Tokyo Court Starts Mt. Gox Bankruptcy
Pro-ceedings—The Boston Globe," *BostonGlobe.com*,
April 25, 2014, https://www.bostonglobe.com
/business/2014/04/25/tokyo-court-starts-gox-bankruptcy
-proceedings/1dcuC1YIYb1jJrd8ut8JjJ/story.html.

19   Metz, "The Rise and Fall of the World's Largest Bitcoin
Exchange."

20   Jon Southurst, "Mt. Gox Files for Bankruptcy, Claims
$63.6 Million Debt," *CoinDesk*, February 28, 2014,
http://www.coindesk.com/mt-gox-files-bankruptcy
-claims-63-6m-debt/.

21   "MtGox Finds 200,000 Missing Bitcoins in Old Wallet,"
BBC News, accessed May 29, 2016, http://www.bbc.com
/news/technology-26677291.

22   Jon Southurst, "Missing Mt Gox Bitcoins Likely an Inside
Job, Say Japanese Police," *CoinDesk*, January 1, 2015,

http://www.coindesk.com/missing-mt-gox-bitcoins
-inside-job-japanese-police/.

23   Tim Hornyak, "Police Blame Fraud for Most of Mt. Gox's
     Missing Bitcoins," *Computerworld*, December 31, 2014,
     http://www.computerworld.com/article/2863167/police
     -blame-fraud-for-most-of-mt-goxs-missing-bitcoins.html.

24   "MtGox Bitcoin Chief Mark Karpeles Charged in Japan,"
     BBC News, September 11, 2015, http://www.bbc.com
     /news/business-34217495.

25   Adrian Chen, "The Underground Website Where You Can
     Buy Any Drug Imaginable," *Gawker*, June 1, 2011,
     http://gawker.com/the-underground-website-where
     -you-can-buy-any-drug-imag-30818160.

26   Sarah Jeong, "The DHS Agent Who Infiltrated Silk Road
     to Take Down Its Kingpin," *Forbes*, January 14, 2015,
     http://www.forbes.com/sites/sarahjeong/2015/01/14
     /the-dhs-agent-who-infiltrated-silk-road-to-take-down
     -its-kingpin/#6250111369dd.

27   Andy Greenberg, "Silk Road Mastermind Ross Ulbricht
     Convicted of All 7 Charges," *WIRED*, February 4, 2015,
     https://www.wired.com/2015/02/silk-road-ross-ulbricht
     -verdict/.

28   Riley Snyder, "California Investor Wins Federal
     Government's Bitcoin Auction," *Los Angeles Times*, July 2,
     2014, http://www.latimes.com/business/technology
     /la-fi-tn-bitcoin-auction-20140702-story.html.

29   John Biggs, "US Marshals to Sell 44,000 BTC at Auction in November," *TechCrunch*, October 5, 2015, http://social.techcrunch.com/2015/10/05/us-marshals -to-sell-44000-btc-at-auction-in-november/.

30   "FAQ—Bitcoin," Bitcoin.org, accessed May 29, 2016, https://bitcoin.org/en/faq.

31   Eric Hughes, "A Cypherpunk's Manifesto," *Electronic Frontier Foundation*, March 9, 1993, https://w2.eff.org /Privacy/Crypto/Crypto_misc/cypherpunk.manifesto.

32   Joichi Ito, "Shenzhen Trip Report—Visiting the World's Manufacturing Ecosystem," *Joi Ito's Web*, September 1, 2014, http://joi.ito.com/weblog/2014/09/01/shenzhen -trip-r.html.

33   "Phantom Series—Intelligent Drones," *DJI*, http://www.dji.com/products/phantom.

34   "The World's First and Largest Hardware Accelerator," *HAX*, https://hax.co/.

Chapter 5: Disobedience over Compliance

1   David A. Hounshell and John Kenly Smith, *Science and Corporate Strategy: Du Pont R and D, 1902–1980* (Cambridge University Press, 1988).

2   Pap Ndiaye, *Nylon and Bombs: DuPont and the March of Modern America* (Baltimore: JHU Press, 2007).

3   Hounshell and Smith, *Science and Corporate Strategy*.

4   Ibid.

5   Gerard Colby, *Du Pont: Behind the Nylon Curtain* (Englewood Cliffs, NJ: Prentice-Hall [1974], 1974).

6   Hounshell and Smith, *Science and Corporate Strategy*.

7   "Wallace Carothers and the Development of Nylon: National Historic Chemical Landmark," *American Chemical Society*, n.d., http://www.acs.org/content/acs/en/education /whatischemistry/landmarks/carotherspolymers.html.

8   Thomas S. Kuhn, *The Structure of Scientific Revolutions: 50th Anniversary Edition*, (University of Chicago Press, 2012).

9   Zachary Crockett, "The Man Who Invented Scotch Tape," *Priceonomics*, December 30, 2014, http://priceonomics .com/the-man-who-invented-scotch-tape/.

10   Tim Donnelly, "9 Brilliant Inventions Made by Mistake,"
     Inc.com, August 15, 2012, http://www.inc.com/tim-donnelly
     /brilliant-failures/9-inventions-made-by-mistake.html.

11   David R. Marsh et al., "The Power of Positive Deviance,"
     BMJ 329, no. 7475 (November 11, 2004): 1177–79,
     doi:10.1136/bmj.329.7475.1177.

12   Tina Rosenberg, "When Deviants Do Good," *New York
     Times*, February 27, 2013, http://opinionator.blogs.nytimes
     .com/2013/02/27/when-deviants-do-good/.

13   David Dorsey, "Positive Deviant," *Fast Company*,
     November 30, 2000, http://www.fastcompany.com/42075
     /positive-deviant.

14   "Austin Hill—Venture Partner @ Montreal Start Up,"
     CrunchBase, accessed May 30, 2016,
     https://www.crunchbase.com/person/austin-hill#/entity.

15   Mathew Ingram, "Austin Hill, Internet Freedom Fighter,"
     The Globe and Mail, October 4, 1999.

16   Joseph Czikk, "'A Straight Out Scam': Montreal Angel
     Austin Hill Recounts First Business at FailCampMTL,"
     Betakit, February 25, 2014, http://www.betakit.com
     /montreal-angel-austin-hill-failed-spectacularly-before
     -later-success/

17   Konrad Yakabuski, "Future Tech: On Guard," *Globe and
     Mail*, August 25, 2000, sec. Metro.

18   David Kalish, "Privacy Software Reason for Concern,"
     Austin American-Statesman, December 14, 1999.

19   Developed by Merrill Flood and Melvin Dresher at the
         RAND Corporation in 1950, and formalized by Princeton
         mathematician Albert W. Tucker, the prisoner's
         dilemma describes a situation in which two participants
         must make a decision without consulting each other,
         but knowing that the outcome of the scenario depends
         partially on the other participant's decision. The classic
         example is that of two prisoners who have been
         offered a chance to confess. If only one of them confesses,
         he orshe will go free while the other goes to prison; if
         both remain silent, they'll be charged with a minor
         crime; if both confess, they will both go to jail, but their
         sentences will be reduced. The most advantageous
         choice is for both participants to remain silent,
         but the most common choice is to confess—neither
         player wants to take the chance that the other will
         confess and send him or her to prison. Variations of the
         prisoner's dilemma are often used to explore questions
         of economics and morality. "Prisoner's Dilemma," *Stanford
         Encyclopedia of Philosophy*, revised August 29, 2014,
         http://plato.stanford.edu/entries/prisoner-dilemma/.

20   Austin Hill, "On Your Permanent Record: Anonymity,
         Pseudonymity, Ephemerality & Bears Omfg!,"
         Medium, March 17, 2014, https://medium.com
         /@austinhill/on-your-permanent-record-f5ab81f9f654#.
         ak8ith7gu.

21   Felix Martin, *Money: The Unauthorized Biography* (New
         York: Knopf Doubleday Publishing Group, 2015).

22   Ibid., 43.

23   Ibid., 55–60.

24 Simon Singh, *The Code Book: The Science of Secrecy from Ancient Egypt to Quantum Cryptography* (New York: Knopf Doubleday Publishing Group, 2011). Kindle Edition, chapter 1: "The Cipher of Mary, Queen of Scots."

25 Ibid.

26 Pierre Berloquin, *Hidden Codes & Grand Designs: Secret Languages from Ancient Times to Modern Day* (New York: Sterling Publishing Company, Inc., 2008).

27 Singh, *The Code Book*.

28 Ibid.

29 Singh, *The Code Book*, chapter 2: "Le Chiffre Indéchiffrable"; Richard A. Mollin, *An Introduction to Cryptography* (Boca Raton, FL: CRC Press, 2000).

30 Singh, *The Code Book*.

31 Singh, *The Code Book*, chapter 6: "Alice and Bob Go Public."

32 C. E. Shannon, "A Mathematical Theory of Communication," *SIGMOBILE Moble Computing Communications Review* 5, no. 1 (January 2001): 3–55, doi:10.1145/584091.584093.

33 C. E. Shannon, "Communication Theory of Secrecy Systems," *Bell System Technical Journal* 28, no. 4 (October 1, 1949): 656–715, doi:10.1002/j.1538-7305.1949.tb00928.x.

34 B. Jack Copeland, *Colossus: The Secrets of Bletchley Park's Code-Breaking Computers* (OUP Oxford, 2006).

35 Russell Kay, "Random Numbers," April 1, 2002.

36 Singh, *The Code Book.*

37 David R. Lide, ed., *A Century of Excellence in Measurements, Standards, and Technology: A Chronicle of Selected NIST Publications 1901–2000*, NIST Special Publication 958 (Washington, D.C.: U.S. Department of Commerce, National Institute of Standards and Technology, 2001).

38 W. Diffie and M. Hellman, "New Directions in Cryptography," *IEEE Transactions in Information Theory* 22, no. 6 (November 1976): 644–54, doi:10.1109 /TIT.1976.1055638.

39 Steven Levy, "Battle of the Clipper Chip," *New York Times Magazine*, June 12, 1994, http://www.nytimes.com /1994/06/12/magazine/battle-of-the-clipper-chip.html.

40 R. L. Rivest, A. Shamir, and L. Adleman, "A Method for Obtaining Digital Signatures and Public-Key Cryptosystems," *Communications of the ACM* 21, no. 2 (February 1978): 120–26, doi:10.1145/359340.359342.

41 AP, "Firm Shuts Down Privacy Feature," *Calgary Herald*, October 9, 2001.

42 CCNMatthews (Canada), "Radialpoint CEO a Finalist for Ernst & Young Entrepreneur of the Year Awards," *MarketWired*, July 29, 2005.

43 Roberto Rocha, "What Goes Around Comes Around; Montreal-Based Akoha.com Encourages Acts of Kindness by Turning Altruism into a Game," *Gazette*, July 14, 2009.

44   The Akoha Team, "Akoha Shutting Down August 15 2011," *Akoha Blog*, August 2, 2011, https://blog.akoha .com/2011/08/02/akoha-shutting-down-august-15-2011/.

45   Michael J. Casey, "Linked-In, Sun Microsystems Founders Lead Big Bet on Bitcoin Innovation," *Moneybeat* blog, *Wall Street Journal*, November 17, 2014, http://blogs.wsj.com /moneybeat/2014/11/17/linked-in-sun-microsystems -founders-lead-big-bet-on-bitcoin-innovation/.

46   "Enabling Blockchain Innovations with Pegged Sidechains," *r/Bitcoin*, Reddit, http://www.reddit.com /r/Bitcoin/comments/2k07oh/enabling_blockchain _innovations_with_pegged/clhak9c.

47   Timothy Leary, "The Cyber-Punk: The Individual as Reality Pilot," *Mississippi Review* 16, no. 2/3 (1988).

48   T.F. Peterson, *Nightwork* (Cambridge, MA.: The MIT Press, 2011), https://mitpress.mit.edu/books/nightwork.

49   While the science on the human microbiome, which includes gut bacteria, is still evolving, there's intriguing evidence that our bacteria have a strong influence not only on our health, but also on our behavior. See, for example, Charles Schmidt, "Mental Health: Thinking from the Gut," *Nature* 518, no. 7540 (February 26, 2015): S12–15, doi:10.1038 /518S13a.; Peter Andrey Smith, "Can the Bacteria in Your Gut Explain Your Mood?," *The New York Times*, June 23, 2015, http://www.nytimes.com/2015/06/28/magazine/can-the -bacteria-in-your-gut-explain-your-mood.html.; and David Kohn, "When Gut Bacteria Changes Brain Function," *The Atlantic*, June 24, 2015, http://www.theatlantic.com/health /archive/2015/06/gut-bacteria-on-the-brain/395918/.

Chapter 6:
Practice over Theory

1   Attributed, and possibly apocryphal.

2   The details in this section come from a visit to Quest to Learn in January 2014.

3   *Quest to Learn (Q2L) — Middle School and High School*, http://www.q2l.org/.

4   Pap Ndiaye, *Nylon and Bombs*, DuPont and the March of Modern America (Baltimore: Johns Hopkins University Press, 2006), 164.

5   Jessica Guynn, "Google Gives Employees 20% Time to Work on Diversity," *USA TODAY*, May 14, 2015, http://www.usatoday.com/story/tech/2015/05/13 /google-twenty-percent-time-diversity/27208475/.

6   And the details in *this* section come from a visit to TwoSigma in December 2013.

7   Dave Winer, "Why You Should Learn to Code," *Scripting News*, February 27, 2013, http://threads2.scripting.com /2013/february/whyyoushouldlearntocode.

8   See, for example, Diana Franklin et al., "Assessment of Computer Science Learning in a Scratch-Based Outreach Program," in *Proceeding of the 44th ACM Technical Symposium on Computer Science Education*, SIGCSE '13 (New York, NY, USA: ACM, 2013), 371–76, doi:10.1145/2445196.2445304.; and Shuchi Grover and

Roy Pea, "Computational Thinking in K–12: A Review of the State of the Field," *Educational Researcher* 42, no. 1 (January 1, 2013): 38–43, doi:10.3102/0013189X12463051.

9   James Gee, interview with Jeff Howe, April 19, 2014.

10   Tim Mansel, "How Estonia Became E-Stonia," *BBC News*, May 16, 2013, http://www.bbc.com/news /business-22317297.

11   Stuart Dredge, "Coding at School: A Parent's Guide to England's New Computing Curriculum," *Guardian*, September 4, 2014, http://www.theguardian.com /technology/2014/sep/04/coding-school-computing -children-programming.

12   Michael Barber et al., "The New Opportunity to Lead: A Vision for Education in Massachusetts in the Next 20 Years" (Massachusetts Business Alliance for Education, 2014), http://www.mbae.org/wp-content /uploads/2014/03/New-Opportunity-To-Lead.pdf.

13   Saad Rizvi, interview with Jeff Howe, January 29, 2014.

14   John Dewey, *Interest and Effort in Education* (New York: Houghton Mifflin, 1913), referenced in Mizuko Ito, "Seamless and Connected—Education in the Digital Age," *HFRP — Harvard Family Research Project*, April 24, 2014, http://www.hfrp.org/publications-resources /browse-our-publications/seamless-and-connected -education-in-the-digital-age.

15   For an overview of recent research in this area, see Andrea Kuszewski, "The Educational Value of Creative

Disobedience," *Scientific American Blog Network*, July 7, 2011, http://blogs.scientificamerican.com/guest-blog /the-educational-value-of-creative-disobedience/; and Mizuko Ito et al., "Connected Learning: An Agenda for Research and Design" (Digital Media and Learning Research Hub, December 31, 2012), http://dmlhub.net /publications/connected-learning-agenda-for-research -and-design/.

16   Joi, his sister Mizuko (Mimi), and Mitch Resnick had a long, wide-ranging, and fascinating discussion about these issues during the Media Lab's Spring 2014 Member Event. The video is available online at *Spring 2014 Member Event: Learning over Education* (MIT Media Lab, 2014), http://www.media.mit.edu/video/view/spring14-2014 -04-23-3.

17   Tania Lombronzo, "'Cheating' Can Be an Effective Learning Strategy," NPR, May 30, 2013, http://www.npr .org/sections/13.7/2013/05/20/185131239/cheating-can -be-an-effective-learning-strategy; Peter Nonacs, "Why I Let My Students Cheat on Their Exam," *Zócalo Public Square*, April 15, 2013, http://www.zocalopublicsquare .org/2013/04/15/why-i-let-my-students-cheat-on-the -final/ideas/nexus/.

18   Dan Pink has written extensively about this issue. See Daniel H. Pink, *Drive: The Surprising Truth About What Motivates Us* (New York: Penguin, 2011); Dan Pink, "The Puzzle of Motivation," 2009, https://www.ted.com/talks /dan_pink_on_motivation.

19   Maria Popova, "Autonomy, Mastery, Purpose: The Science of What Motivates Us, Animated," *Brain Pickings*,

http://www.brainpickings.org/index.php/2013/05/09
/daniel-pink-drive-rsa-motivation/.

20   Faith Wallis, *Medieval Medicine: A Reader* (University of
Toronto Press, 2010).

Chapter 7:
Diversity over Ability

1 Firas Khatib et al., "Critical Structure of a Monometric Retroviral Protease Solved by Folding Game Players," *Nature Structural and Molecular Biology* 18 (2011): 1175–77, http://www.nature.com/nsmb/journal/v18/n10/full /nsmb.2119.html; "Mason Pfizer Monkey Virus," *Microbe Wiki*, http://microbewiki.kenyon.edu/index.php/Mason _pfizer_monkey_virus.

2 "Solve Puzzles for Science," *Foldit*, accessed June 1, 2016, http://fold.it/portal/.

3 Ewan Callaway, "Video Gamers Take on Protein Modellers," *Nature Newsblog*, accessed June 1, 2016, http:// blogs.nature.com/news/2011/09/tk.html.

4 "Welcome to Eterna!," http://eterna.cmu.edu/eterna_page .php?page=me_tab.

5 An earlier version of this section, including the quotes from Zoran Popović and Adrien Treuille, appeared in *Slate*. Jeff Howe, "The Crowdsourcing of Talent," *Slate*, February 27, 2012, http://www.slate.com /articles/technology/future_tense/2012/02/foldit _crowdsourcing_and_labor_.html.

6 Jeff Howe, "The Rise of Crowdsourcing," *WIRED*, June 1, 2006, http://www.wired.com/2006/06/crowds/.

7 Todd Wasserman, "Oxford English Dictionary Adds 'Crowdsourcing,' 'Big Data,'" *Mashable*, June 13, 2013,

http://mashable.com/2013/06/13/dictionary-new
-words-2013/.

8   "Longitude Found: John Harrison," *Royal Museums
Greenwich*, October 7, 2015, http://www.rmg.co.uk
/discover/explore/longitude-found-john-harrison.

9   Michael Franklin, "A Globalised Solver Network to Meet
the Challenges of the 21st Century," *InnoCentive Blog*,
April 15, 2016, http://blog.innocentive.com/2016/04/15
/globalised-solver-network-meet-challenges-21st-century/.

10   Karim R. Lakhani et al., "The Value of Openness in
Scientific Problem Solving" (Cambridge, MA: Harvard
Business School, January 2007), http://hbswk.hbs.edu
/item/the-value-of-openness-in-scientific-problem
-solving.

11   Scott E. Page, *The Difference: How the Power of Diversity
Creates Better Groups, Firms, Schools, and Societies*
(Princeton, NJ: Princeton University Press, 2008).

12   Katherine W. Phillips, "How Diversity Makes Us
Smarter," *Scientific American*, October 1, 2014.
www.scientificamerican.com/how-diversity-makes
-us-smarter/.

13   Kerwin Charles and Ming-Ching Luoh, "Male
Incarceration, the Marriage Market, and Female
Outcomes," *The Review of Economics and Statistics*, 92,
no. 3 (2010); 614–627.

14   Four years later, the number of Germans approving of
racial persecution held steady at 5 percent, though only
26 percent were now willing to express their *disapproval*,

compared to 63 percent in 1938. Sarah Ann Gordon, *Hitler, Germans, and the "Jewish Question"* (Princeton, NJ: Princeton University Press, 1984), 262–63.

15　Obergefell v. Hodges, 135 S. Ct. 2071 (Supreme Court of the United States 2015).

16　The American Society of Newspaper Editors (ASNE) publishes an annual concensus measuring diversity in newspaper newsrooms. For an excellent analysis of the relationship between media diversity and the Great Recession, see Riva Gold's *Atlantic* magazine article, "Newsroom Diversity: A Casualty of Journalism's Financial Crisis." (July 2013) httpp://www.theatlantic.com /national/archive/2013/07/newsroom-diversity-a -casualty-of-journalisms-financial-crisis/277622/.

Chapter 8:
Resilience over Strength

1   "YouTube—Broadcast Yourself.," *Internet Archive Wayback Machine*, April 28, 2005, https://web.archive.org /web/20050428014715/http://www.youtube.com/.

2   Jim Hopkins, "Surprise! There's a Third YouTube Co-Founder," *USA Today*, October 11, 2006, http://usatoday30 .usatoday.com/tech/news/2006-10-11-youtube-karim_x .htm.

3   Amy-Mae Elliott, "10 Fascinating YouTube Facts That May Surprise You," *Mashable*, February 19, 2011, http://mashable.com/2011/02/19/youtube-facts/.

4   Keith Epstein, "The Fall of the House of Schrader," *Keith Epstein. Investigation | Communication | Insight*, April 23, 2001, http://www.kepstein.com/2001/04/23/the-fall-of -the-house-of-schrader/.

5   Ellen McCarthy, "After the Glamour, a Modest Return," *Washington Post*, July 18, 2005, sec. Business, http://www .washingtonpost.com/wp-dyn/content/article/2005 /07/17/AR2005071700718.html.

6   While not everyone agrees that an immune-system approach to network security is realistic, it's become increasingly mainstream over the past few years. Nicole Eagan, "What the Human Body Teaches Us about Cyber Security," *World Economic Forum*, August 20, 2015, https://www.weforum.org/agenda/2015/08/good -immune-system-wards-off-cyber-threats/; Shelly Fan,

"How Artificial Immune Systems May Be the Future
of Cybersecurity," *Singularity HUB*, December 27, 2015,
http://singularityhub.com/2015/12/27/cyberimmunity
-ai-based-artificial-immune-systems-may-be
-cybersecurity-of-the-future/; "Workshop on Bio-Inspired
Security, Trust, Assurance and Resilience (BioSTAR 2016)"
(37th IEEE Symposium on Security and Privacy, IEEE
S&P 2016 Workshop), San Jose, CA, May 26, 2016),
http://biostar.cybersecurity.bio/.

7   In *The Code Book*, Simon Singh gives an example in which
Alice and Bob each start with a bucket of yellow paint. Alice
adds a liter of purple to hers, Bob adds a liter of red, and then
they swap buckets. Alice now adds another liter of purple
to Bob's bucket, while Bob adds a liter of red to Alice's. Now
Bob and Alice each have an identical bucket of murky brown
paint, but Eve (the eavesdropper) won't be able to reproduce
the color, even if she has access to the pigments they used.
She could, of course, feed the color information into a
computer, which would be able to calculate potential mixes,
but imagine that instead of three colors, the bucket contains a
million colors, or a billion, or 100 quadrillion. Even the most
powerful processor might take longer to isolate the individual
pigments than the sun has left to burn. Singh, *The Code Book*,
Kindle edition, chapter 6: "Alice and Bob Go Public."

8   While Rivest, Shamir, and Adleman are generally credited
with creating the first functional asymmetric cipher, no
one at the time knew that James Ellis, Clifford Cocks, and
Malcolm Williamson, cryptographers at GCHQ in the
United Kingdom, had already developed a very similar
approach. However, as their work was not made public
until 1997, it did not greatly influence the development of
public key cryptography. Ibid.

9   Amy Thomson and Cornelius Rahn, "Russian Hackers
    Threaten Power Companies, Researchers Say," *Bloomberg
    News*, July 1, 2014, http://www.bloomberg.com/news
    /articles/2014-06-30/symantec-warns-energetic-bear
    -hackers-threaten-energy-firms.

10 Martin Giles, "Defending the Digital Frontier," *Economist*,
    July 12, 2014, http://www.economist.com/news/special
    -report/21606416-companies-markets-and-countries-are
    -increasingly-under-attack-cyber-criminals.

11 Forrest, Hofmeyr, and Edwards, "The Complex Science
    of Cyber Defense," *Harvard Business Review*, June 24, 2013,
    https://hbr.org/2013/06/embrace-the-complexity-of-cybe.

12 "The World's Firt All-Machine Hacking Tournament,"
    http://www.cybergrandchallenge.com.

13 Stephanie Forrest, Steven Hofmeyr, and Benjamin
    Edwards, "The Complex Science of Cyber Defense."

14 John M. Barry, *The Great Influenza: The Epic Story of the
    Deadliest Plague in History* (New York: Penguin, 2005), 267.

15 Stephanie Forrest, Steven Hofmeyr, and Benjamin
    Edwards, "The Complex Science of Cyber Defense."

16 Ibid.

17 Andrea Peterson, "Why One of Cybersecurity's Thought
    Leaders Uses a Pager instead of a Smart Phone," *Washington
    Post*, August 11, 2014, https://www.washingtonpost.com
    /news/the-switch/wp/2014/08/11/why-one-of-cybersecuritys
    -thought-leaders-uses-a-pager-instead-of-a-smart-phone/.

Chapter 9:
Systems over Objects

1 Communication with Joi Ito.

2 Interview with Jeff Howe.

3 Ferris Jabr and *Scientific American* staff, "Know Your Neurons: What Is the Ration of Glia to Neurons in the Brain?" *Scientific American*, June 3, 2012.

4 Paul Reber, "What Is the Memory Capacity of the Human Brain?," *Scientific American*, May 1, 2010, http://www .scientificamerican.com/article/what-is-the-memory-capacity/.

5 Nate, "How Much Is A Petabyte?," *Mozy Blog*, July 2, 2009, https://mozy.com/blog/misc/how-much-is-a-petabyte/.

6 Mark Fischetti, "Computers versus Brains," *Scientific American*, November 1, 2011, http://www .scientificamerican.com/article/computers-vs-brains/.

7 Elwyn Brooks White, *Here Is New York* (New York Review of Books, 1949), 19.

8 Edward Boyden, "A History of Optogenetics: The Development of Tools for Controlling Brain Circuits with Light," *F1000 Biology Reports* 3 (May 3, 2011), doi:10.3410/B3-11.

9 Boyden, "A History of Optogenetics."

10 "Edward Boyden Wins 2016 Breakthrough Prize in Life Sciences," *MIT News*, November 9, 2015, http://news.mit

.edu/2015/edward-boyden-2016-breakthrough-prize-life
-sciences-1109.

11   John Colapinto, "Lighting the Brain," *New Yorker*, May 18,
2015, http://www.newyorker.com/magazine/2015/05/18
/lighting-the-brain.

12   Quinn Norton, "Rewiring the Brain: Inside the New
Science of Neuroengineering," *WIRED*, March 2, 2009,
http://www.wired.com/2009/03/neuroengineering1/.

13   Katherine Bourzac, "In First Human Test of Optogenetics,
Doctors Aim to Restore Sight to the Blind," *MIT Technology
Review*, February 19, 2016, https://www.technologyreview
.com/s/600696/in-first-human-test-of-optogenetics
-doctors-aim-to-restore-sight-to-the-blind/.

14   Anne Trafton, "Seeing the Light," *MIT News*, April 20,
2011, http://news.mit.edu/2011/blindness-boyden-0420.

15   Karl Deisseroth, "Optogenetics: Controlling the Brain
with Light [Extended Version]," *Scientific American*,
October 20, 2010, http://www.scientificamerican.com
/article/optogenetics-controlling/.

16   Ibid.

17   Ernst Bamberg, "Optogenetics," *Max-Planck-Gesellschaft*,
2010, https://www.mpg.de/18011/Optogenetics.

18   Udi Nussinovitch and Lior Gepstein, "Optogenetics for
in Vivo Cardiac Pacing and Resynchronization Therapies,"
Nature Biotechnology 33, no. 7 (July 2015): 750–54,
doi:10.1038/nbt.3268.

19   Deisseroth, "Optogenetics: Controlling the Brain with Light [Extended Version]."

20   "1985 | Timeline of Computer History," *Computer History Museum*, accessed June 7, 2016, http://www.computerhistory.org/timeline/1985/.

21   Quoted in Tom Collins, *The Legendary Model T Ford: The Ultimate History of America's First Great Automobile* (Fort Collins, CO.: Krause Publications, 2007), 155.

22   Henry Ford, *My Life and Work* (New York: Doubleday, 1922), 73.

23   David Gartman, "Tough Guys and Pretty Boys: The Cultural Antagonisms of Engineering and Aesthetics in Automotive History," *Automobile in American Life and Society*, accessed June 7, 2016, http://www.autolife.umd .umich.edu/Design/Gartman/D_Casestudy/D _Casestudy3.htm.

24   Elizabeth B-N Sanders, "From User-Centered to Participatory Design Approaches," *Design and the Social Sciences: Making Connections*, 2002, 1–8.

25   Quoted in Drew Hansen, "Myth Busted: Steve Jobs Did Listen to Customers," *Forbes*, December 19, 2013, http://www.forbes.com/sites/drewhansen/2013/12/19 /myth-busted-steve-jobs-did-listen-to-customers/.

26   Sanders, "From User-Centered to Participatory Design Approaches."

Conclusion

1   And the less said about the "blood-vomiting game" of 1835 the better.

2   Sensei's Library, "Excellent Move," last edited May 31, 2016, http://senseis.xmp.net/?Myoshu.

3   That sounds unlikely, doesn't it? And yet, it's true. For an accessible explanation of the math involved, see Eliene Augenbraun, "Epic Math Battles: Go versus Atoms," *Scientific American 60-Second Science Video*, May 19, 2016, http://www.scientificamerican.com/video/epic-math -battles-go-versus-atoms.

4   Xiangchuan Chen, Daren Zhang, Xiaochu Zhang, Zhihao Li, Xiaomei Meng, Sheng He, Xiaoping Hu, "A Functional MRI Study of High-Level Cognition: II. The Game of GO," *Cognitive Brain Research*, 16, issue 1 (March 2003): 32–37, ISSN 0926-6410, http://dx.doi.org/10.1016/S0926 -6410(02)00206-9.

5   Rémi Coulom, "Efficient Selectivity and Backup Operators in Monte-Carlo Tree Search." *Computers and Games, 5th International Conference, CG 2006, Turin, Italy, May 29–31, 2006, revised papers*, H. Jaap van den Herik, Paolo Ciancarini, H. H. L. M. Donkers, eds., Springer, 72–8, http://citeseerx.ist.psu.edu/viewdoc /summary?doi=10.1.1.81.6817

6   David Silver, Aja Huang, Chris J. Maddison, Arthur Guez, Laurent Sifre, George Van Den Driessche, Julian Schrittwieser et al., "Mastering the Game of Go with

Deep Neural Net-works and Tree Search," *Nature* 529, no. 7587 (2016): 484–489.

7 Elizabeth Gibney, "Go Players React to Computer Defeat," *Nature News*, January 27, 2016, http://www.nature.com /news/go-players-react-to-computer-defeat-1.19255.

8 Mark Zuckerberg, Facebook post dated January 27, 2016, https://www.facebook.com/zuck/posts /10102619979696481?comment _id=10102620696759481&comment _tracking=%7B%22tn%22%3A%22R0%22%7D.

9 Cade Metz, "In Two Moves, AlphaGo and Lee Sedol Redefined the Future," *Wired*, March 16, 2016, http://www.wired.com/2016/03/two-moves-alphago-lee -sedol-redefined-future/.

10 Cade Metz, "The Sadness and Beauty of Watching Google's AI Play Go," *Wired,* March 11, 2016, http://www.wired.com/2016/03/sadness-beauty -watching-googles-ai-play-go/.

11 In 2016, the Super Bowl drew 111.9 million viewers, compared to 280 million for the video of Sedol's matches against AlphaGo. Frank Pallotta and Brian Stelter, "Super Bowl 50 Audience Is Third Largest in TV History," *CNN Money*, February 8, 2016, http:// money.cnn.com/2016/02/08/media/super-bowl -50-ratings/.

12 Baek Byung-yeul, "Lee-AlphaGo Match Puts Go Under Spotlight," *Korea Times*, March 10, 2016,

http://www.koreatimes.co.kr/www/news/nation
/2016/04/663_200122.html.

13   Iyad Rahwan, "Society-in-the-Loop: Programming the
Algorithmic Social Contract," Medium, August 13, 2016.
http://medium.com/mit-media-lab/society-in-the-loop
-54ffd71cd802#.2mxobntqk.

14   Yochai Benkler, "Coase's Penguin, or, Linux and the
Nature of the Firm," *Yale Law Journal* (2002): 369–446.

15   Melanie Mitchell, *Complexity: A Guided Tour* (New York:
Oxford University Press, 2009), ix.

About the Authors

Joichi "Joi" Ito has been recognized for his work as an activist, entrepreneur, venture capitalist, and advocate of emergent democracy, privacy, and Internet freedom. As director of the MIT Media Lab, he is currently exploring how radical new approaches to science and technology can transform society in substantial and positive ways. Ito has served as both board chair and CEO of Creative Commons, and sits on the boards of Sony Corporation, the John S. and James L. Knight Foundation, the John D. and Catherine T. MacArthur Foundation, the New York Times Company, and the Mozilla Foundation. Ito's honors include *TIME* magazine's "Cyber-Elite" listing in 1997 (at age thirty-one) and selection as one of the "Global Leaders for Tomorrow" by the World Economic Forum (2001). In 2008, *BusinessWeek* named him one of the "25 Most Influential People on the Web." In 2011, he received the Lifetime Achievement Award from the Oxford Internet Institute. In 2013, he received an honorary DLitt from the New School in New York City, and in 2015 an honorary Doctor of Humane Letters degree from Tufts University. In 2014, he was inducted into the SXSW Interactive Hall of Fame; also in 2014, he was one of the recipients of the Golden Plate award from the Academy of Achievement.

Jeff Howe is an assistant professor at Northeastern University and the coordinator of its Media Innovation program. A longtime contributing editor at *Wired*, he coined the term "crowdsourcing" in a 2006 article for that magazine. In 2008 he published a book with Random House that looked more deeply at the phenomenon of massive online collaboration. Called *Crowdsourcing: How the Power of the Crowd Is Driving the Future of Business*, it has been translated into ten languages. He was a Nieman Fellow at Harvard University during the 2009–2010 academic year, and is currently a visiting scholar at the MIT Media Lab. He has written for the *Washington Post*, Newyorker.com, the *New York Times*, *Time*, *Newsweek*, and many other publications. He lives in Cambridge, Massachusetts, with his wife and two children.